Experiment Central

*Understanding Scientific Principles
Through Projects*

Experiment Central

Understanding Scientific Principles
Through Projects
Second Edition

VOLUME 5: PL-SO

M. Rae Nelson
Kristine Krapp, editor

U·X·L
A part of Gale, Cengage Learning

GALE
CENGAGE Learning

Detroit • New York • San Francisco • New Haven, Conn • Waterville, Maine • London

GALE
CENGAGE Learning

Experiment Central
Understanding Scientific
Principles Through Projects
Second Edition
M. Rae Nelson

Project Editor: Kristine Krapp

Managing Editor: Debra Kirby

Rights Acquisition and Management:
Margaret Abendroth, Robyn Young

Composition: Evi Abou-El-Seoud, Mary
Beth Trimper

Manufacturing: Wendy Blurton

Product Manager: Julia Furtaw

Product Design: Jennifer Wahi

© 2010 Gale, Cengage Learning

For product information and technology assistance, contact us at
Gale Customer Support, 1-800-877-4253.
For permission to use material from this text or product, submit all requests online at **www.cengage.com/permissions.**
Further permissions questions can be e-mailed to
permissionrequest@cengage.com

Cover photographs: Images courtesy of Dreamstime, Photos.com, and iStockPhoto.

While every effort has been made to ensure the reliability of the information presented in this publication, Gale, a part of Cengage Learning, does not guarantee the accuracy of the data contained herein. Gale accepts no payment for listing; and inclusion in the publication of any organization, agency, institution, publication, service, or individual does not imply endorsement of the editors or publisher. Errors brought to the attention of the publisher and verified to the satisfaction of the publisher will be corrected in future editions.

Library of Congress Cataloging-in-Publication Data

Experiment central : understanding scientific principles through projects. --
2nd ed. / M. Rae Nelson, Kristine Krapp, editors.   p. cm. --
Includes bibliographical references and index.
ISBN 978-1-4144-7613-1 (set) -- ISBN 978-1-4144-7614-8 (vol. 1) --
ISBN 978-1-4144-7615-5 (vol. 2) -- ISBN 978-1-4144-7616-2 (vol. 3) --
ISBN 978-1-4144-7617-9 (vol. 4) -- ISBN 978-1-4144-7618-6 (vol. 5) --
ISBN 978-1-4144-7619-3 (vol. 6)
1. Science--Experiments--Juvenile literature. I. Nelson, M. Rae. II. Krapp, Kristine M.

Q164.E96 2010
507.8--dc22   2009050304

Gale
27500 Drake Rd.
Farmington Hills, MI, 48331-3535

978-1-4144-7613-1 (set)	1-4144-7613-2 (set)
978-1-4144-7614-8 (vol. 1)	1-4144-7614-0 (vol. 1)
978-1-4144-7615-5 (vol. 2)	1-4144-7615-9 (vol. 2)
978-1-4144-7616-2 (vol. 3)	1-4144-7616-7 (vol. 3)
978-1-4144-7617-9 (vol. 4)	1-4144-7617-5 (vol. 4)
978-1-4144-7618-6 (vol. 5)	1-4144-7618-3 (vol. 5)
978-1-4144-7619-3 (vol. 6)	1-4144-7619-1 (vol. 6)

This title is also available as an e-book.
ISBN-13: 978-1-4144-7620-9 (set)
ISBN-10: 1-4144-7620-5 (set)
Contact your Gale sales representative for ordering information.

Printed by China Translation & Printing Services Limited,
Guangdong Province, China. 1st printing. 05/2010
1 2 3 4 5 6 7 14 13 12 11 10

Table of Contents

Experiment Central, 2nd edition

Reader's Guide

Experiment Central: Understanding Scientific Principles Through Projects provides in one resource a wide variety of science experiments covering nine key science curriculum fields—astronomy, biology, botany, chemistry, ecology, food science, geology, meteorology, and physics—spanning the earth sciences, life sciences, and physical sciences.

Experiment Central, 2nd edition combines, expands, and updates the original four-volume and two-volume UXL sets. This new edition includes 20 new chapters, 60 new experiments, and more than 35 enhanced experiments. Each chapter explores a scientific subject and offers experiments or projects that utilize or reinforce the topic studied. Chapters are alphabetically arranged according to scientific concept, including: Air and Water Pollution, Color, Eclipses, Forensic Science, Genetics, Magnetism, Mountains, Periodic Table, Renewable Energy, Storms and Water Cycle. Two to three experiments or projects are included in each chapter.

Entry format

Chapters are presented in a standard, easy-to-follow format. All chapters open with an explanatory overview section designed to introduce students to the scientific concept and provide the background behind a concept s discovery or important figures who helped advance the study of the field.

Each experiment is divided into eight standard sections to help students follow the experimental process clearly from beginning to end. Sections are:

- Purpose/Hypothesis
- Level of Difficulty

- Materials Needed
- Approximate Budget
- Timetable
- Step-by-Step Instructions
- Summary of Results
- Change the Variables

Chapters also include a "Design Your Own Experiment" section that allows students to apply what they have learned about a particular concept and to create their own experiments. This section is divided into:

- How to Select a Topic Relating to this Concept
- Steps in the Scientific Method
- Recording Data and Summarizing the Results
- Related Projects

Special Features

A "Words to Know" sidebar provides definitions of terms used in each chapter. A cumulative glossary collected from all the "Words to Know" sections is included in the beginning of each volume.

The "Experiments by Scientific Field" section categorizes experiments by scientific curriculum area. This section cumulates all experiments across the six-volume series.

The Parent's and Teacher's Guide recommends that a responsible adult always oversee a student's experiment and provides several safety guidelines for all students to follow.

Standard sidebars accompany experiments and projects.

- "What Are the Variables?" explains the factors that may have an impact on the outcome of a particular experiment.
- "How to Experiment Safely" clearly explains any risks involved with the experiment and how to avoid them.
- "Troubleshooter's Guide" presents problems that a student might encounter with an experiment, possible causes of the problem, and ways to remedy the problem.

Over 450 photos enhance the text; approximately 450 custom illustrations show the steps in the experiments.

Four indexes cumulate information from all the experiments in this six-volume set, including:

- Budget Index categorizes the experiments by approximate cost.
- Level of Difficulty Index lists experiments according to "easy," "moderate," or "difficult," or a combination thereof.
- Timetable Index categorizes each experiment by the amount of time needed to complete it, including setup and follow-through time.
- General Subject Index provides access to all major terms, people, places, and topics covered in the set.

Acknowledgments

The author wishes to acknowledge and thank Laurie Curtis, teacher/researcher; Cindy O'Neill, science educator; and Joyce Nelson, chemist, for their contributions to this edition as consultants.

Comments and Suggestions

We welcome your comments on *Experiment Central*. Please write: Editors, *Experiment Central*, U*X*L, 27500 Drake Rd. Farmington Hills, MI 48331-3535; call toll-free: 1-800-347-4253; or visit us at www.gale.cengage.com.

Parent's and Teacher's Guide

The experiments and projects in *Experiment Central* have been carefully constructed with issues of safety in mind, but your guidance and supervision are still required. Following the safety guidelines that accompany each experiment and project (found in the "How to Experiment Safely" sidebar box), as well as putting to work the safe practices listed below, will help your child or student avoid accidents. Oversee your child or student during experiments, and make sure he or she follows these safety guidelines:

- Always wear safety goggle is there is any possiblity of sharp objects, small particles, splashes of liquid, or gas fumes getting in someone's eyes.

- Always wear protective gloves when handling materials that could irritate the skin.

- Never leave an open flame, such as a lit candle, unattended. Never wear loose clothing around an open flame.

- Follow instructions carefully when using electrical equipment, including batteries, to avoid getting shocked.

- Be cautious when handling sharp objects or glass equipment that might break. Point scissors away from you and use them carefully.

- Always ask for help in cleaning up spills, broken glass, or other hazardous materials.

- Always use protective gloves when handling hot objects. Set them down only on a protected surface that will not be damaged by heat.

- Always wash your hands thoroughly after handling material that might contain harmful microorganisms, such as soil and pond water.

- Do not substitute materials in an experiment without asking a knowledgeable adult about possible reactions.

- Do not use or mix unidentified liquids or powders. The result might be an explosion or poisonous fumes.

- Never taste or eat any substances being used in an experiment.

- Always wear old clothing or a protective apron to avoid staining your clothes.

Experiments by Scientific Field

Chapter name in brackets, followed by experiment name. The numeral before the colon indicates volume; numbers after the colon indicate page number.

CHEMISTRY

ECOLOGY

FOOD SCIENCE

GEOLOGY

Words to Know

A

Abdomen: The third segment of an insect body.

Abscission: Barrier of special cells created at the base of leaves in autumn.

Absolute dating: The age of an object correlated to a specific fixed time, as established by some precise dating method.

Acceleration: The rate at which the velocity and/or direction of an object is changing with respect to time.

Acid: Substance that when dissolved in water is capable of reacting with a base to form salts and release hydrogen ions.

Acid rain: A form of precipitation that is significantly more acidic than neutral water, often produced as the result of industrial processes and pollution.

Acoustics: The science concerned with the production, properties, and propagation of sound waves.

Acronym: A word or phrase formed from the first letter of other words.

Active solar energy system: A solar energy system that uses pumps or fans to circulate heat captured from the Sun.

Additive: A chemical compound that is added to foods to give them some desirable quality, such as preventing them from spoiling.

Adhesion: Attraction between two different substances.

Adhesive: A substance that bonds or adheres two substances together.

Aeration: Mixing a gas, like oxygen, with a liquid, like water.

Aerobic: A process that requires oxygen.

Aerodynamics: The study of the motion of gases (particularly air) and the motion and control of objects in the air.

Agar: A nutrient rich, gelatinous substance that is used to grow bacteria.

Air: Gaseous mixture that covers Earth, composed mainly of nitrogen (about 78%) and oxygen (about 21%) with lesser amounts of argon, carbon dioxide, and other gases.

Air density: The ratio of the mass of a substance to the volume it occupies.

Air mass: A large body of air that has similar characteristics.

Air pressure: The force exerted by the weight of the atmosphere above a point on or above Earth's surface.

Alga/Algae: Single-celled or multicellular plants or plant-like organisms that contain chlorophyll, thus making their own food by photosynthesis. Algae grow mainly in water.

Alignment: Adjustment in a certain direction or orientation.

Alkali metals: The first group of elements in the periodic table, these metals have a single electron in the outermost shell.

Alkaline: Having a pH of more than 7.

Alleles: One version of the same gene.

Alloy: A mixture of two or more metals with properties different from those metals of which it is made.

Amine: An organic compound derived from ammonia.

Amino acid: One of a group of organic compounds that make up proteins.

Amnesia: Partial or total memory loss.

Amperage: A measurement of current. The common unit of measure is the ampere or amp.

Amphibians: Animals that live on land and breathe air but return to the water to reproduce.

Amplitude: The maximum displacement (difference between an original position and a later position) of the material that is vibrating. Amplitude can be thought of visually as the highest and lowest point of a wave.

Anaerobic: A process that does not require oxygen.

Anal fin: Fin on the belly of a fish, used for balance.

Anatomy: The study of the structure of living things.

Anemometer: A device that measures wind speed.

Angiosperm: A flowering plant that has its seeds produced within an ovary.

Animalcules: Life forms that Anton van Leeuwenhoek named when he first saw them under his microscope; they later became known as protozoa and bacteria.

Anther: The male reproductive organs of the plant, located on the tip of a flower's stamen.

Anthocyanin: Red pigment found in leaves, petals, stems, and other parts of a plant.

Antibiotic: A substance produced by or derived from certain fungi and other organisms, that can destroy or inhibit the growth of other microorganisms.

Antibiotic resistance: The ability of microorganisms to change so that they are not killed by antibiotics.

Antibody: A protein produced by certain cells of the body as an immune (disease-fighting) response to a specific foreign antigen.

Antigen: A substance that causes the production of an antibody when injected directly into the body.

Antioxidants: Used as a food additive, these substances can prevent food spoilage by reducing the food's exposure to air.

Aquifer: Underground layer of sand, gravel, or spongy rock that collects water.

Arch: A curved structure that spans an opening and supports a weight above the opening.

Artesian well: A well in which water is forced out under pressure.

Asexual reproduction: A reproductive process that does not involve the union of two individuals in the exchange of genetic material.

Astronomers: Scientists who study the positions, motions, and composition of stars and other objects in the sky.

Astronomy: The study of the physical properties of objects and matter outside Earth's atmosphere.

Atmosphere: Layers of air that surround Earth.

Experiment Central, 2nd edition

Atmospheric pressure: The pressure exerted by the atmosphere at Earth's surface due to the weight of the air.

Atom: The smallest unit of an element, made up of protons and neutrons in a central nucleus surrounded by moving electrons.

Atomic mass: Also known as atomic weight, the average mass of the atoms in an element; the number that appears under the element symbol in the periodic table.

Atomic number: The number of protons (or electrons) in an atom; the number that appears over the element symbol in the periodic table.

Atomic symbol: The one- or two-letter abbreviation for a chemical element.

Autotroph: An organism that can build all the food and produce all the energy it needs with its own resources.

Auxins: A group of plant hormones responsible for patterns of plant growth.

Axis: An imaginary straight line around which an object, like a planet, spins or turns. Earth's axis is a line that goes through the North and South Poles.

B

Bacteria: Single-celled microorganisms that live in soil, water, plants, and animals that play a key role in the decay of organic matter and the cycling of nutrients. Some are agents of disease.

Bacteriology: The scientific study of bacteria, their characteristics, and their activities as related to medicine, industry, and agriculture.

Barometer: An instrument for measuring atmospheric pressure, used especially in weather forecasting.

Base: Substance that when dissolved in water is capable of reacting with an acid to form salts and release hydrogen ions; has a pH of more than 7.

Base pairs: In DNA, the pairing of two nucleotides with each other: adenine (A) with thymine (T), and guanine (G) with cytosine (C).

Beam: A straight, horizontal structure that spans an opening and supports a weight above the opening.

Bedrock: Solid layer of rock lying beneath the soil and other loose material.

Beriberi: A disease caused by a deficiency of thiamine and characterized by nerve and gastrointestinal disorders.

Biochemical oxygen demand (BOD5): The amount of oxygen microorganisms use over a five-day period in 68°F (20°C) water to decay organic matter.

Biodegradable: Capable of being decomposed by biological agents.

Biological variables: Living factors such as bacteria, fungi, and animals that can affect the processes that occur in nature and in an experiment.

Bioluminescence: The chemical phenomenon in which an organism can produce its own light.

Biomass: Organic materials that are used to produce usable energy.

Biomes: Large geographical areas with specific climates and soils, as well as distinct plant and animal communities that are interdependent.

Biomimetics: The development of materials that are found in nature.

Biopesticide: Pesticide produced from substances found in nature.

Bivalve: Bivalves are characterized by shells that are divided into two parts or valves that completely enclose the mollusk like the clam or scallop.

Blanching: A cooking technique in which the food, usually vegetables and fruits, are briefly cooked in boiling water and then plunged into cold water.

Blood pattern analysis: The study of the shape, location, and pattern of blood in order to understand how it got there.

Blueshift: The shortening of the frequency of light waves toward the blue end of the visible light spectrum as they travel towards an observer; most commonly used to describe movement of stars towards Earth.

Boiling point: The temperature at which a substance changes from a liquid to a gas or vapor.

Bond: The force that holds two atoms together.

Bone joint: A place in the body where two or more bones are connected.

Bone marrow: The spongy center of many bones in which blood cells are manufactured.

Bone tissue: A group of similar cells in the bone with a common function.

Bony fish: The largest group of fish, whose skeleton is made of bone.

Boreal: Northern.

Botany: The branch of biology involving the scientific study of plant life.

Braided rivers: Wide, shallow rivers with multiple channels and pebbly islands in the middle.

Buoyancy: The tendency of a liquid to exert a lifting effect on a body immersed in it.

By-product: A secondary substance produced as the result of a physical or chemical process, in addition to the main product.

C

Calcium carbonate: A substance that is secreted by a mollusk to create the shell it lives in.

Calibration: To standardize or adjust a measuring instrument so its measurements are correct.

Cambium: The tissue below the bark that produces new cells, which become wood and bark.

Camouflage: Markings or coloring that help hide an animal by making it blend into the surrounding environment.

Cancellous bone: Also called spongy bone, the inner layer of a bone that has cells with large spaces in between them filled with marrow.

Canning: A method of preserving food using airtight, vacuum-sealed containers and heat processing.

Capillary action: The tendency of water to rise through a narrow tube by the force of adhesion between the water and the walls of the tube.

Caramelization: The process of heating sugars to the point at which they break down and lead to the formation of new compounds.

Carbohydrate: A compound consisting of carbon, hydrogen, and oxygen found in plants and used as a food by humans and other animals.

Carbonic acid: A weak acid that forms from the mixture of water and carbon dioxide.

Carnivore: A meat-eating organism.

Carotene: Yellow-orange pigment in plants.

Cartilage: The connective tissue that covers and protects the bones.

Cartilaginous fish: The second largest group of fish whose skeleton is made of cartilage

Cast: In paleontology, the fossil formed when a mold is later filled in by mud or mineral matter.

Catalase: An enzyme found in animal liver tissue that breaks down hydrogen peroxide into oxygen and water.

Catalyst: A compound that starts or speeds up the rate of a chemical reaction without undergoing any change in its own composition.

Caudal fin: Tail fin of a fish used for fast swimming.

Cave: Also called cavern, a hollow or natural passage under or into the ground large enough for a person to enter.

Celestial bodies: Describing planets or other objects in space.

Cell membrane: The layer that surrounds the cell, but is inside the cell wall, allowing some molecules to enter and keeping others out of the cell.

Cell theory: All living things have one or more similar cells that carry out the same functions for the living process.

Cell wall: A tough outer covering over the cell membrane of bacteria and plant cells.

Cells: The basic unit for living organisms; cells are structured to perform highly specialized functions.

Centrifugal force: The apparent force pushing a rotating body away from the center of rotation.

Centrifuge: A device that rapidly spins a solution so that the heavier components will separate from the lighter ones.

Centripetal force: Rotating force that moves towards the center or axis.

Cerebral cortex: The outer layer of the brain.

Channel: A shallow trench carved into the ground by the pressure and movement of a river.

Chemical change: The change of one or more substances into other substances.

Chemical energy: Energy stored in chemical bonds.

Chemical property: A characteristic of a substance that allows it to undergo a chemical change. Chemical properties include flammability and sensitivity to light.

Chemical reaction: Any chemical change in which at least one new substance is formed.

Chemosense: A sense stimulated by specific chemicals that cause the sensory cell to transmit a signal to the brain.

Chitin: Substance that makes up the exoskeleton of crustaceans.

Chlorophyll: A green pigment found in plants that absorbs sunlight, providing the energy used in photosynthesis, or the conversion of carbon dioxide and water to complex carbohydrates.

Chloroplasts: Small structures in plant cells that contain chlorophyll and in which the process of photosynthesis takes place.

Chromatography: A method for identifying the components of a substance based on their characteristic colors.

Chromosome: A structure of DNA found in the cell nucleus.

Cilia: Hairlike structures on olfactory receptor cells that sense odor molecules.

Circuit: The complete path of an electric current including the source of electric energy.

Circumference: The distance around a circle.

Clay: Type of soil comprising the smallest soil particles.

Cleavage: The tendency of a mineral to split along certain planes.

Climate: The average weather that a region experiences over a long period.

Coagulation: The clumping together of particles in a mixture, often because the repelling force separating them is disrupted.

Cohesion: Attraction between like substances.

Cold blooded: When an animals body temperature rises or falls to match the environment.

Collagen: A protein in bone that gives the bone elasticity.

Colloid: A mixture containing particles suspended in, but not dissolved in, a dispersing medium.

Colony: A mass of microorganisms that have been bred in a medium.

Colorfast: The ability of a material to keep its dye and not fade or change color.

Coma: Glowing cloud of gas surrounding the nucleus of a comet.

Combustion: Any chemical reaction in which heat, and usually light, is produced. It is commonly the burning of organic substances during which oxygen from the air is used to form carbon dioxide and water vapor.

Comet: An icy body orbiting in the solar system, which partially vaporizes when it nears the Sun and develops a diffuse envelope of dust and gas as well as one or more tails.

Comet head: The nucleus and the coma of a comet.

Comet nucleus: The core or center of a comet. (Plural: Comet nuclei.)

Comet tail: The most distinctive feature of comets; comets can display two basic types of tails: one gaseous and the other largely composed of dust.

Compact bone: The outer, hard layer of the bone.

Complete metamorphosis: Metamorphosis in which a larva becomes a pupa before changing into an adult form.

Composting: The process in which organic compounds break down and become dark, fertile soil called humus.

Compression: A type of force on an object where the object is pushed or squeezed from each end.

Concave: Hollowed or rounded inward, like the inside of a bowl.

Concave lens: A lens that is thinner in the middle than at the edges.

Concentration: The amount of a substance present in a given volume, such as the number of molecules in a liter.

Condensation: The process by which a gas changes into a liquid.

Conduction: The flow of heat through a solid.

Conductivity: The ability of a material to carry an electrical current.

Conductor: A substance able to carry an electrical current.

Cones: Cells in the retina that can perceive color.

Confined aquifer: An aquifer with a layer of impermeable rock above it where the water is held under pressure.

Coniferous: Refers to trees, such as pines and firs, that bear cones and have needle-like leaves that are not shed all at once.

Conservation of energy: The law of physics that states that energy can be transformed from one form to another, but can be neither created nor destroyed.

Constellations: Patterns of stars in the night sky. There are eighty-eight known constellations.

Continental drift: The theory that continents move apart slowly at a predictable rate.

Contract: To shorten, pull together.

Control experiment: A set-up that is identical to the experiment but is not affected by the variable that will be changed during the experiment.

Convection: The circulatory motion that occurs in a gas or liquid at a nonuniform temperature owing to the variation of its density and the action of gravity.

Convection current: A circular movement of a fluid in response to alternating heating and cooling.

Convex: Curved or rounded outward, like the outside of a ball.

Convex lens: A lens that is thicker in the middle than at the edges.

Coprolites: The fossilized droppings of animals.

Coriolis force: A force that makes a moving object appear to travel in a curved path over the surface of a spinning body.

Corona: The outermost atmospheric layer of the Sun.

Corrosion: An oxidation-reduction reaction in which a metal is oxidized (reacted with oxygen) and oxygen is reduced, usually in the presence of moisture.

Cotyledon: Seed leaves, which contain the stored source of food for the embryo.

Crater: An indentation caused by an object hitting the surface of a planet or moon.

Crest: The highest point reached by a wave.

Cross-pollination: The process by which pollen from one plant pollinates another plant of the same species.

Crust: The hard outer shell of Earth that floats upon the softer, denser mantle.

Crustacean: A type of arthropod characterized by hard and thick skin, and having shells that are jointed. This group includes the lobster, crab, and crayfish.

Crystal: Naturally occurring solid composed of atoms or molecules arranged in an orderly pattern that repeats at regular intervals.

Crystal faces: The flat, smooth surfaces of a crystal.

Crystal lattice: The regular and repeating pattern of the atoms in a crystal.

Cultures: Microorganisms growing in prepared nutrients.

Cumulonimbus cloud: The parent cloud of a thunderstorm; a tall, vertically developed cloud capable of producing heavy rain, high winds, and lightning.

Current: The flow of electrical charge from one point to another.

Currents: The horizontal and vertical circulation of ocean waters.

Cyanobacteria: Oxygen-producing, aquatic bacteria capable of manufacturing its own food; resembles algae.

Cycles: Occurrence of events that take place on a regular, repeating basis.

Cytology: The branch of biology concerned with the study of cells.

Cytoplasm: The semifluid substance inside a cell that surrounds the nucleus and other membrane-enclosed organelles.

D

Decanting: The process of separating a suspension by waiting for its heavier components to settle out and then pouring off the lighter ones.

Decibel (dB): A unit of measurement for the amplitude of sound.

Deciduous: Plants that lose their leaves during some season of the year, and then grow them back during another season.

Decompose: To break down into two or more simpler substances.

Decomposition: The breakdown of complex molecules of dead organisms into simple nutrients that can be reutilized by living organisms.

Decomposition reaction: A chemical reaction in which one substance is broken down into two or more substances.

Deficiency disease: A disease marked by a lack of an essential nutrient in the diet.

Degrade: Break down.

Dehydration: The removal of water from a material.

Denaturization: Altering an enzyme so it no longer works.

Density: The mass of a substance divided by its volume.

Density ball: A ball with the fixed standard of 1.0 gram per milliliter, which is the exact density of pure water.

Deoxyribonucleic acid (DNA): Large, complex molecules found in the nuclei of cells that carry genetic information for an organism's development; double helix. (Pronounced DEE-ox-see-rye-bo-noo-klay-ick acid)

Dependent variable: The variable in an experiment whose value depends on the value of another variable in the experiment.

Deposition: Dropping of sediments that occurs when a river loses its energy of motion.

Desert: A biome with a hot-to-cool climate and dry weather.

Desertification: Transformation of arid or semiarid productive land into desert.

Dewpoint: The point at which water vapor begins to condense.

Dicot: Plants with a pair of embryonic seeds that appear at germination.

Diffraction: The bending of light or another form of electromagnetic radiation as it passes through a tiny hole or around a sharp edge.

Diffraction grating: A device consisting of a surface into which are etched very fine, closely spaced grooves that cause different wavelengths of light to reflect or refract (bend) by different amounts.

Diffusion: Random movement of molecules that leads to a net movement of molecules from a region of high concentration to a region of low concentration.

Disinfection: Using chemicals to kill harmful organisms.

Dissolved oxygen: Oxygen molecules that have dissolved in water.

Distillation: The process of separating liquids from solids or from other liquids with different boiling points by a method of evaporation and condensation, so that each component in a mixture can be collected separately in its pure form.

DNA fingerprinting: A technique that uses DNA fragments to identify the unique DNA sequences of an individual.

DNA replication: The process by which one DNA strand unwinds and duplicates all its information, creating two new DNA strands that are identical to each other and to the original strand.

DNA (deoxyribonucleic acid): Large, complex molecules found in nuclei of cells that carry genetic information for an organism's development.

Domain: Small regions in iron that possess their own magnetic charges.

Dominant gene: A gene that passes on a certain characteristic, even when there is only one copy (allele) of the gene.

Doppler effect: The change in wavelength and frequency (number of vibrations per second) of either light or sound as the source is moving either towards or away from the observer.

Dormant: A state of inactivity in an organism.

Dorsal fin: The fin located on the back of a fish, used for balance.

Double helix: The shape taken by DNA (deoxyribonucleic acid) molecules in a nucleus.

Drought: A prolonged period of dry weather that damages crops or prevents their growth.

Dry cell: A source of electricity that uses a non-liquid electrolyte.

Dust tail: One of two types of tails a comet may have, it is composed mainly of dust and it points away from the Sun.

Dye: A colored substance that is used to give color to a material.

Dynamic equilibrium: A situation in which substances are moving into and out of cell walls at an equal rate.

E

Earthquake: An unpredictable event in which masses of rock suddenly shift or rupture below Earth's surface, releasing enormous amounts of energy and sending out shockwaves that sometimes cause the ground to shake dramatically.

Eclipse: A phenomenon in which the light from a celestial body is temporarily cut off by the presence of another.

Ecologists: Scientists who study the interrelationship of organisms and their environments.

Ecosystem: An ecological community, including plants, animals and microorganisms, considered together with their environment.

Efficiency: The amount of power output divided by the amount of power input. It is a measure of how well a device converts one form of power into another.

Effort: The force applied to move a load using a simple machine.

Elastomers: Any of various polymers having rubbery properties.

Electric charge repulsion: Repulsion of particles caused by a layer of negative ions surrounding each particle. The repulsion prevents coagulation and promotes the even dispersion of such particles through a mixtures.

Electrical energy: Kinetic energy resulting from the motion of electrons within any object that conducts electricity.

Electricity: A form of energy caused by the presence of electrical charges in matter.

Electrode: A material that will conduct an electrical current, usually a metal; used to carry electrons into or out of a battery.

Electrolyte: Any substance that, when dissolved in water, conducts an electric current.

Electromagnetic spectrum: The complete array of electromagnetic radiation, including radio waves (at the longest-wavelength end), microwaves, infrared radiation, visible light, ultraviolet radiation, X rays, and gamma rays (at the shortest-wavelength end).

Electromagnetism: A form of magnetic energy produced by the flow of an electric current through a metal core. Also, the study of electric and magnetic fields and their interaction with charges and currents.

Electron: A subatomic particle with a single negative electrical change that orbits the nucleus of an atom.

Electroplating: The process of coating one metal with another metal by means of an electrical current.

Electroscope: A device that determines whether an object is electrically charged.

Element: A pure substance composed of just one type of atom that cannot be broken down into anything simpler by ordinary chemical means.

Elevation: Height above sea level.

Elliptical: An orbital path which is egg-shaped or resembles an elongated circle.

Elongation: The percentage increase in length that occurs before a material breaks under tension.

Embryo: The seed of a plant, which through germination can develop into a new plant.

Embryonic: The earliest stages of development.

Endothermic reaction: A chemical reaction that absorbs heat or light energy, such as photosynthesis, the production of food by plant cells.

Energy: The ability to cause an action or to perform work.

Entomology: The study of insects.

Environmental variables: Nonliving factors such as air temperature, water, pollution, and pH that can affect processes that occur in nature and in an experiment.

Enzyme: Any of numerous complex proteins produced by living cells that act as catalysts, speeding up the rate of chemical reactions in living organisms.

Enzymology: The science of studying enzymes.

Ephemerals: Plants that lie dormant in dry soil for years until major rainstorms occur.

Epicenter: The location where the seismic waves of an earthquake first appear on the surface, usually almost directly above the focus.

Equilibrium: A balancing or canceling out of opposing forces, so that an object will remain at rest.

Erosion: The process by which topsoil is carried away by water, wind, or ice action.

Ethnobotany: The study of how cultures use plants in everyday life.

Eukaryotic: Multicellular organism whose cells contain distinct nuclei, which contain the genetic material. (Pronounced yoo-KAR-ee-ah-tic)

Euphotic zone: The upper part of the ocean where sunlight penetrates, supporting plant life, such as phytoplankton.

Eutrophication: The process by which high nutrient concentrations in a body of water eventually cause the natural wildlife to die.

Evaporation: The process by which liquid changes into a gas.

Exoskeleton: A hard outer covering on animals, which provide protection and structure.

Exothermic reaction: A chemical reaction that releases heat or light energy, such as the burning of fuel.

Experiment: A controlled observation.

Extremophiles: Bacteria that thrive in environments too harsh to support most life forms.

F

False memory: A memory of an event that never happened or an altered memory from what happened.

Family: A group of elements in the same column of the periodic table or in closely related columns of the table. A family of chemical compounds share similar structures and properties.

Fat: A type of lipid, or chemical compound used as a source of energy, to provide insulation and to protect organs in an animal body.

Fat-soluble vitamins: Vitamins such as A, D, E, and K that can be dissolved in the fat of plants and animals.

Fault: A crack running through rock as the result of tectonic forces.

Fault blocks: Pieces of rock from Earth's crust that press against each other and cause earthquakes when they suddenly shift or rupture from the pressure.

Fault mountain: A mountain that is formed when Earth's plates come together and cause rocks to break and move upwards.

Fermentation: A chemical reaction in which enzymes break down complex organic compounds (for example, carbohydrates and sugars) into simpler ones (for example, ethyl alcohol).

Filament: In a flower, stalk of the stamen that bears the anther.

Filtration: The mechanical separation of a liquid from the undissolved particles floating in it.

Fireball: Meteors that create an intense, bright light and, sometimes, an explosion.

First law of motion (Newton's): An object at rest or moving in a certain direction and speed will remain at rest or moving in the same motion and speed unless acted upon by a force.

Fish: Animals that live in water who have gills, fins, and are cold blooded.

Fixative: A substance that mixes with the dye to hold it to the material.

Flagella: Whiplike structures used by some organisms for movement. (Singular: flagellum.)

Flammability: The ability of a material to ignite and burn.

Flower: The reproductive part of a flowering plant.

Fluid: A substance that flows; a liquid or gas.

Fluorescence: The emission of visible light from an object when the object is bombarded with electromagnetic radiation, such as ultraviolet rays. The emission of visible light stops after the radiation source has been removed.

Focal length: The distance from the lens to the point where the light rays come together to a focus.

Focal point: The point at which rays of light converge or from which they diverge.

Focus: The point within Earth where a sudden shift or rupture occurs.

Fold mountain: A mountain that is formed when Earth's plates come together and push rocks up into folds.

Food webs: Interconnected sets of food chains, which are a sequence of organisms directly dependent on one another for food.

Force: A physical interaction (pushing or pulling) tending to change the state of motion (velocity) of an object.

Forensic science: The application of science to the law and justice system.

Fortified: The addition of nutrients, such as vitamins or minerals, to food.

Fossil: The remains, trace, or impressions of a living organism that inhabited Earth more than ten thousand years ago.

Fossil fuel: A fuel such as coal, oil, or natural gas that is formed over millions of years from the remains of plants and animals.

Fossil record: The documentation of fossils placed in relationship to one another; a key source to understand the evolution of life on Earth.

Fracture: A mineral's tendency to break into curved, rough, or jagged surfaces.

Frequency: The rate at which vibrations take place (number of times per second the motion is repeated), given in cycles per second or in hertz (Hz). Also, the number of waves that pass a given point in a given period of time.

Friction: A force that resists the motion of an object, resulting when two objects rub against one another.

Front: The area between air masses of different temperatures or densities.

Fuel cell: A device that uses hydrogen as the fuel to produce electricity and heat with water as a byproduct.

Fulcrum: The point at which a lever arm pivots.

Fungi: Kingdom of various single-celled or multicellular organisms, including mushrooms, molds, yeasts, and mildews, that do not contain chlorophyll.

Funnel cloud: A fully developed tornado vortex before it has touched the ground.

Fusion: Combining of nuclei of two or more lighter elements into one nucleus of a heavier element; the process stars use to produce energy to produce light and support themselves against their own gravity.

G

Galaxy: A large collection of stars and clusters of stars containing anywhere from a few million to a few trillion stars.

Gastropod: The largest group of mollusks; characterized by a single shell that is often coiled in a spiral. Snails are gastropods.

Gene: A segment of a DNA (deoxyribonucleic acid) molecule contained in the nucleus of a cell that acts as a kind of code for the production of some specific protein. Genes carry instructions for the formation, functioning, and transmission of specific traits from one generation to another.

Generator: A device that converts mechanical energy into electrical energy,

Genetic engineering: A technique that modifies the DNA of living cells in order to make them change its characteristics. Also called genetic modification.

Genetic material: Material that transfers characteristics from a parent to its offspring.

Geology: The study of the origin, history and structure of Earth.

Geothermal energy: Energy from deep within Earth.

Geotropism: The tendency of roots to bend toward Earth.

Germ theory of disease: The theory that disease is caused by micro-organisms or germs, and not by spontaneous generation.

Germination: First stage in development of a plant seed.

Gibbous moon: A phase of the Moon when more than half of its surface is lighted.

Gills: Special organ located behind the head of a fish that takes in oxygen from the water.

Glacier: A large mass of ice formed from snow that has packed together and which moves slowly down a slope under its own weight.

Global warming: Warming of Earth's atmosphere as a result of an increase in the concentration of gases that store heat, such as carbon dioxide.

Glucose: A simple sugar broken down in cells to produce energy.

Gnomon: The perpendicular piece of the sundial that casts the shadow.

Golgi body: An organelles that sorts, modifies, and packages molecules.

Gravity: Force of attraction between objects, the strength of which depends on the mass of each object and the distance between them.

Greenhouse effect: The warming of Earth's atmosphere due to water vapor, carbon dioxide, and other gases in the atmosphere that trap heat radiated from Earth's surface.

Greenhouse gases: Gases that absorb infrared radiation and warm the air before the heat energy escapes into space.

Greenwich Mean Time (GMT): The time at an imaginary line that runs north and south through Greenwich, England, used as the standard for time throughout the world.

Groundwater: Water that soaks into the ground and is stored in the small spaces between the rocks and soil.

Group: A vertical column of the periodic table that contains elements possessing similar chemical characteristics.

H

Hardwood: Wood from angiosperm, mostly deciduous, trees.

Heartwood: The inner layers of wood that provide structure and have no living cells.

Heat: A form of energy produced by the motion of molecules that make up a substance.

Heat capacity: The measure of how well a substance stores heat.

Heat energy: The energy produced when two substances that have different temperatures are combined.

Heliotropism: The tendency of plants to turn towards the Sun throughout the day.

Herbivore: A plant-eating organism.

Hertz (Hz): The unit of measurement of frequency; a measure of the number of waves that pass a given point per second of time.

Heterogeneous: Different throughout.

Heterotrophs: Organisms that cannot make their own food and that must, therefore, obtain their food from other organisms.

High air pressure: An area where the air is cooler and more dense, and the air pressure is higher than normal.

Hippocampus: A part of the brain associated with learning and memory.

Homogenous: The same throughout.

Hormones: Chemicals produced in the cells of plants and animals that control bodily functions.

Hue: The color or shade.

Humidity: The amount of water vapor (moisture) contained in the air.

Humus: Fragrant, spongy, nutrient-rich decayed plant or animal matter.

Hydrologic cycle: Continual movement of water from the atmosphere to Earth's surface through precipitation and back to the atmosphere through evaporation and transpiration.

Hydrologists: Scientists who study water and its cycle.

Hydrology: The study of water and its cycle.

Hydrometer: An instrument that determines the specific gravity of a liquid.

Hydrophilic: A substance that is attracted to and readily mixes with water.

Hydrophobic: A substance that is repelled by and does not mix with water.

Hydropower: Energy produced from capturing moving water.

Hydrotropism: The tendency of roots to grow toward a water source.

Hypertonic solution: A solution with a higher concentration of materials than a cell immersed in the solution.

Hypha: Slender, cottony filaments making up the body of multicellular fungi. (Plural: hyphae)

Hypothesis: An idea in the form of a statement that can be tested by observation and/or experiment.

Hypotonic solution: A solution with a lower concentration of materials than a cell immersed in the solution.

I

Igneous rock: Rock formed from the cooling and hardening of magma.

Immiscible: Incapable of being mixed.

Imperfect flower: Flowers that have only the male reproductive organ (stamen) or the female reproductive organs (pistil).

Impermeable: Not allowing substances to pass through.

Impurities: Chemicals or other pollutants in water.

Inclined plane: A simple machine with no moving parts; a slanted surface.

Incomplete metamorphosis: Metamorphosis in which a nymph form gradually becomes an adult through molting.

Independent variable: The variable in an experiment that determines the final result of the experiment.

Indicator: Pigments that change color when they come into contact with acidic or basic solutions.

Inertia: The tendency of an object to continue in its state of motion.

Infrared radiation: Electromagnetic radiation of a wavelength shorter than radio waves but longer than visible light that takes the form of heat.

Inner core: Very dense, solid center of Earth.

Inorganic: Not containing carbon; not derived from a living organism.

Insect: A six-legged invertebrate whose body has three segments.

Insoluble: A substance that cannot be dissolved in some other substance.

Insulated wire: Electrical wire coated with a non-conducting material such as plastic.

Insulation: A material that is a poor conductor of heat or electricity.

Insulator: A material through which little or no electrical current or heat energy will flow.

Interference fringes: Bands of color that fan out around an object.

Internal skeleton: An animal that has a backbone.

Invertebrate: An animal that lacks a backbone or internal skeleton.

Ion: An atom or groups of atoms that carry an electrical charge—either positive or negative—as a result of losing or gaining one or more electrons.

Ion tail: One of two types of tails a comet may have, it is composed mainly of charged particles and it points away from the Sun.

Ionic conduction: The flow of an electrical current by the movement of charged particles, or ions.

Isobars: Continuous lines that connect areas with the same air pressure.

Isotonic solutions: Two solutions that have the same concentration of solute particles and therefore the same osmotic pressure.

J

Jawless fish: The smallest group of fishes, who lacks a jaw.

K

Kinetic energy: The energy of an object or system due to its motion.

Kingdom: One of the five classifications in the widely accepted classification system that designates all living organisms into animals, plants, fungi, protists, and monerans.

L

Labyrinth: A lung-like organ located above the gills that allows the fish to breathe in oxygen from the air.

Lactobacilli: A strain of bacteria.

Landfill: A method of disposing of waste materials by placing them in a depression in the ground or piling them in a mound. In a sanitary landfill, the daily deposits of waste materials are covered with a layer of soil.

Larva: Immature form (wormlike in insects; fishlike in amphibians) of an organism capable of surviving on its own. A larva does not resemble the parent and must go through metamorphosis, or change, to reach its adult stage.

Lava: Molten rock that occurs at the surface of Earth, usually through volcanic eruptions.

Lava cave: A cave formed from the flow of lava streaming over solid matter.

Leach: The movement of dissolved minerals or chemicals with water as it percolates, or oozes, downward through the soil.

Leaching: The movement of dissolved chemicals with water that is percolating, or oozing, downward through the soil.

Leavening agent: A substance used to make foods like dough and batter to rise.

Leeward: The side away from the wind or flow direction.

Lens: A piece of transparent material with two curved surfaces that bend rays of light passing through it.

Lichen: An organism composed of a fungus and a photosynthetic organism in a symbiotic relationship.

Lift: Upward force on the wings of an aircraft created by differences in air pressure on top of and underneath the wings.

Ligaments: Tough, fibrous tissue connecting bones.

Light: A form of energy that travels in waves.

Light-year: Distance light travels in one year in the vacuum of space, roughly 5.9 trillion miles (9.5 trillion kilometers).

The Local Group: A cluster of thirty galaxies, including the Milky Way, pulled together by gravity.

Long-term memory: The last category of memory in which memories are stored away and can last for years.

Low air pressure: An area where the air is warmer and less dense, and the air pressure is lower than normal.

Luminescent: Producing light through a chemical process.

Luminol: A compound used to detect blood.

Lunar eclipse: An eclipse that occurs when Earth passes between the Sun and the Moon, casting a shadow on the Moon.

Luster: A glow of reflected light; a sheen.

M

Machine: Any device that makes work easier by providing a mechanical advantage.

Macrominerals: Minerals needed in relatively large quantities.

Macroorganisms: Visible organisms that aid in breaking down organic matter.

Magma: Molten rock deep within Earth that consists of liquids, gases, and particles of rocks and crystals. Magma underlies areas of volcanic activity and at Earth's surface is called lava.

Magma chambers: Pools of bubbling liquid rock that are the source of energy causing volcanoes to be active.

Magma surge: A swell or rising wave of magma caused by the movement and friction of tectonic plates, which heats and melts rock, adding to the magma and its force.

Magnet: A material that attracts other like materials, especially metals.

Magnetic circuit: A series of magnetic domains aligned in the same direction.

Magnetic field: The space around an electric current or a magnet in which a magnetic force can be observed.

Magnetism: A fundamental force in nature caused by the motion of electrons in an atom.

Maillard reaction: A reaction caused by heat and sugars and resulting in foods browning and flavors.

Mammals: Animals that have a backbone, are warm blooded, have mammary glands to feed their young and have or are born with hair.

Mantle: Thick dense layer of rock that underlies Earth's crust and overlies the core; also soft tissue that is located between the shell and an animal's inner organs. The mantle produces the calcium carbonate substance that create the shell of the animal.

Manure: The waste matter of animals.

Mass: Measure of the total amount of matter in an object. Also, an object's quantity of matter as shown by its gravitational pull on another object.

Matter: Anything that has mass and takes up space.

Meandering river: A lowland river that twists and turns along its route to the sea.

Medium: A material that contains the nutrients required for a particular microorganism to grow.

Melting point: The temperature at which a substance changes from a solid to a liquid.

Memory: The process of retaining and recalling past events and experiences.

Meniscus: The curved surface of a column of liquid.

Metabolism: The process by which living organisms convert food into energy and waste products.

Metamorphic rock: Rock formed by transformation of pre-existing rock through changes in temperature and pressure.

Metamorphosis: Transformation of an immature animal into an adult.

Meteor: An object from space that becomes glowing hot when it passes into Earth's atmosphere; also called shooting star.

Meteor shower: A group of meteors that occurs when Earth's orbit intersects the orbit of a meteor stream.

Meteorites: A meteor that is large enough to survive its passage through the atmosphere and hit the ground.

Meteoroid: A piece of debris that is traveling in space.

Meteorologist: Scientist who studies the weather and the atmosphere.

Microbiology: Branch of biology dealing with microscopic forms of life.

Microclimate: A unique climate that exists only in a small, localized area.

Microorganisms: Living organisms so small that they can be seen only with the aid of a microscope.

Micropyle: Seed opening that enables water to enter easily.

Microvilli: The extension of each taste cell that pokes through the taste pore and first senses the chemicals.

Milky Way: The galaxy in which our solar system is located.

Mimicry: A characteristic in which an animal is protected against predators by resembling another, more distasteful animal.

Mineral: An inorganic substance found in nature with a definite chemical composition and structure. As a nutrient, it helps build bones and soft tissues and regulates body functions.

Mixture: A combination of two or more substances that are not chemically combined with each other and that can exist in any proportion.

Mnemonics: Techniques to improve memory.

Mold: In paleontology, the fossil formed when acidic water dissolves a shell or bone around which sand or mud has already hardened.

Molecule: The smallest particle of a substance that retains all the properties of the substance and is composed of one or more atoms.

Mollusk: An invertebrate animal usually enclosed in a shell, the largest group of shelled animals.

Molting: A process by which an animal sheds its skin or shell.

Monocot: Plants with a single embryonic leaf at germination.

Monomer: A small molecule that can be combined with itself many times over to make a large molecule, the polymer.

Moraine: Mass of boulders, stones, and other rock debris carried along and deposited by a glacier.

Mordant: A substance that fixes the dye to the material.

Mountain: A landform that stands well above its surroundings; higher than a hill.

Mucus: A thick, slippery substance that serves as a protective lubricant coating in passages of the body that communicate with the air.

Multicellular: Living things with many cells joined together.

Muscle fibers: Stacks of long, thin cells that make up muscle; there are three types of muscle fiber: skeletal, cardiac, and smooth.

Mycelium: In fungi, the mass of threadlike, branching hyphae.

N

Nanobots: A nanoscale robot.

Nanometer: A unit of length; this measurement is equal to one-billionth of a meter.

Nanotechnology: Technology that involves working and developing technologies on the nanometer (atomic and molecular) scale.

Nansen bottles: Self-closing containers with thermometers that draw in water at different depths.

Nebula: Bright or dark cloud, often composed of gases and dust, hovering in the space between the stars.

Nectar: A sweet liquid, found inside a flower, that attracts pollinators.

Neutralization: A chemical reaction in which the mixing of an acidic solution with a basic (alkaline) solution results in a solution that has the properties of neither an acid nor a base.

Neutron: A subatomic particle with a mass of about one atomic mass unit and no electrical charge that is found in the nucleus of an atom.

Newtonian fluid: A fluid that follows certain properties, such as the viscosity remains constant at a given temperature.

Niche: The specific location and place in the food chain that an organism occupies in its environment.

Noble gases: Also known as inert or rare gases; the elements argon, helium, krypton, neon, radon, and xenon, which are nonreactive gases and form few compounds with other elements.

Non-Newtonian fluid: A fluid whose property do not follow Newtonian properties, such as viscosity can vary based on the stress.

Nonpoint source: An unidentified source of pollution, which may actually be a number of sources.

Nucleation: The process by which crystals start growing.

Nucleotide: The basic unit of a nucleic acid. It consists of a simple sugar, a phosphate group, and a nitrogen-containing base. (Pronounced noo-KLEE-uh-tide.)

Nucleus: The central part of the cell that contains the DNA; the central core of an atom, consisting of protons and (usually) neutrons.

Nutrient: A substance needed by an organism in order for it to survive, grow, and develop.

Nutrition: The study of the food nutrients an organism needs in order to maintain well-being.

Nymph: An immature form in the life cycle of insects that go through an incomplete metamorphosis.

O

Objective lens: In a refracting telescope, the lens farthest away from the eye that collects the light.

Oceanographer: A person who studies the chemistry of the oceans, as well as their currents, marine life, and the ocean floor.

Oceanography: The study of the chemistry of the oceans, as well as their currents, marine life, and the ocean bed.

Olfactory: Relating to the sense of smell.

Olfactory bulb: The part of the brain that processes olfactory (smell) information.

Olfactory epithelium: The patch of mucous membrane at the top of the nasal cavity that contains the olfactory (smell) nerve cells.

Olfactory receptor cells: Nerve cells in the olfactory epithelium that detect odors and transmit the information to the brain.

Oort cloud: Region of space beyond our solar system that theoretically contains about one trillion inactive comets.

Optics: The study of the nature of light and its properties.

Orbit: The path followed by a body (such as a planet) in its travel around another body (such as the Sun).

Organelle: A membrane-enclosed structure that performs a specific function within a cell.

Organic: Containing carbon; also referring to materials that are derived from living organisms.

Oscillation: A repeated back-and-forth movement.

Osmosis: The movement of fluids and substances dissolved in liquids across a semipermeable membrane from an area of its greater concentration to an area of its lesser concentration until all substances involved reach a balance.

Experiment Central, 2nd edition

Outer core: A liquid core that surrounds Earth's solid inner core; made mostly of iron.

Ovary: In a plant, the base part of the pistil that bears ovules and develops into a fruit.

Ovule: Structure within the ovary that develops into a seed after fertilization.

Oxidation: A chemical reaction in which oxygen reacts with some other substance and in which ions, atoms, or molecules lose electrons.

Oxidation state: The sum of an atom's positive and negative charges.

Oxidation-reduction reaction: A chemical reaction in which one substance loses one or more electrons and the other substance gains one or more electrons.

Oxidizing agent: A chemical substance that gives up oxygen or takes on electrons from another substance.

P

Paleontologist: Scientist who studies the life of past geological periods as known from fossil remains.

Papain: An enzyme obtained from the fruit of the papaya used as a meat tenderizer, as a drug to clean cuts and wounds, and as a digestive aid for stomach disorders.

Papillae: The raised bumps on the tongue that contain the taste buds.

Parent material: The underlying rock from which soil forms.

Partial solar/lunar eclipse: An eclipse in which our view of the Sun/ Moon is only partially blocked.

Particulate matter: Solid matter in the form of tiny particles in the atmosphere. (Pronounced par-TIK-you-let.)

Passive solar energy system: A solar energy system in which the heat of the Sun is captured, used, and stored by means of the design of a building and the materials from which it is made.

Pasteurization: The process of slow heating that kills bacteria and other microorganisms.

Peaks: The points at which the energy in a wave is maximum.

Pectin: A natural carbohydrate found in fruits and vegetables.

Pectoral fin: Pair of fins located on the side of a fish, used for steering.

Pedigree: A diagram that illustrates the pattern of inheritance of a genetic trait in a family.

Pelvic fin: Pair of fins located toward the belly of a fish, used for stability.

Pendulum: A free-swinging weight, usually consisting of a heavy object attached to the end of a long rod or string, suspended from a fixed point.

Penicillin: A mold from the fungi group of microorganisms; used as an antibiotic.

Pepsin: Digestive enzyme that breaks down protein.

Percolate: To pass through a permeable substance.

Perfect flower: Flowers that have both male and female reproductive organs.

Period: A horizontal row in the periodic table.

Periodic table: A chart organizing elements by atomic number and chemical properties into groups and periods.

Permeable: Having pores that permit a liquid or a gas to pass through.

Permineralization: A form of preservation in which mineral matter has filled in the inner and outer spaces of the cell.

Pest: Any living thing that is unwanted by humans or causes injury and disease to crops and other growth.

Pesticide: Substance used to reduce the abundance of pests.

Petal: Leafy structure of a flower just inside the sepals; they are often brightly colored and have many different shapes.

Petrifaction: Process of turning organic material into rock by the replacement of that material with minerals.

pH: A measure of the acidity or alkalinity of a solution referring to the concentration of hydrogen ions present in a liter of a given fluid. The pH scale ranges from 0 (greatest concentration of hydrogen ions and therefore most acidic) to 14 (least concentration of hydrogen ions and therefore most alkaline), with 7 representing a neutral solution, such as pure water.

Pharmacology: The science dealing with the properties, reactions, and therapeutic values of drugs.

Phases: Changes in the portion of the Moon's surface that is illuminated by light from the Sun as the Moon revolves around Earth.

Phloem: The plant tissue that carries dissolved nutrients through the plant.

Phosphorescence: The emission of visible light from an object when the object is bombarded with electromagnetic radiation, such as ultraviolet rays. The object stores part of the radiation energy and the emission of visible light continues for a period ranging from a fraction of a second to several days after the radiation source has been removed.

Photoelectric effect: The phenomenon in which light falling upon certain metals stimulates the emission of electrons and changes light into electricity.

Photosynthesis: Chemical process by which plants containing chlorophyll use sunlight to manufacture their own food by converting carbon dioxide and water to carbohydrates, releasing oxygen as a by-product.

Phototropism: The tendency of a plant to grow toward a source of light.

Photovoltaic cells: A device made of silicon that converts sunlight into electricity.

Physical change: A change in which the substance keeps its molecular identity, such as a piece of chalk that has been ground up.

Physical property: A characteristic that you can detect with your senses, such as color and shape.

Physiologist: A scientist who studies the functions and processes of living organisms.

Phytoplankton: Microscopic aquatic plants that live suspended in the water.

Pigment: A substance that displays a color because of the wavelengths of light that it reflects.

Pili: Short projections that assist bacteria in attaching to tissues.

Pistil: Female reproductive organ of flowers that is composed of the stigma, style, and ovary.

Pitch: A property of a sound, determined by its frequency; the highness or lowness of a sound.

Plant extract: The juice or liquid essence obtained from a plant by squeezing or mashing it.

Plasmolysis: Occurs in walled cells in which cytoplasm, the semifluid substance inside a cell, shrivels and the membrane pulls away from the cell wall when the vacuole loses water.

Plates: Large regions of Earth's surface, composed of the crust and uppermost mantle, which move about, forming many of Earth's major geologic surface features.

Platform: The horizontal surface of a bridge on which traffic travels.

Pnematocysts: Stinging cells.

Point source: An identified source of pollution.

Pollen: Dust-like grains or particles produced by a plant that contain male sex cells.

Pollinate: The transfer of pollen from the male reproductive organs to the female reproductive organs of plants.

Pollination: Transfer of pollen from the male reproductive organs to the female reproductive organs of plants.

Pollinator: Any animal, such as an insect or bird, that transfers the pollen from one flower to another.

Pollution: The contamination of the natural environment, usually through human activity.

Polymer: Chemical compound formed of simple molecules (known as monomers) linked with themselves many times over.

Polymerization: The bonding of two or more monomers to form a polymer.

Polyvinyl acetate: A type of polymer that is the main ingredient of white glues.

Pore: An opening or space.

Potential energy: The energy of an object or system due to its position.

Precipitation: Any form of water that falls to Earth, such as rain, snow, or sleet.

Predator: An animal that hunts another animal for food.

Preservative: An additive used to keep food from spoiling.

Primary colors: The three colors red, green, and blue; when combined evenly they produce white light and by combining varying amounts can produce the range of colors.

Prism: A piece of transparent material with a triangular cross-section. When light passes through it, it causes different colors to bend different amounts, thus separating them into a rainbow of colors.

Probe: The terminal of a voltmeter, used to connect the voltmeter to a circuit.

Producer: An organism that can manufacture its own food from nonliving materials and an external energy source, usually by photosynthesis.

Product: A compound that is formed as a result of a chemical reaction.

Prokaryote: A cell without a true nucleus, such as a bacterium.

Prominences: Masses of glowing gas, mainly hydrogen, that rise from the Sun's surface like flames.

Propeller: Radiating blades mounted on a rapidly rotating shaft, which moves aircraft forward.

Protein: A complex chemical compound consisting of many amino acids attached to each other that are essential to the structure and functioning of all living cells.

Protists: Members of the kingdom Protista, primarily single-celled organisms that are not plants or animals.

Proton: A subatomic particle with a single positive charge that is found in the nucleus of an atom.

Protozoa: Single-celled animal-like microscopic organisms that live by taking in food rather than making it by photosynthesis. They must live in the presence of water.

Pulley: A simple machine made of a cord wrapped around a wheel.

Pupa: The insect stage of development between the larva and adult in insects that go through complete metamorphosis.

R

Radiation: Energy transmitted in the form of electromagnetic waves or subatomic particles.

Radicule: Seed's root system.

Radio wave: Longest form of electromagnetic radiation, measuring up to 6 miles (9.6 kilometers) from peak to peak.

Radioisotope dating: A technique used to date fossils, based on the decay rate of known radioactive elements.

Radiosonde balloons: Instruments for collecting data in the atmosphere and then transmitting that data back to Earth by means of radio waves.

Radon: A radioactive gas located in the ground; invisible and odorless, radon is a health hazard when it accumulates to high levels inside homes and other structures where it is breathed.

Rain shadow: Region on the side of the mountain that receives less rainfall than the area windward of the mountain.

Rancidity: Having the condition when food has a disagreeable odor or taste from decomposing oils or fats.

Reactant: A compound present at the beginning of a chemical reaction.

Reaction: Response to an action prompted by stimulus.

Recessive gene: A gene that produces a certain characteristic only two both copies (alleles) of the gene are present.

Recycling: The use of waste materials, also known as secondary materials or recyclables, to produce new products.

Redshift: The lengthening of the frequency of light waves toward the red end of the visible light spectrum as they travel away from an observer; most commonly used to describe movement of stars away from Earth.

Reduction: A process in which a chemical substance gives off oxygen or takes on electrons.

Reed: A tall woody perennial grass that has a hollow stem.

Reflection: The bouncing of light rays in a regular pattern off the surface of an object.

Reflector telescope: A telescope that directs light from an opening at one end to a concave mirror at the far end, which reflects the light back to a smaller mirror that directs it to an eyepiece on the side of the tube.

Refraction: The bending of light rays as they pass at an angle from one transparent or clear medium into a second one of different density.

Refractor telescope: A telescope that directs light through a glass lens, which bends the light waves and brings them to a focus at an eyepiece that acts as a magnifying glass.

Relative age: The age of an object expressed in relation to another like object, such as earlier or later.

Relative density: The density of one material compared to another.

Rennin: Enzyme used in making cheese.

Resistance: A partial or complete limiting of the flow of electrical current through a material. The common unit of measure is the ohm.

Respiration: The physical process that supplies oxygen to living cells and the chemical reactions that take place inside the cells.

Resultant: A force that results from the combined action of two other forces.

Retina: The light-sensitive part of the eyeball that receives images and transmits visual impulses through the optic nerve to the brain.

Ribosome: A protein composed of two subunits that functions in protein synthesis (creation).

Rigidity: The amount an object will deflect when supporting a weight. The less it deflects for a given amount of weight, the greater its rigidity.

River: A main course of water into which many other smaller bodies of water flow.

Rock: Naturally occurring solid mixture of minerals.

Rods: Cells in the retina that are sensitive to degrees of light and movement.

Root hairs: Fine, hair-like extensions from the plant's root.

Rotate: To turn around on an axis or center.

Runoff: Water that does not soak into the ground or evaporate, but flows across the surface of the ground.

S

Salinity: The amount of salts dissolved in water.

Saliva: Watery mixture with chemicals that lubricates chewed food.

Sand: Granular portion of soil composed of the largest soil particles.

Sapwood: The outer wood in a tree, which is usually a lighter color.

Saturated: In referring to solutions, a solution that contains the maximum amount of solute for a given amount of solvent at a given temperature.

Saturation: The intensity of a color.

Scanning tunneling microscope: A microscope that can show images of surfaces at the atomic level by scanning a probe over a surface.

Scientific method: Collecting evidence and arriving at a conclusion under carefully controlled conditions.

Screw: A simple machine; an inclined plane wrapped around a cylinder.

Scurvy: A disease caused by a deficiency of vitamin C, which causes a weakening of connective tissue in bone and muscle.

Sea cave: A cave in sea cliffs, formed most commonly by waves eroding the rock.

Second law of motion (Newton's): The force exerted on an object is proportional to the mass of the object times the acceleration produced by the force.

Sediment: Sand, silt, clay, rock, gravel, mud, or other matter that has been transported by flowing water.

Sedimentary rock: Rock formed from compressed and solidified layers of organic or inorganic matter.

Sedimentation: A process during which gravity pulls particles out of a liquid.

Seed crystal: Small form of a crystalline structure that has all the facets of a complete new crystal contained in it.

Seedling: A small plant just starting to grow into its mature form.

Seismic belt: Boundaries where Earth's plates meet.

Seismic waves: Vibrations in rock and soil that transfer the force of an earthquake from the focus into the surrounding area.

Seismograph: A device that detects and records vibrations of the ground.

Seismology: The study and measurement of earthquakes.

Seismometer: A seismograph that measures the movement of the ground.

Self-pollination: The process in which pollen from one part of a plant fertilizes ovules on another part of the same plant.

Semipermeable membrane: A thin barrier between two solutions that permits only certain components of the solutions, usually the solvent, to pass through.

Sensory memory: Memory that the brain retains for a few seconds.

Sepal: The outermost part of a flower; typically leaflike and green.

Sexual reproduction: A reproductive process that involves the union of two individuals in the exchange of genetic material.

Shear stress: An applied force to a give area.

Shell: A region of space around the center of the atom in which electrons are located; also, a hard outer covering that protects an animal living inside.

Short-term memory: Also known as working memory, this memory was transferred here from sensory memory.

Sidereal day: The time it takes for a particular star to travel around and reach the same position in the sky; about four minutes shorter than the average solar day.

Silt: Medium-sized soil particles.

Simple machine: Any of the basic structures that provide a mechanical advantage and have no or few moving parts.

Smog: A form of air pollution produced when moisture in the air combines and reacts with the products of fossil fuel combustion. Smog is characterized by hazy skies and a tendency to cause respiratory problems among humans.

Softwood: Wood from coniferous trees, which usually remain green all year.

Soil: The upper layer of Earth that contains nutrients for plants and organisms; a mixture of mineral matter, organic matter, air, and water.

Soil horizon: An identifiable soil layer due to color, structure, and/or texture.

Soil profile: Combined soil horizons or layers.

Solar collector: A device that absorbs sunlight and collects solar heat.

Solar day: Called a day, the time between each arrival of the Sun at its highest point.

Solar eclipse: An eclipse that occurs when the Moon passes between Earth and the Sun, casting a shadow on Earth.

Solar energy: Any form of electromagnetic radiation that is emitted by the Sun.

Solubility: The tendency of a substance to dissolve in some other substance.

Soluble: A substance that can be dissolved in some other substance.

Solute: The substance that is dissolved to make a solution and exists in the least amount in a solution, for example sugar in sugar water.

Solution: A mixture of two or more substances that appears to be uniform throughout except on a molecular level.

Solvent: The major component of a solution or the liquid in which some other component is dissolved, for example water in sugar water.

Specific gravity: The ratio of the density of a substance to the density of pure water.

Specific heat capacity: The energy required to raise the temperature of 1 kilogram of the substance by 1 degree Celsius.

Speleologist: One who studies caves.

Speleology: Scientific study of caves and their plant and animal life.

Spelunkers: Also called cavers, people who explore caves for a hobby.

Spiracles: The openings on an insects side where air enters.

Spoilage: The condition when food has taken on an undesirable color, odor, or texture.

Spore: A small, usually one-celled, reproductive body that is capable of growing into a new organism.

Stalactite: Cylindrical or icicle-shaped mineral deposit projecting downward from the roof of a cave. (Pronounced sta-LACK-tite.)

Stalagmite: Cylindrical or icicle-shaped mineral deposit projecting upward from the floor of a cave. (Pronounced sta-LAG-mite.)

Stamen: Male reproductive organ of flowers that is composed of the anther and filament.

Standard: A base for comparison.

Star: A vast clump of hydrogen gas and dust that produces great energy through fusion reactions at its core.

Static electricity: A form of electricity produced by friction in which the electric charge does not flow in a current but stays in one place.

Stigma: Top part of the pistil upon which pollen lands and receives the male pollen grains during fertilization.

Stomata: Pores in the epidermis (surface) of leaves.

Storm: An extreme atmospheric disturbance, associated with strong damaging winds, and often with thunder and lightning.

Storm chasers: People who track and seek out storms, often tornadoes.

Stratification: Layers according to density; applies to fluids.

Streak: The color of the dust left when a mineral is rubbed across a rough surface.

Style: Stalk of the pistil that connects the stigma to the ovary.

Subatomic: Smaller than an atom. It usually refers to particles that make up an atom, such as protons, neutrons, and electrons.

Sublime: The process of changing a solid into a vapor without passing through the liquid phase.

Substrate: The substance on which an enzyme operates in a chemical reaction.

Succulent: Plants that live in dry environments and have water storage tissue.

Sundial: A device that uses the position of the Sun to indicate time.

Supersaturated: Solution that is more highly concentrated than is normally possible under given conditions of temperature and pressure.

Supertaster: A person who is extremely sensitive to specific tastes due to a greater number of taste buds.

Supplements: A substance intended to enhance the diet.

Surface area: The total area of the outside of an object; the area of a body of water that is exposed to the air.

Surface tension: The attractive force of molecules to each other on the surface of a liquid.

Surface water: Water in lakes, rivers, ponds, and streams.

Suspension: A temporary mixture of a solid in a gas or liquid from which the solid will eventually settle out.

Swim bladder: Located above the stomach, takes in air when the fish wants to move upwards and releases air when the fish wants to move downwards.

Symbiosis: A pattern in which two or more organisms live in close connection with each other, often to the benefit of both or all organisms.

Synthesis reaction: A chemical reaction in which two or more substances combine to form a new substance.

Synthesize: To make something artificially, in a laboratory or chemical plant, that is generally not found in nature.

Synthetic: A substance that is synthesized, or manufactured, in a laboratory; not naturally occurring.

Synthetic crystals: Artificial or manmade crystals.

T

Taiga: A large land biome mostly dominated by coniferous trees.

Taste buds: Groups of taste cells located on the papillae that recognize the different tastes.

Taste pore: The opening at the top of the taste bud from which chemicals reach the taste cells.

Tectonic: Relating to the forces and structures of the outer shell of Earth.

Tectonic plates: Huge flat rocks that form Earth's crust.

Telescope: A tube with lenses or mirrors that collect, transmit, and focus light.

Temperate: Mild or moderate weather conditions.

Temperature: The measure of the average energy of the molecules in a substance.

Tendon: Tough, fibrous connective tissue that attaches muscle to bone.

Tensile strength: The force needed to stretch a material until it breaks.

Terminal: A connection in an electric circuit; usually a connection on a source of electric energy such as a battery.

Terracing: A series of horizontal ridges made in a hillside to reduce erosion.

Testa: A tough outer layer that protects the embryo and endosperm of a seed from damage.

Theory of special relativity: Theory put forth by Albert Einstein that time is not absolute, but it is relative according to the speed of the observer's frame of reference.

Thermal conductivity: A number representing a material's ability to conduct heat.

Thermal energy: Kinetic energy caused by the movement of molecules due to temperature.

Thermal inversion: A region in which the warmer air lies above the colder air; can cause smog to worsen.

Thermal pollution: The discharge of heated water from industrial processes that can kill or injure water life.

Thiamine: A vitamin of the B complex that is essential to normal metabolism and nerve function.

Thigmotropism: The tendency for a plant to grow toward a surface it touches.

Third law of motion (Newton's): For every action there is an equal and opposite reaction.

Thorax: The middle segment of an insect body; the legs and wings are connected to the thorax.

Tides: The cyclic rise and fall of seawater.

Titration: A procedure in which an acid and a base are slowly mixed to achieve a neutral substance.

Topsoil: The uppermost layers of soil containing an abundant supply of decomposed organic material to supply plants with nutrients.

Tornado: A violently rotating, narrow column of air in contact with the ground and usually extending from a cumulonimbus cloud.

Total solar/lunar eclipse: An eclipse in which our view of the Sun/Moon is totally blocked.

Toxic: Poisonous.

Trace element: A chemical element present in minute quantities.

Trace minerals: Minerals needed in relatively small quantities.

Translucent: Permits the passage of light.

Transpiration: Evaporation of water in the form of water vapor from the stomata on the surfaces of leaves and stems of plants.

Troglobite: An animal that lives in a cave and is unable to live outside of one.

Troglophile: An animal that lives the majority of its life cycle in a cave but is also able to live outside of the cave.

Trogloxene: An animal that spends only part of its life cycle in a cave and returns periodically to the cave.

Tropism: The growth or movement of a plant toward or away from a stimulus.

Troposphere: The lowest layer of Earth's atmosphere, ranging to an altitude of about 9 miles (15 km) above Earth's surface.

Trough: The lowest point of a wave. (Pronounced trawf.)

Tsunami: A large wave of water caused by an underwater earthquake.

Tuber: An underground, starch-storing stem, such as a potato.

Tundra: A treeless, frozen biome with low-lying plants.

Turbine: A spinning device used to transform mechanical power from energy into electrical energy.

Turbulence: Air disturbance that affects an aircraft's flight.

Turgor pressure: The force that is exerted on a plant's cell wall by the water within the cell.

Tyndall effect: The effect achieved when colloidal particles reflect a beam of light, making it visible when shined through such a mixture.

U

Ultraviolet: Electromagnetic radiation (energy) of a wavelength just shorter than the violet (shortest wavelength) end of the visible light spectrum and thus with higher energy than the visible light.

Unconfined aquifer: An aquifer under a layer of permeable rock and soil.

Unicellular: Living things that have one cell. Protozoans are unicellular, for example.

Unit cell: The basic unit of the crystalline structure.

Universal law of gravity: The law of physics that defines the constancy of the force of gravity between two bodies.

Updraft: Warm, moist air that moves away from the ground.

Upwelling: The process by which lower-level, nutrient-rich waters rise upward to the ocean's surface.

V

Vacuole: An enclosed, space-filling sac within plant cells containing mostly water and providing structural support for the cell.

Van der Waals' force: An attractive force between two molecules based on the positive and negative side of the molecule.

Variable: Something that can affect the results of an experiment.

Vegetative propagation: A form of asexual reproduction in which plants are produced that are genetically identical to the parent.

Velocity: The rate at which the position of an object changes with time, including both the speed and the direction.

Veneer: Thin slices of wood.

Viable: The capability of developing or growing under favorable conditions.

Vibration: A regular, back-and-forth motion of molecules in the air.

Viscosity: The measure of a fluid's resistance to flow; its flowability.

Visible spectrum: The range of individual wavelengths of radiation visible to the human eye when white light is broken into its component colors as it passes through a prism or by some other means.

Vitamin: A complex organic compound found naturally in plants and animals that the body needs in small amounts for normal growth and activity.

Volatilization: The process by which a liquid changes (volatilizes) to a gas.

Volcano: A conical mountain or dome of lava, ash, and cinders that forms around a vent leading to molten rock deep within Earth.

Voltage: Also called potential difference; a measurement of the amount of electric energy stored in a mass of electric charges compared to the energy stored in some other mass of charges. The common unit of measure is the volt.

Voltmeter: An instrument for measuring the amperage, voltage, or resistance in an electrical circuit.

Volume: The amount of space occupied by a three-dimensional object; the amplitude or loudness of a sound.

Vortex: A rotating column of a fluid such as air or water.

Waste stream: The waste materials generated by the population of an area, or by a specific industrial process, and removed for disposal.

Water (hydrologic) cycle: The constant movement of water molecules on Earth as they rise into the atmosphere as water vapor, condense into droplets and fall to land or bodies of water, evaporate, and rise again.

Water clock: A device that uses the flow of water to measure time.

Water table: The level of the upper surface of groundwater.

Water vapor: Water in its gaseous state.

Water-soluble vitamins: Vitamins such as C and the B-complex vitamins that dissolve in the watery parts of plant and animal tissues.

Waterline: The highest point to which water rises on the hull of a ship. The portion of the hull below the waterline is under water.

Wave: A means of transmitting energy in which the peak energy occurs at a regular interval; the rise and fall of the ocean water.

Wavelength: The distance between the peak of a wave of light, heat, or other form of energy and the next corresponding peak.

Weather: The state of the troposphere at a particular time and place.

Weather forecasting: The scientific predictions of future weather patterns.

Weathered: Natural process that breaks down rocks and minerals at Earth's surface into simpler materials by physical (mechanical) or chemical means.

Wedge: A simple machine; a form of inclined plane.

Weight: The gravitational attraction of Earth on an object; the measure of the heaviness of an object.

Wet cell: A source of electricity that uses a liquid electrolyte.

Wetlands: Areas that are wet or covered with water for at least part of the year.

Wheel and axle: A simple machine; a larger wheel(s) fastened to a smaller cylinder, an axle, so that they turn together.

Work: The result of a force moving a mass a given distance. The greater the mass or the greater the distance, the greater the work involved.

Xanthophyll: Yellow pigment in plants.

Xerophytes: Plants that require little water to survive.

Xylem: Plant tissue consisting of elongated, thick-walled cells that transport water and mineral nutrients. (Pronounced ZY-lem.)

Yeast: A single-celled fungi that can be used to as a leavening agent.

Plant Anatomy

Plants come in all shapes and sizes, from floating water plants about the size of a pencil dot to trees towering hundreds of feet high. Travel to anywhere on Earth and you will spot some type of plant, even in the extreme cold and hot environments. All animals, from bugs to people, depend upon plants to live. They supply oxygen and food, both directly and indirectly.

There are an estimated 500,000 different types of plants with a wide variety of features. But in general, plants share a similar anatomy (structure).

At the root of it The root of a plant is an organ that plays many roles. In general, most plant roots lie underground. They anchor the plant, keeping it from being tossed into the air on gusty days. Roots are how most plants absorb water and nutrients. Nutrients in the soil dissolve in water. The root hairs, hundreds of fine hairs on the root, absorb the water through a process called osmosis. Osmosis is the movement of water from an area where there is a high concentration of water to an area of low water concentration through a cell membrane. The membrane encircles the cell and allows only some substances to pass into the cell.

Roots also take in oxygen. Although plants produce oxygen, they also need some oxygen to live in a process called respiration. Soil contains pockets of oxygen. In some plants, roots lie near the ground where there is a richer supply of oxygen. Trees that live in or near the mud, where there is little oxygen, sometimes have roots above ground to gather oxygen.

Plants that have their roots in the air are called epiphytes. Epiphytes often live on another

Roots are how most plants absorb water and nutrients.
ILLUSTRATION BY TEMAH NELSON.

Cacti store water in its stem and use it little by little in order to survive the dry conditions of the desert. FIELD MARK PUBLICATIONS.

plant, collecting water and nutrients from the runoff or rain. Epiphytes that live in humid environments can take in the water and nutrients from the air.

Some epiphytes have adapted to slow their growth when there is little water. Other plants have shallow roots that thread out extensively so they can quickly suck up water close to the surface.

Holding it all together Stems pick up where the root meets the ground, holding the plant up and supporting its structure. The larger the plant, the thicker the stem. Larger plants can also have multiple stems, with shoots branching off from one another. Stems can be soft and flexible, allowing the plant to bend. Other plants, such as trees, have stems that are hard and woody.

Water and nutrients absorbed from the roots move through the stem and up the plant through tube-like structures. The tubes that carry the water are called xylem. The xylem is made of dead cells and has thick walls. The tubes that carry the food are called phloem. The phloem is made of living cells and have thin walls.

Stems can also store water and food. Many cacti, for example, store water in its stem and use it little by little. In some plants, stems act as reproductive shoots. Potatoes grow from the underground parts of a stem, acting as food storage and reproductive organs.

Making food and oxygen The point at which the leaf joins the stem is called the node. The water and nutrients move from the root into the veins of the leaves. The substances move from the larger leaf veins to smaller offshoots in the leaf.

Leaves are where the plant produces its food in a process called photosynthesis. To make its food or energy, plants need water, carbon dioxide (a gas in the air), and energy from the sun. The same compound in plants that supplies its green color, chlorophyll, is also responsible for collecting the sun's energy.

The products of photosynthesis results in sugars and oxygen. The sugars are what the plant uses for food and the oxygen is released into the air. In photosynthesis, plants take in more carbon dioxide and release more oxygen than the amount of oxygen they need in respiration. That means plants end up producing more oxygen than they consume.

A leaf's surface has microscopic openings called stomata, named after the Greek word for mouth. The stomata open and close regularly to exchange gases, such as oxygen and carbon dioxide. The plant will also lose its water in the form of water vapor when the stomata are open. In plants, this loss of water is called transpiration. For most plants transpiration occurs primarily on the leaves. Water can also escape from leaves in the form of liquid. When a plant takes in too much water, the water can escape through pores in the leaves.

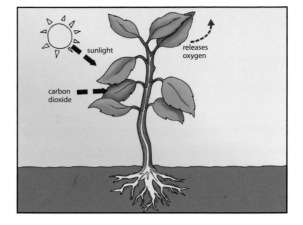

To make its food or energy, plants need water, carbon dioxide (a gas in the air), and energy from the sun.
ILLUSTRATION BY TEMAH NELSON.

All shapes and sizes The structure and type of leaf depends upon the plant's environment. Cacti are found in deserts, which are extremely dry. Leaves of a cactus are few and small to keep it from losing water. Shaped like sharp needles, the leaves also keep hungry or thirsty animals away.

Where a leaf sits on the stem helps determine how much sunlight it will get. In some plants the leaves spiral up a stem and in others they sit on opposite sides of the stem. Another leaf arrangement, called the whorl, is when several leaves shoot out from the same point.

Because capturing the sun's energy is essential for a plant's survival, plants living in low sunlight areas have made several adaptations. These can be plants that live low to the ground or deep inside a lush forest. In some plants, the stalks of the lower leaves reach longer than the ones

Where a leaf sits on the stem helps determine how much sunlight it will get.
ILLUSTRATION BY TEMAH NELSON.

above it. This is one reason why there are many cone-shaped plants, such as pine trees. Some leaves on upper parts have holes or notches that allow the sunlight to shine through. Leaves can arrange themselves into mosaics, such as an ivy-covered wall or leaves growing around trees. In these leaf patterns the arrangement allows each leaf to be exposed to the sun. There are other plants that have adapted to the shade by growing wide, large leaves.

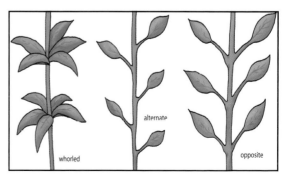

WORDS TO KNOW

Anatomy: The study of the structure of living things.

Chlorophyll: A green pigment found in plants that absorbs sunlight, providing the energy used in photosynthesis.

Control experiment: A setup that is identical to the experiment, but is not affected by the variable that acts on the experimental group.

Hypothesis: An idea in the form of a statement that can be tested by observation and/or experiment.

Osmosis: The movement of fluids and substances dissolved in liquids across a semi-permeable membrane from an area of greater concentration to an area of lesser concentration until all substances involved reach a balance.

Photosynthesis: Chemical process by which plants containing chlorophyll use sunlight to manufacture their own food by converting carbon dioxide and water into carbohydrates, releasing oxygen as a by-product.

Phloem: The plant tissue that carries dissolved nutrients through the plant.

Respiration: The process of an organism using oxygen for its life processes.

Root hairs: Fine, hair-like extensions from the plant's root.

Stomata: Pores in the epidermis (surface) of leaves.

Transpiration: Evaporation of water in the form of water vapor from the stomata on the surfaces of leaves and stems of plants.

Variable: Something that can affect the results of an experiment.

Xylem: Plant tissue consisting of elongated, thick-walled cells that transport water and mineral nutrients. (Pronounced ZY-lem.)

EXPERIMENT 1

Plant Hormones: What is the affect of hormones on root and stem growth?

Purpose/Hypothesis Gibberellic acid is a group of growth hormones that are produced naturally in plants. Gibberellic acid plays a role in how plants develop and grow. In this experiment, you will test the affect of giving plants Gibberellic acid at different points of its life cycle to evaluate how the hormone affects the root and stem growth. You will apply Gibberellic acid during the seed stage for one experimental set-up and shortly after the plant has sprouted for the second set-up. By measuring the stem length and comparing root growth, you will be able to see how the hormone has affected development.

Because Gibberellic acid is dissolved is in a water solution, this experiment will also help you observe how plants take in essential nutrients through water.

Before you begin, make an educated guess about the outcome of this experiment based on your knowledge of plant growth and hormones. This educated guess, or prediction, is your hypothesis. A hypothesis should explain these things:

- the topic of the experiment
- the variable you will change
- the variable you will measure
- what you expect to happen

A hypothesis should be brief, specific, and measurable. It must be something you can test through further investigation. Your experiment will prove or disprove whether your hypothesis is correct. Here is one possible hypothesis for this experiment: "Plants that receive hormones at the youngest stage, as a seed, will show more stem and root growth than the other plants."

In this case, the variable you will change is the stage in the growth cycle that Gibberellic acid is given to the plant. The variable you will measure is the plant stem and root growth.

Conducting a control experiment will help you isolate each variable and measure the changes in the dependent variable. Only one variable will change between the control and the experimental plants, and that is the Gibberellic acid. For the control, you will not apply any Gibberellic acid to the plant. At the end of the experiment you will compare this group of plants to the others.

Level of Difficulty Moderate, due to the time involved.

Materials Needed

- 1 packages of seeds: radishes, peas, and geraniums work well
- 1 peat pellet or similar type starter pot, with a cover (available at gardening stores); or 3 small pots with potting soil
- Gibberellic acid (available at some gardening stores or science supply stores)
- fingernail polish remover (with acetone)
- 2 plastic bottles
- distilled water

What Are the Variables?

Variables are anything that might affect the results of an experiment. Here are the main variables in this experiment:

- environmental temperature
- time given for experiment
- type of plant
- how the growth hormone is applied
- soil nutrient content

In other words, the variables in this experiment are everything that might affect the growth of the plant. If you change more than one variable at the same time, you will not be able to tell which variable impacted the plant's root and stem growth.

How to Experiment Safely

There are no safety hazards in this experiment. Wash your hands and clean up your work area after you have planted the seeds.

- ruler
- 2 stirring spoons
- measuring cup

Approximate Budget $15.

Timetable 20 minutes preparation time; five minutes daily for approximately six weeks.

Step-by-Step Instructions

1. Mark one pot "Group 1;" the second pot "Group 2;" and the third pot "Control."

2. Tear two small pieces of wax paper and place a large pinch of Gibberellic acid (GA) on each sheet. Try to have the same amount of GA on each sheet. If you have a sensitive gram scale you can weigh the sheets to make sure they are equal. Pour one pinch of GA in one bottle and the second pinch of GA in the second bottle. Add two to four drops of fingernail polish to each bottle and swirl until the Gibberellic acid is dissolved.

3. Add a cup of distilled water to the first bottle and mix with a spoon. This is the GA solution you will use to water Group 1.

4. Add a cup of distilled water to the second bottle and set aside. This is the GA solution you will use to water Group 2.

5. Plant the seeds as directed. You should plant at least two seeds in each Group and in the Control group.

6. Water Group 1 as directed using the mixed GA solution. Water Group 2 and the Control seeds with plain water.

7. Cover (if you have one) and set aside in a warm environment. Continue watering the seeds as needed. Use the GA solution for Group 1 until all the water is used and then use only water.

Step 2: Add two to four drops of fingernail polish to each bottle and swirl until the Gibberellic acid is dissolved. ILLUSTRATION BY TEMAH NELSON.

8. When the seeds germinate, use a ruler to measure the growth. You may want to sketch the growth.

9. When Group 2 has grown approximately 0.79 in (2 centimeters), mix the second bottle of GA solution with a spoon and begin watering these young plants with the GA water. Continue watering Group 2 with its GA solution until the solution is gone and then switch back to plain water.

10. Check on the plants every day and water when needed. After approximately five to six weeks measure stem and root growth.

11. To measure stem growth: Use a ruler to compare the height of each stem and make a note.

12. To measure root growth: Carefully, lift the Group 1 plants out of the pots and immerse in a container of warm water. Allow the plants to soak for 15 minutes and gently rub the soil off the roots. Set these plants aside and mark them as Group 1. Repeat this same process for the Group 2 and Control plants.

13. Use a ruler to measure the longest roots for each of the plants. You may want to draw the root growth.

14. When you have finished with your analysis and experiment, you can replant the plants and continue growing them.

Step 9: Mix the second bottle of GA solution with a spoon and begin watering these plants with the GA water. ILLUSTRATION BY TEMAH NELSON.

Step 13: Use a ruler to measure the longest roots for each of the plants. ILLUSTRATION BY TEMAH NELSON.

Summary of Results If you had two plants grow in each group, average the stem height for the group. Look at how the two experimental plants compare to the Control plants. If you have made sketches or drawings during the experiment, compare how each of the groups compares to the control during the experiment. You may want to create a graph to record the germination and height of each group. Did the seeds given Gibberellic acid show more or less growth than the young plants? If you want to continue following the plant's growth, you can measure

Troubleshooter's Guide

Below are some problems that may arise during this experiment, some possible causes, and some ways to remedy the problem.

Problem: All the plants grew about the same and at the same rate.

Possible cause: The Gibberellic acid may not have been dissolved in the water. Gibberellic acid does not dissolve in water but it does dissolve in acetone (fingernail polish remover) or alcohol. Make sure the nail polish remover you used contains acetone. If it does not, you can use several drops of rubbing alcohol and mix it thoroughly with the GA.

Problem: None of the seeds sprouted.

Possible cause: There can be several reasons why your plants did not grow. Check to make sure you are using nutrient-rich soil and make sure you did not over water them. You may want to ask the advice of a friend or adult who grows plants. If none of the seeds germinated the seeds may all have been unhealthy. Purchase another bag of seeds and repeat the experiment.

flowering and leaf growth. You may need to transfer the young plants to a larger pot.

Change the Variables One variable you can change is the type of plant. Not all plants respond the same way to Gibberellic acid. Choose plants that flower, for example, and measure how the growth hormone affects flowering? You could also change the concentration of Gibberellic acid, using both more and less concentrated GA solutions. Another variable you could change is how the growth hormone is applied. In this experiment you added it to the soil. What would happen if you sprayed the water on the leaves?

EXPERIMENT 2
Water Uptake: How do different plants differ in their water needs?

Purpose/Hypothesis The amount of water plants need to live depends upon the type of plant. Different plants take in different amount of water at various times. Some plants need a constant supply of water and cannot survive in extremely dry soil. Other plants take in their water in spurts, drying out before they need more water.

In this experiment, you will be measuring how different plants take in water through its roots. You will use a form of potometer, which can measure the rate of water uptake. The main reason for water uptake by a plant is transpiration. You will test young plants with different size leaves: One has broader, larger leaves relative to the other plant, which has small little leaves. When testing different plants, you will need to try and keep the plants as similar as possible, in both size and leaves.

To begin this experiment, use what you know about plant anatomy to make an educated guess about how the different plants will take up water. This educated guess, or prediction, is your hypothesis. A hypothesis should explain these things:

- the topic of the experiment
- the variable you will change

- the variable you will measure
- what you expect to happen

A hypothesis should be brief, specific, and measurable. It must be something you can test through observation. Your experiment will prove or disprove whether your hypothesis is correct. Here is one possible hypothesis for this experiment: "The plant with the broadest and largest leaves will take up the most water."

In this case, the variable you will change is the type of plant, and the variable you will measure is the amount of water taken up by the plant, during the day and night, over several days.

Level of Difficulty Moderate to Difficult. (This experiment takes patience and an attention to detail.)

Materials Needed

- 2 clamps (available at hardware stores)
- pothos seeds (also called devil's ivy; you can try other plants with large, broad leaves)
- sweat pea seeds (you can also try other plants with small leaves)
- 1, 10-section peat pellet or similar type starter pot with a cover (available at gardening stores); you can replace this with 2 to 3 cups of potting soil and an egg carton
- ring stand (available at science supplies stores; a vertical wooden paper towel holder also works well.)
- plastic tubing with a 1/4-inch diameter opening, about 3 feet (available at hardware stores)
- scissors
- 1 ml. plastic pipette, 1/4-inch diameter (available from science supply stores)
- Vaseline (petroleum jelly)
- plastic wrap
- small bowl
- knife or scissors
- toothpicks
- copper wire, chopsticks, or other thin long item

What Are the Variables?

Variables are anything that might affect the results of an experiment. Here are the main variables in this experiment:

- the type of plant
- the amount of plant used
- the amount of sun or temperature
- the amount of time before water uptake is measured
- the humidity
- the amount of wind

In other words, the variables in this experiment are everything that might affect the water uptake of the plants. If you change more than one variable, you will not be able to tell which variable most affected the plants' need for water.

How to Experiment Safely

Be careful when cutting the tubing with the scissors. Have an adult help you cut the plastic pipette with a knife or scissors

Approximate Budget $20.

Timetable Approximately two hours working time; total time three to four weeks. Note: this experiment asks for measurements in 12-hour increments. Try to begin the experiment in the morning or evening.

Step-by-Step Instructions

1. Follow the direction for the peat pellet or add soil to the sections in the egg carton and plant several seeds of both plants.

2. Continue caring for the plant according to the instructions until at least one of each type of plant is approximately 2 to 3 inches (5–8 centimeters) tall. (The second experimental plant will have three more days to grow so it can be a slightly smaller than the first experimental plant.)

3. Fill a small bowl with warm water. Gently, lift the section of soil holding one of the plants and set it in the bowl. Use your fingers to carefully remove the dirt, making sure not to harm the roots.

4. Attach both clamps to the ring stand, one towards the top and one in the middle.

5. Cut the plastic pipette about half an inch from the bottom to widen it. You made need to have an adult use a knife.

6. Place the pipette into the plastic tube. It should fit snugly and not move around.

7. Attach the pipette to the middle clamp and the plastic tube to the top clamp. The plastic tube should go to about the top of the ring stand. Cut off any extra tubing.

8. Fill the tube with water until water moves up to the 1ml. mark on the pipette.

9. Carefully set the plant's roots into the tube. You may need a toothpick or other small object to poke down the roots.

10. To seal the plant from the air, tape plastic wrap around the opening between the roots and tube. Spread petroleum jelly

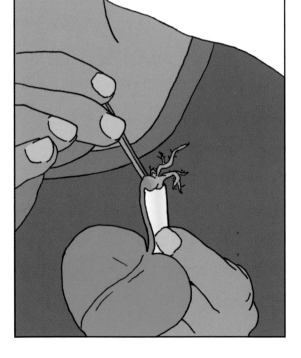

Step 9: Carefully set the plant's roots into the tube. ILLUSTRATION BY TEMAH NELSON.

on any openings between the plant and the plastic wrap.

11. Make sure the water mark is at the 1 ml. mark and there are no bubbles. You may need to add more water if any spilled. Use a long, thin utensil or wire to poke in the water and pop any bubbles.

12. Set a small plastic cup or deep bottle cap on the end of the open end of the pipette.

13. Note the time and water level on a chart.

14. In 12-hour increments, note the water level over the next two to three days.

15. Repeat Steps 8–14 for the second type of plant. Try to match the number of leaves and height of the first plant.

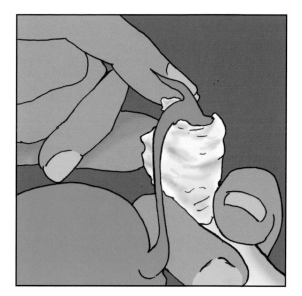

Step 10: Tape plastic wrap around the opening between the roots and tube. ILLUSTRATION BY TEMAH NELSON.

Step 14: In 12 hour increments, note the water level over the next 2 to 3 days. ILLUSTRATION BY TEMAH NELSON.

Summary of Results Graph the water uptake for each of the plants, broken into the 12-hour periods of day and night. Did the plant with the larger leaf need more water? Was there a pattern to when either plant took in water? Summarize your results in writing.

Change the Variables There are many ways you can vary this experiment. Once you have the setup for the potometer, you can examine how environmental conditions affect water uptake and loss. You can use a fan for wind, or test humidity. How does the amount of indoor light or Sun affect different plants?

Design Your Own Experiment

How to Select a Topic Relating to this Concept There are many aspects of plant anatomy you can further explore, either as a project or as an experiment. Look around at what plants are growing in your local area. Consider how plants growing near streets and human activity differ from the plants growing in more remote

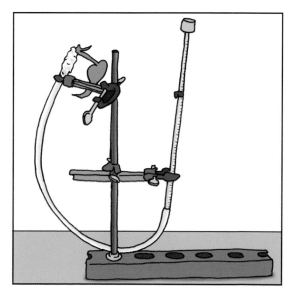

Troubleshooter's Guide

Here is a problem that may arise in this experiment, a possible cause, and a way to remedy it.

Problem: The water was almost used up.

Possible cause: The seal that locked the plant stem into the tube may not have been tight, which would have allowed water to evaporate into the air. Try the experiment again, making sure to use enough plastic wrap and Vaseline.

Problem: The two tests were extremely different.

Possible cause: There may have been bubbles in the liquids. Bubbles are air that take the place of the water. Repeat the experiment, looking carefully for bubbles as you fill the tubing and making sure to pop all bubbles.

areas. As you observe the different types of plants, examine the properties of the leaves and stems.

Check the Further Readings section for this topic, and talk with a teacher or gardener to help you formulate a topic. You might want to visit a local greenhouse (nursery) to see a wide variety of plants.

Steps in the Scientific Method To do an original experiment, you need to plan carefully and think things through. Otherwise, you might not be sure what question you're answering, what you are or should be measuring, or what your findings prove or disprove.

Here are the steps in designing an experiment:

- State the purpose of—and the underlying question behind—the experiment you propose to do.
- Recognize the variables involved, and select one that will help you answer the question at hand.
- State a testable hypothesis, an educated guess about the answer to your question.
- Decide how to change the variable you selected.
- Decide how to measure your results.

Recording Data and Summarizing the Results Your data should include charts and graphs such as the one you did for these experiments. They should be clearly labeled and easy to read. You may also want to include photographs and drawings of your experimental setup and results, which will help other people visualize the steps in the experiment.

If you are preparing an exhibit, you may want to display your results, such as any experimental setup you designed. If you have completed a nonexperimental project, explain clearly what your research question was and illustrate your findings.

Related Projects Plant anatomy is a broad topic. You can take advantage of the many species of plants to conduct an experiment that highlights one aspect of the anatomy. You could compare the characteristics and behavior of a desert plant, such as a cactus, with a water plant. You could study the adaptations of the leaves and roots of different plant species. You could also investigate in more detail how water transpires from leaves by examining a plant under a microscope.

Another related project could focus on how water allows a plant to acquire its essential nutrients. Plants will usually get their nutrients from the soil, once the nutrients dissolve in water and are pulled into the plant. Some plants do not need soil to get their nutrients. Hydroponics is the technique of growing plants in water that contains dissolved nutrients. A hydroponics experiment could vary the nutrients in the water or the plants.

For More Information

Andrew Rader Studios. "Plant Basics." *Rader's Biology4kids.com.* http://www.biology4kids.com/files/plants_main.html (accessed on April 9, 2008). Information on plant biology and structures.

Black, David, and Anthony Huxley. *Plants.* New York: Facts on File, 1985. Readable scientific introduction to plants.

Bruce, Anne. "Water movement through a plant." *Microscopy–UK.* http://www.microscopy-uk.org.uk/mag/artmar00/watermvt.html (accessed on April 9, 2008). Explains how water moves through plants; includes informative pictures.

Missouri Botanical Garden. *Biology of Plants.* http://www.mbgnet.net/bioplants (accessed on April 9, 2008). Basic information about plant biology and life.

PlantingScience. http://www.plantingscience.org (accessed on April 9, 2008). Examples of student research projects, images, and resources to collect plant information.

Suzuki, David and Kathy Vanderlinden. *Eco-Fun.* Vancouver: BC: Greystone Books, 2001. Project and experiments related to plants and the environment.

Taylor, Barbara. *Inside Guides: Incredible Plants.* New York: DK Publishing, 1997. Large illustrations and clear information on the parts of a plant.

Plants and Water

Water enters a plant through the plant's root hairs. The root hairs absorb the water through a process called osmosis.
COPYRIGHT © KELLY
A. QUIN.

Plants are a diverse group of organisms that include over 250,000 species. They live in a range of environmental conditions, from mountaintops to the ocean floor. They can claim the world's largest organism, a redwood tree that can stretch to a height of 364 feet (110 meters), and the world's oldest organism, the 4,700-year-old bristlecone pine tree.

Without plants, life on Earth as it is now could not exist. Plants make their own food by photosynthesis, a process that uses the energy of the Sun to make sugar and oxygen. Humans and other organisms use the oxygen released by photosynthesis to survive. Plants are also used for food, shelter, and protection by organisms in every known environment.

Plants depend on water for several essential functions. Water is needed for photosynthesis and to help transport nutrients through a plant's system. Most growing plants contain about 90% water. This water maintains the plant's internal temperature and provides it structure. Without water or with too much water, a plant dies. How plants take in water and what they do with it is essential for their survival.

Rooting water flow Water enters a plant through the plant's root hairs, hundreds of fine hairs that extend out from the root. These hairs suck in the water that lies between the soil particles. Most of the nutrients that a plant needs are dissolved in this water. The root hairs absorb the water through a process called osmosis. Osmosis is the movement of water from an area where there is a high concentration of water to an area of low water concentration through the cell membrane, the layer that encircles and holds the parts of a cell together. The cell's membrane is semipermeable, meaning it allows some things to pass through the membrane and prevents others from passing.

Once inside the root hair, the plant uses osmosis to move the water into the xylem (pronounced ZY-lem). The xylem are long tubes or vessels made up of bundles of dead cells with tough cell walls. Xylem vessels transport water to all parts of the plant, from the root to the leaves. Water in the xylem is mainly drawn upwards through osmosis because there is a continual need for water in the outer leaves of a plant. Water in leaves is constantly evaporating or turning into water vapor. Water vapor is water in its gas state. The low concentration of water in the leaves pulls the water upwards.

In plants, this loss of water is called transpiration. For most plants transpiration occurs primarily on the leaves. A leaf's surface has tiny pores called stomata that open and close regularly to exchange gases, such as oxygen and carbon dioxide. When stomata are open, the plant loses water or transpires.

Like evaporation, transpiration occurs more rapidly in hot, dry weather. In most plants there are more stomata located on the underside of the leaves. This ensures the plant will not lose too much water since it is transpiring on the side facing away from the sun. Some plants have tiny hairs that protect them from transpiring too much. Other plants are protected from excess water loss by a waxy film covering the outer layer of the leaves. Desert plants have thorns in place of leaves to avoid losing too much water.

Standing up straight Aside from providing a plant's basic food and water requirements, water maintains a plant cell's structure and shape. The visible sign that a plant has taken in enough water is when it stands up straight and shows no sign of limpness.

In a plant cell the membrane is surrounded by a rigid cell wall. Inside the cell wall in the center of the plant cell there is a large, liquid compartment called a vacuole (pronounced VAK-yoo-ole). Vacuoles transport and store nutrients, waste products, and other molecules. A vacuole is also the area in the cell

Osmosis is the movement of water through the cell membrane from an area of high water concentration to an area of low water concentration. GALE GROUP.

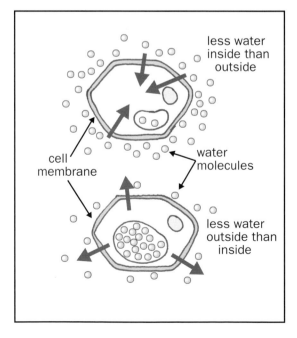

less water inside than outside

cell membrane

water molecules

less water outside than inside

where water collects. When water enters the vacuole, it causes pressure to build inside the cell. The pressure of the vacuole pushing outwards on the cells is called turgor pressure. The strong cell walls keep the buildup of water from bursting the cell, which results in increased pressure.

Turgor pressure of all the neighboring cells is what allows a plant to stand upright. If a plant does not have enough water in its cells there is nothing pressing against the cell walls. This phenomenon causes plasmolysis, meaning when a cell has lost its water, and wilting results. Plasmolysis frequently occurs in plants left in hot sunny windows and not given enough water. As long as the cells are still living the turgor pressure can be increased. Watering the plant will cause the cells to take in water and the vacuoles again press against the wall to straighten the plant.

Turgor pressure also impacts transpiration as it affects whether the stomata (singular: stoma) open. A stoma is surrounded by two guard cells. When water enters these surrounding cells, the turgor pressure causes them to swell and creates an opening between them, which is the stoma. When the turgor pressure decreases, the cells relax and the stomata close.

Adapting to dry environments In places where water is a rare resource, such as deserts, plants have had to adapt to survive in the dry, hot environment. These plants usually have special methods of storing and conserving water. The desert cacti, for example, have few or no leaves, which reduces transpiration. Some desert plants have deep roots to pull up water deep in the sand. Other plants have shallow roots that thread out extensively so they can quickly suck up water close to the surface.

Desert plants can store water in their stems, leaves, or thick roots. For example, the old man cactus has a layer of hair that helps it to store water. This hair can also keep it from losing water by lessening the drying effects of the wind.

Some desert plants are dormant, not active, during dry periods, and then spring to life when

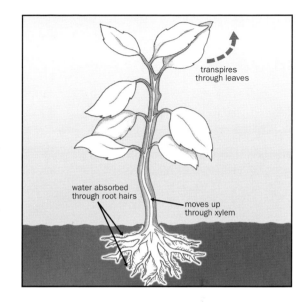

The plant uses osmosis to move the water into the xylem. Xylem vessels transport water to all parts of the plant, from the roots to the leaves. GALE GROUP.

Turgor pressure is what allows a plant to stand upright. GALE GROUP.

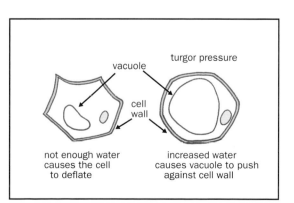

A wilting plant is a sure sign of plasmolysis, meaning the plant is in need of water. COPYRIGHT © KELLY A. QUIN.

Turgor pressure causes guard cells to open the stoma, causing transpiration to occur. GALE GROUP.

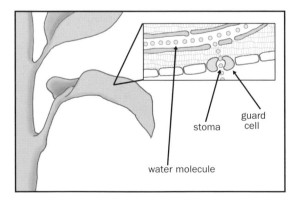

water molecule

stoma

guard cell

it rains. To avoid the heat of the Sun, many plants move into action during the night hours. For example, the Sonoran Desert's saguaro only opens its white flowers at night.

Some desert plants have adapted by having smaller or no leaves. On others leaves will have a thick covering that is coated with a waxy substance to reduce water loss. Hair on the leaves of plants helps to reduce the evaporation of moisture from the surface of leaves by reflecting sunlight.

EXPERIMENT 1

Water Flow: How do varying solutions of water affect the amount of water a plant takes in and its turgor pressure?

Purpose/Hypothesis To maintain a stable environment, plants move water in and out of their cells until the concentration of water molecules is equal on both sides of the cell membrane. Osmosis causes the water to flow from a region of high concentration to a region of low concentration. As the plant cells takes in more water, the turgor pressure increases; when the plant cells take in less water, the turgor pressure decreases.

Changing the concentration of the particles, or solutes, dissolved in water will change the amount of water present. Adding salt to water, for example, makes the water have a high concentration of solutes, which is called a hypertonic solution. A low-solute concentration is called a hypotonic solution. In osmosis, cells will try to equalize the concentration of the solute molecules. A cell placed in a hypotonic solution will draw water into its cells to equalize the solute molecules. A cell in a hypertonic solution will move water out of the cell to make the solutes more equal.

In this experiment, you will examine the movement of water in a plant. This experiment will investigate how varying concentrations of salt water affect the amount of water that enters or leaves a plant's cells. You will place a flower in three colored-water solutions, two of which contain different concentrations of salt. You will

900

WORDS TO KNOW

Cell membrane: The layer that surrounds the cell, but is inside the cell wall, allowing some molecules to enter and keeping others out of the cell.

Cell wall: A tough outer covering over the cell membrane of bacteria and plant cells.

Dormant: A state of inactivity in an organism.

Control experiment: A setup that is identical to the experiment, but is not affected by the variable that acts on the experimental group.

Hypothesis: An idea in the form of a statement that can be tested by observation and/or experiment.

Osmosis: The movement of fluids and substances dissolved in liquids across a semi-permeable membrane from an area of greater concentration to an area of lesser concentration until all substances involved reach a balance.

Photosynthesis: Chemical process by which plants containing chlorophyll use sunlight to manufacture their own food by converting carbon dioxide and water into carbohydrates, releasing oxygen as a by-product.

Plasmolysis: Occurs in walled cells in which cytoplasm, the semifluid substance inside a cell, shrivels and the membrane pulls away from the cell wall when the vacuole loses water.

Root hairs: Fine, hairlike extensions from the plant's root.

Stomata: Pores in the epidermis (surface) of leaves.

Transpiration: Evaporation of water in the form of water vapor from the stomata on the surfaces of leaves and stems of plants.

Turgor pressure: The force that is exerted on a plant's cell wall by the water within the cell.

Vacuole: An enclosed, space-filling sac within plant cells containing mostly water and providing structural support for the cell.

Variable: Something that can affect the results of an experiment.

Xylem: Plant tissue consisting of elongated, thick-walled cells that transport water and mineral nutrients. (Pronounced ZY-lem.)

measure the movement of water in three ways: observing the plant's turgor pressure, observing the water movement in the plant, and weighing the flowers before and after they are placed in the water.

Before you begin, make an educated guess about the outcome of this experiment based on your knowledge of plant cells and turgor pressure. This educated guess, or prediction, is your hypothesis. A hypothesis should explain these things:

- the topic of the experiment
- the variable you will change
- the variable you will measure
- what you expect to happen

What Are the Variables?

Variables are anything that might affect the results of an experiment. Here are the main variables in this experiment:

- the amount of salt
- the type of plant
- the water
- time of experiment
- environmental conditions

In other words, the variables in this experiment are everything that might affect the amount of water the plant draws in or out of its cells. If you change more than one variable, you will not be able to tell which variable impacted the water uptake.

A hypothesis should be brief, specific, and measurable. It must be something you can test through further investigation. Your experiment will prove or disprove whether your hypothesis is correct. Here is one possible hypothesis for this experiment: "Water with a low concentration of salt will flow into a plant's cells and cause an increase in turgor pressure and weight; water with a high concentration of salt will flow out of a plant's cells and cause a decrease in turgor pressure and weight."

In this case, the variable you will change is the amount of salt in the water. The variable you will measure is how much water the plant has drawn into its cells.

Conducting a control experiment will help you isolate each variable and measure the changes in the dependent variable. Only one variable will change between the control and the experimental plants, and that is the amount of salt. For the control, you will place the flower in plain water. At the end of the experiment you will compare this plant with each of the others.

Note: When making a solid-liquid solution (solid/liquid), it is standard to use weight/weight (grams/grams) or weight/volume (grams/milliliters). With water, 1 gram of water equals 1 milliliter. In this experiment, teaspoons and tablespoons are used to measure the solid.

Step 9: Leave the flowers undisturbed eight to twelve hours. GALE GROUP.

Level of Difficulty Easy to Moderate.

Materials Needed

- 4 clear plastic cups
- 3 white carnation flowers
- blue food coloring, concentrated
- salt
- measuring spoons
- scale
- sharp knife or plant shears
- marking pen

Approximate Budget $7.

Timetable 45 minutes for setup and followup; 8 to 12 hours waiting.

Step-by-Step Instructions

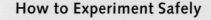

How to Experiment Safely

Handle the knife or scissors carefully when cutting the stems.

1. Make a 40% weight/weight (gram/gram) solution of salt water. One gram of water equals 1 milliliter of water. Add 7 tablespoons (96 grams) of salt to 1 cup (240 milliliters or 240 grams) of warm water. If you have a gram scale you can measure 40 grams of salt and add that with 100 grams of warm water. Add the salt slowly and stir after each addition. The salt should be completely dissolved in the water. Label the cup "40%."

2. To make a 20% solution of salt water, add 3.5 tablespoons (46 grams) of salt to 1 cup (240 milliliters or 240 grams) of warm water. If you have a gram scale you can measure 20 grams of salt and add that to 100 grams of water. Label the cup "20%."

3. Allow the water to cool to room temperature.

4. Fill up a cup with plain water. Label the cup "Control."

5. Stir several drops of blue dye into each cup for a strong blue color.

6. Carefully cut each carnation's stem under cool running water.

7. Dry off the stems and weigh each flower.

8. Place one carnation in each of the cups of water.

9. Leave the flowers undisturbed 8 to 12 hours.

10. In a chart, describe the turgor pressure of each flower relative to the 20 percent salt concentration. Weigh each flower and note in the chart. Examine the blue water's movement and note whether the water has entered each flower.

Step 10: Data chart for Experiment 1. GALE GROUP.

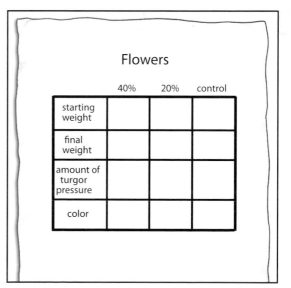

Summary of Results Examine the chart. Has the water entered some flower or flowers more than others? If the blue water is not visible in the white flower of the carnation, you may want to carefully cut the bottom part of the stem to see if the water has entered the flower. Observe the stem's bottom of each flower and the petals of

Troubleshooter's Guide

Below are some problems that may arise during this experiment, some possible causes, and some ways to remedy the problem.

Problem: The water did not go move at all or barely moved into any of the carnations.

Possible cause: You may have started out with a flower that was dead. Purchase another flower and repeat the experiment.

Possible cause: You may have crushed the stem when you cut it. Try the experiment again, making sure to cut the stem under cool water. Cutting under water prevents the flowers from taking in air instead of water.

Problem: The flower was heavier and the turgor pressure increased but water did not go appear to enter the plant.

Possible cause: The water may have moved into the plant but you were not able to see it because the color was not strong enough. Make sure you are using a nonsweetened concentrated dye. Blue ink works well also. Repeat the experiment, making sure the water is a rich blue color.

the carnations. Look at the before and after weights of each flower. How do the test flowers compare to the control flowers? In any flower that took up the water, describe how the water entered the petals. Write a paragraph describing your results and explanations of what occurred.

Change the Variables You can vary this experiment several ways:

- Change the type of flower or plant you use. Celery stalks, with leaves, and white-colored flowers with large stems work well.

- Alter the solute you put in the water to another substance, such as sugar.

- Decrease or increase the amount of time the plant is sitting in the solution.

- Change the environmental conditions of the plant by placing one flower under a heat lamp or out in the sun, and another in a cool, dark place.

EXPERIMENT 2

Transpiration: How do different environmental conditions affect plants' rates of transpiration?

Purpose/Hypothesis All plants transpire. The rate of transpiration depends on a plant's physical properties and its environmental conditions. As transpiration occurs mainly on the leaf, a general rule is that plants with larger leaves will transpire more than plants with smaller leaves.

In this experiment, you will examine the environmental factors that affect a plant's transpiration rate. Using the same type and size plants, you will vary the amount of heat and wind each plant receives. You will place one plant in a warm environment, a second plant in a windy environment, and a third plant in a cool, calm environment.

Before you begin, make an educated guess about the outcome of this experiment based on your knowledge of plants and transpiration. This educated guess, or prediction, is your hypothesis. A hypothesis should explain these things:

- the topic of the experiment
- the variable you will change
- the variable you will measure
- what you expect to happen

A hypothesis should be brief, specific, and measurable. It must be something you can test through further investigation. Your experiment will prove or disprove whether your hypothesis is correct. Here is one possible hypothesis for this experiment: "Plants that receive more heat and wind will transpire at a greater rate than plants in a cool, calm environment."

In this case, the variable you will change is the environment of the plant. The variable you will measure is the amount of water the plant transpires.

Conducting a control experiment will help you isolate each variable and measure the changes in the dependent variable. Only one variable will change between the control and the experimental plants, and that is the change to its environment. For the control, you will place the plant in a standard indoor environment. At the end of the experiment you will compare this plant with each of the others.

What Are the Variables?

Variables are anything that might affect the results of an experiment. Here are the main variables in this experiment:

- environmental conditions, temperature and wind
- time given for experiment
- type of plant
- leaf size
- leaf shape
- soil content

In other words, the variables in this experiment are everything that might affect the amount of water that the plant transpires. If you change more than one variable at the same time, you will not be able to tell which variable impacted the plant's rate of transpiration.

Level of Difficulty Moderate.

Materials Needed

- four potted plants with large leaves; make sure the leaves are not waxy or hairy: geraniums, caladiums, coleus, and philodendrons work well
- four plastic sandwich bags
- wire ties
- small fan
- four small dry sponges
- scale

Approximate Budget $15.

How to Experiment Safely

This experiment poses no safety hazards. For the plants' health, when you have completed the experiment remove the plastic sandwich bags and care for the plant as directed.

Timetable 1 hour preparation time; 24 hours waiting.

Step-by-Step Instructions

1. Assign each plant a number. On each plant, place a sandwich bag over a group of three to four leaves. Choose leaves that are of equal dimensions.
2. Fasten each bag securely on the stem with a wire tie.
3. Place one plant in the direct sunlight or under a heat lamp. Place one plant in a dark, covered area. Place the third plant in front of the fan and turn the fan on low. Leave the control plant indoors and set it aside.
4. After 24 hours note the results of any water in the bags.
5. Weigh a dry sponge and record the weight.
6. Carefully, soak up all the water in the bag with the sponge. Reweigh the sponge and record the weight.
7. Repeat Steps 5 and 6 for every plant, using a new sponge each time.

Summary of Results Create a data table to record your observations. Subtract the weight of the dry sponge from the final weight of the wet

Step 3: Place each plant in a different environmental condition. GALE GROUP.

sponge to calculate the weight of the water each plant transpired. Was your hypothesis correct? For additional information, you could determine the area of each of the leaves and calculate the rate of transpiration for the entire plant. Hypothesize what adaptations outside plants could make to transpire less, compared to the characteristics of indoor plants.

Change the Variables There are several ways that you can change this experiment. One variable you can change is the type of plant. Choose another plant with a broader leaf. With a larger bag, you can also conduct the transpiration experiment on trees. You can lengthen the amount of time the plants transpire. You can also alter the environmental conditions, such as producing a humid environment or a dry environment.

Design Your Own Experiment

How to Select a Topic Relating to this Concept
You come into contact with plants every day through your diet and environment. Observe the plants that are around you as you prepare to design an experiment. You could also visit a greenhouse and examine the different species of plants available.

Check the Further Readings section and talk with your science teacher to learn more about plants and water. You could also talk with a botanist in your area or a professional who works with plants.

Steps in the Scientific Method To conduct an original experiment, you need to plan carefully and think things through. Otherwise, you might not be sure what question you are answering, what you are or should be measuring, or what your findings prove or disprove.

Here are the steps in designing an experiment:

- State the purpose of—and the underlying question behind—the experiment you propose to do.
- Recognize the variables involved and select one that will help you answer the question at hand.

Troubleshooter's Guide

Below are some problems that may arise during this experiment, some possible causes, and some ways to remedy the problem.

Problem: Some of the bags did not contain moisture.

Possible cause: The bags may not have been sealed tightly and the water vapor escaped. You can try to seal the bag with a rubber band or fasten the tie tightly. Repeat the experiment, checking that there are no leaks or holes in the bag.

Problem: It looked like there was water in the bags, but it weighed nothing.

Possible cause: Your scale may not be sensitive enough to register the weight. If possible, borrow a more sensitive scale from your school and repeat the experiment. You could also note the results visually.

Desert plants, such as the organ pipe cactus, have developed special methods of storing and conserving water to survive in the dry, hot environment.
FIELD MARK PUBLICATIONS.

- State your hypothesis, an educated guess about the answer to your question.
- Decide how to change the variable you selected.
- Decide how to measure your results.

Recording Data and Summarizing the Results
Your data should include charts and graphs such as the one you did for these experiments. They should be clearly labeled and easy to read. You may also want to include photographs and drawings of your experimental setup and results, which will help other people visualize the steps in the experiment.

If you are preparing an exhibit, you may want to display your results, such as any experimental setup you designed. If you have completed a nonexperimental project, explain clearly what your research question was and illustrate your findings.

Related Projects You can take advantage of the many species of plants to conduct an experiment with plants and water. For example, you could compare the characteristics and behavior of a desert plant, such as a cactus, with a water plant. How does transpiration differ in the two species of plants? You could study the adaptations related to transpiration in a variety of plant species. Covering one side of a leaf with petroleum jelly will allow you to determine where transpiration occurs in a plant's leaves. You could also investigate in more detail how water flows into a plant by examining parts of a plant's stem, leaves, roots, and cells under a powerful microscope.

Another related project could focus on how water allows a plant to acquire its essential nutrients. Plants will usually get their nutrients from the soil, once the nutrients dissolve in water and are pulled into the plant. Some plants do not need soil to get their nutrients. Hydroponics is the technique of growing plants in water that contains dissolved nutrients. A hydroponics experiment could vary the nutrients in the water or the plants.

For More Information

Andrew Rader Studios. "Plant Basics." *Rader's Biology4kids.com.* http://www.biology4kids.com/files/plants_main.html (accessed on February 8, 2008). Information on plant biology and structures.

Black, David, and Anthony Huxley. *Plants.* New York: Facts on File, 1985. Readable scientific introduction to plants.

Bruce, Anne. "Water movement through a plant." *Microscopy–UK.* http://www.microscopy-uk.org.uk/mag/artmar00/watermvt.html (accessed on February 12, 2008). Explains how water moves through plants; includes informative pictures.

"Cell Expansion and Differentiation." *Ohio State University: Horticulture and Crop Science in Virtual Perspective.* http://www.hcs.ohio-state.edu/hcs300/cell3.htm (accessed on February 12, 2008). Illustrations on turgor pressure and the cell wall.

Missouri Botanical Garden. *Biology of Plants.* http://www.mbgnet.net/bioplants (accessed on February 6, 2008). Basic information about plant biology and life.

United States Department of Agriculture. *Plant's Database.* http://plants.usda.gov/ (accessed on February 6, 2008). Provides a list of plants in every state, along with images of many plants.

United States Department of Agriculture Forest Service. *Celebrating Wildflowers.* http://www.fs.fed.us/wildflowers/index.shtml (accessed on February 16, 2008). Variety of information on a wide range of plants.

Polymers

Polymers are everywhere, both inside us and around us. The word comes from the Greek words *poly,* meaning "many," and *meros,* meaning "parts." A polymer is a material composed of long string of repeating molecular units. They can contain a chain of hundreds to thousands of these units, in the shape of a single straight chain or multiple branching chains. The type and number of the repeating units, along with how the polymer connects to other polymers, determine the physical properties of that polymer.

Polymers are valuable in both nature and industry because they can have great strength and durability, yet be lightweight. There are both natural and synthetic, or manmade, polymers. Proteins, silk, and starches are polymers found in nature. Understanding how polymers function in the natural world has led not only to advancements in biology, but also to the development of synthetic polymers that have revolutionized numerous products and fields. Space science depends on synthetic polymers for their space vehicles and equipment. In medicine polymers are used in heart valves, artificial skin, and organ replacements. Plastic bags, nylon, rugs, and fabrics are examples of synthetic polymers that people commonly use.

Chain properties One of the first polymers created was due to the popular sport of billiards in the late 1800s. At that time, billiard balls were made of ivory, a material in short supply even then. An American inventor won a contest to find a material to replace the ivory. He took the basic structural material that makes up plant cell walls and treated it with chemicals. The result was the polymer celluloid—a shiny, hard material that could be molded when hot. This type of plastic became commonly used in X-ray film and motion picture film. In the early 1900s the first synthetic polymer from a nonnatural substance was developed. That was soon followed by the first synthetic fiber, rayon. Companies

Silly Putty is a synthetic rubber polymer. AP/WIDE WORLD

began to get involved in developing polymers, and the study of polymers began in earnest.

Polymers start off from tiny units called monomers. To make a polymer, monomers are strung together like beads to form a long polymer chain. A polymer can be made up of billions or trillions of monomers. The chemical reaction that makes polymers from monomers is called polymerization.

Each bead on the chain is the basic unit. In many cases, the chain links on a polymer are made up of only carbon atoms. The carbon-carbon bond is a strong one and this gives these polymers strength. In other cases, the chain units are made of nitrogen, oxygen, and/or silicon.

Many classes of polymers are made of just carbon and hydrogen. In these polymers, carbon makes up the basic links in the chain, and hydrogen atoms are bonded along the carbon backbone. For example, the common plastic polyethylene, which is found in grocery bags, juice containers, and bottles, is one such polymer. Composed of the monomer ethylene, polyethylene is composed of a chain of carbon atoms bonded together, with each carbon atom attached to two hydrogen atoms.

Monomers string together like beads on a string to form a polymer. GALE GROUP.

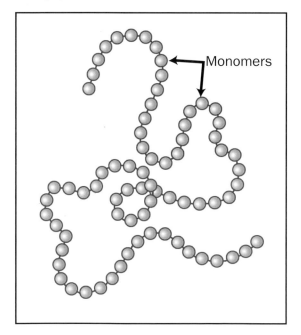

Monomers

What kind is it? Because there are so many different kinds of polymers, there are also many different ways to classify them, depending on their properties. There are some polymers that are flexible and others are that are hard. Elastomers are polymers that have an elastic or rubbery behavior. They can be stretched or bent, but spring back to their original shape. Other polymers, such as a fishing line, are hard and difficult to stretch. Some polymers can be heated and reheated repeatedly. Others will undergo a permanent chemical change if they are heated, which will alter their properties.

One way polymers are differentiated is according to their mechanical properties, such as tensile strength. A polymer's tensile strength is the force needed to stretch a material until it breaks. Elongation is another mechanical property. A polymer's elongation is the percentage increase in length that occurs before it breaks under tension.

Physical properties of polymers are another way to group them. The chain length of a polymer plays a major role in the polymer's physical properties and behavior. One factor that affects tensile strength is the chain length or the molecular weight. As a general rule, polymers with a higher molecular weight produce stiffer, stronger, and denser materials. The greater the molecular weight, the higher the tensile strength.

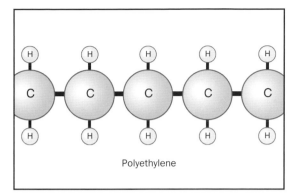

Many polymers are made of hydrogen atoms bonded along a carbon backbone. GALE GROUP.

How the chains are arranged also affects the physical properties of a polymer. The chains in a polymer can tangle up with each other, like a plate of spaghetti. This makes many polymers incredibly durable. The chains can be either linear (straight), branched, or cross-linked.

Getting rid of polymers The positive qualities in polymers—their durability, strength, and lightness—bring with them the challenge of how to get rid of many of these products. Enormous quantities of disposable, synthetic polymers are produced every year in the United States alone.

Plastic wrap, food containers, and bags are synthetic polymers commonly used in the average household. COPYRIGHT © KELLY A. QUIN.

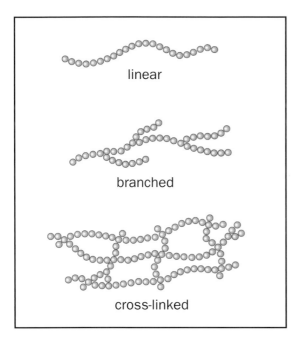

linear

branched

cross-linked

The arrangement of a polymer chain has an impact on its physical properties. GALE GROUP.

The production of these materials is causing concerns for the environment.

Many of the products are plastics and are not biodegradable, meaning that they do not break down naturally and quickly into the raw materials of nature. Plastic soda can rings, for example, can take an estimated 400 years to break down!

Recycling these plastics will help reduce the amount of garbage in the environment. When plastics are recycled they are reprocessed and made into new products. Yet different methods are used to recycle different materials, and there can be multiple polymers in a person's garbage. Most plastics and bottles are made from six polymers. The plastics industry has developed a chart to distinguish the six polymers from each other: A specific number is written in a three-arrow triangle that is imprinted on most plastic products. Polymers' physical properties, such as density, are also used to separate the different types. People are encouraged to recycle and separate their plastic containers. In the meantime, researchers are working to develop polymers with improved biodegradability.

EXPERIMENT 1

Polymer Strength: What are the tensile properties of certain polymers that make them more durable than others?

Purpose/Hypothesis Tensile strength is one key test that researchers conduct on polymers. A polymer's tensile strength depends on what molecules make up the polymer, as well as the orientation of the polymers. Polymers align themselves as long chains. These chains are aligned parallel to each other and tangle together in many synthetic polymers. When pulled lengthwise, these chains can stretch a great distance before breaking. However, widthwise it is only the entanglements that hold the polymers together. In this direction the polymer will break much more easily. Companies make many synthetic polymers by manufacturing the long chains of polymers parallel to each other along the length of the product. This results in a strong bond length-wise, from top to bottom, and a weak bond widthwise, from left to right.

In this experiment you will test in what direction the orientation of the polymer is strongest: lengthwise or widthwise. The polymer you will use will be any plastic bag. Most plastic bags are made of the polymer polyethylene. To test a polymer's tensile strength, one end of the polymer is held stationary while a force is applied to the other end until the sample breaks. Before the sample breaks it elongates, or lengthens.

Tensile testing is usually done on samples shaped like a "dogbone." The size of the sample can vary, but the shape is important. Almost all the elongation will occur in the narrow section of the dogbone. Elongation occurs in the thinnest section because it is the weakest.

You will test plastic samples in both directions by taping one end of the samples to a stationary object and attaching a weight to the opposite end. You will increase the weight incrementally, measuring the plastic's elongation after each addition of the weight, until the plastic breaks. Samples should always break in the thinnest section, the middle of the dogbone. For increased accuracy, you will conduct three trials for both the lengthwise and widthwise direction.

To begin this experiment make an educated guess, or prediction, of what you think will occur based on your knowledge of polymer strength and orientation. This educated guess, or prediction, is your hypothesis. A hypothesis should explain these things:

- the topic of the experiment
- the variable you will change
- the variable you will measure
- what you expect to happen

A hypothesis should be brief, specific, and measurable. It must be something you can test through further investigation. Your experiment will prove or disprove whether your hypothesis is correct. Here is one possible hypothesis for this experiment: "The plastic bag cut in the

A mound of plastic products awaits reprocessing at a Des Moines, Iowa, recycling facility. AP/WIDE WORLD

WORDS TO KNOW

Biodegradable: Capable of being decomposed by biological agents.

Control experiment: A setup that is identical to the experiment, but is not affected by the variable that acts on the experimental group.

Elastomers: Any of various polymers having rubbery properties.

Elongation: The percentage increase in length that occurs before a material breaks under tension.

Hypothesis: An idea in the form of a statement that can be tested by observation and/or experiment.

Monomer: A small molecule that can be combined with itself many times over to make a large molecule, the polymer.

Polymer: Chemical compound formed of simple molecules (known as monomers) linked with themselves many times over.

Polymerization: The bonding of two or more monomers to form a polymer.

Synthetic: Something that is made artificially, in a laboratory or chemical plant, but is generally not found in nature.

Tensile strength: The force needed to stretch a material until it breaks.

Variable: Something that can affect the results of an experiment.

What Are the Variables?

Variables are anything that might affect the results of an experiment. Here are the main variables in this experiment:

- the type of plastic bag (polymer) used
- the amount of weight
- the direction the polymer is cut
- the size of the cut polymer
- the shape of the cut polymer

In other words, variables in this experiment are everything that might affect the amount of weight the polymer can hold. If you change more than one variable, you will not be able to tell which variable impacted the polymer's strength.

lengthwise direction will support far more weight than the sample cut widthwise."

In this experiment the variable you will change will be the orientation of the polymer chains, and the variable you will measure will be the amount of weight the polymer can hold before it breaks.

Level of Difficulty Difficult.

Materials Needed

- bar to hold the clothes hanger or plastic sample (clothing rod works well).
- sturdy clothes hanger with a stiff, straight section across the bottom (wood or very stiff metal)
- 2 plastic garbage bags (white or light color)
- scissors

- wide duct tape
- a 2-liter empty plastic bottle
- string
- wastebasket or bucket to catch plastic bottle
- water
- funnel
- measuring cup
- piece of 8.5-inch by 11-inch (216-millimeter by 280-millimeter) paper
- marking pen

Approximate Budget $8.

Timetable 1 hour.

Step-by-Step Instructions

1. Trace the template of the dogbone (refer to the illustration) on the paper and cut out the paper.
2. To determine the lengthwise direction of the bag, stretch the bag gently in each direction and determine which way has the least pull. This is the lengthwise direction. It is not always the top-to-bottom direction of the bag. Mark the "top" and the "bottom" with the marking pen.
3. Lay the plastic bag in the lengthwise, top-to-bottom, direction and place the paper template over the bag. Cut out the plastic bag, making sure the cuts are smooth.
4. Repeat Step 3 two more times so that you have three dogbone-shaped pieces of plastic. Mark each piece with an "L" for lengthwise.
5. Repeat Steps 2 and 3 in the crosswise direction. Mark each piece with a "C" for crosswise.

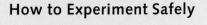

How to Experiment Safely

Be careful when using the scissors.

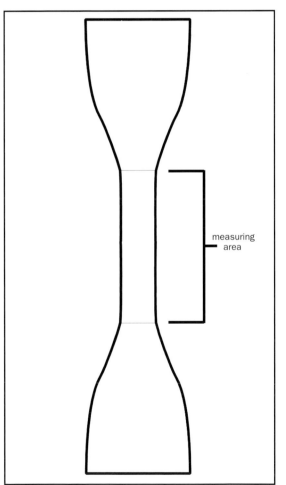

Step 1: The dogbone template.
GALE GROUP.

measuring area

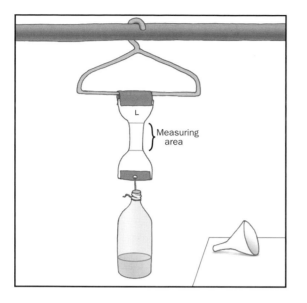

Steps 7 and 8: Setup for Experiment 1. GALE GROUP.

6. On each of your samples draw a line across the beginning and end of the mid-section of the bone. This will be the area you will measure.

7. Attach one end of a plastic sample to the hanger with duct tape, wrapping the tape firmly around the hanger.

8. Attach another piece of duct tape to the bottom of the plastic. In the center of this bottom piece of duct tape make a small hole. Put a string around the neck of the 2-liter bottle and attach the other end of the string through the hole. Tie with a double knot.

9. Measure the length between the top and bottom marks on the bag and write it down.

10. Place the wastebasket or bucket on the floor directly under the bottle. Carefully pour ¼ cup of water (60 milliliters) into the bottle using a funnel. Measure the length between the top and bottom marks on the bag again and write it down.

11. Continue adding ¼ cup (60 milliliters) of water, measuring the stretch or elongation of the sample after every water addition until the sample breaks. Note your results.

12. Repeat Steps 7 through 11 for each of the remaining five sample bags.

Summary of Results Average the three trials of elongation for both the lengthwise and crosswise polymer orientations. Construct a chart where Column 1 is the weight of the water, Column 2 is the length of the sample, and Column 3 is the percent elongation. The percent elongation is the length of the end sample minus the original length of the sample divided by the original length of sample. Multiply that number times 100 to get the percent. Percent elongation = [(finished sample length–original sample length) divided by original sample length] × 100.

Plot a graph of the results with the amount of water on the y-axis and the percent elongation on the x-axis. Did the samples break at different weights? Clearly label your graph. Did the samples break at different weights? Did the lengthwise or crosswise sample break first? Write a brief explanation of your results.

Change the Variables You can vary this experiment in several ways. Try using different types of plastic, such as a food wrapper compared to a thick plastic garbage bag. You could experiment with cutting the bag in the diagonal direction. Cut out different sizes of the dogbone, using the same direction and plastic. Does this impact the plastic's elongation?

EXPERIMENT 2

Polymer Slime: How will adding more of a polymer change the properties of a polymer "slime"?

Purpose/Hypothesis The objective of this experiment is to create a cross-linked polymer and observe the physical properties of adding increased polymer chains. Guar gum is used as a thickening agent in foods. The guar contains a polymer called polysaccharide. Polysaccharide is a large molecule composed of carbon, oxygen, and hydrogen atoms joined together in long chains, which makes it long and flexible. Because it is a linear polymer that is not cross-linked, guar gum pours like a thick solution.

In order to form a "slime" the linear polysaccharide must be cross-linked to form a three-dimensional network. This creates stronger bonds between the separate chains. Borax has sodium borate as the active ingredient. Sodium borate is the cross-linking agent, meaning that it creates the interconnecting bonds between the carbon and oxygen atoms that link the linear polymer chains together.

In this experiment you will determine how the amount of a polymer alters the properties of a mixture. You will make three different polymer slimes with varying amounts of polysaccharide. The borax will cross-link

Troubleshooter's Guide

Below are some problems that may arise during this experiment, some possible causes, and some ways to remedy the problem.

Problem: The plastics break at the top or bottom.

Possible cause: There could be a slight tear or cut in the plastic. If it breaks anywhere but the middle you will need to repeat the experiment.

Problem: The widthwise-labeled dogbone was stronger.

Possible cause: You may have mislabeled the plastics when you first stretched the bag to determine the lengthwise direction. Repeat the experiment, making sure to pull gently on the bag to determine which direction pulls the least amount.

Problem: The elongation for the three trials varied greatly.

Possible cause: You may have changed more than one variable. Make sure you used the same sturdy hanger for each trial. Was one a thin metal hanger that bent? Could you have mismeasured the water or spilled some as you were pouring? Repeat the experiment, making sure all the variables are equal.

What Are the Variables?

Variables are anything that might affect the results of an experiment. Here are the main variables in this experiment:

- the amount of borax used
- the amount of guar gum
- the amount of water used
- the temperature of the mixture
- any added food coloring

In other words, the variables in this experiment are everything that might affect the properties of the slime. If you change more than one variable at the same time, you will not be able to tell which variable had the most effect on the slime's physical properties.

the polysaccharides. After you have made the three different slimes, you will conduct tests to compare the firmness and elasticity of the slimes.

Before you begin, make an educated guess about the outcome of this experiment based on your knowledge of polymers and their properties. This educated guess, or prediction, is your hypothesis. A hypothesis should explain these things:

- the topic of the experiment
- the variable you will change
- the variable you will measure
- what you expect to happen

A hypothesis should be brief, specific, and measurable. It must be something you can test through further investigation. Your experiment will prove or disprove whether your hypothesis is correct. Here is one possible hypothesis for this experiment: "Increasing the amount of polymer in the slime will give the polymer greater firmness and elasticity."

In this case, the variable you will change is the amount of polymer you add to your slime. The variables you will measure are the slime's firmness and elasticity.

When making a solid-liquid solution (solid/liquid), it is standard to use weight/weight (grams/grams) or weight/volume (grams/milliliters). With water, 1 gram of water equals 1 milliliter. In this experiment, teaspoons and tablespoons are used to measure the solid.

Level of Difficulty Moderate.

Materials Needed

- borax (found in supermarkets in the laundry section)
- guar gum (a thickener agent; found in health food stores)
- water
- four stirring rods or spoons
- measuring spoons
- scale or measuring cup
- resealable bags
- food coloring (optional)

- four clear mixing bowls [to see if the materials dissolved]
- marking pen
- masking tape
- latex gloves

Approximate Budget $10.

Timetable 45 minutes.

Step-by-Step Instructions

1. Pour one-half of a cup (120 milliliters or 120 grams) of water into a bowl.
2. Add 1 teaspoon of borax (sodium borate) to the water and stir until completely dissolved. The solution should be clear.
3. Label the solution "Borax."
4. Measure out one-third of a cup (80 milliliters or 80 grams) of water into a second bowl or measuring cup.
5. Add ¼ teaspoon of guar gum to the solution while stirring. Continue stirring until completely dissolved. The guar gum will suspend in the liquid so this solution will not be clear.
6. Label the solution on the tape: "¼ teaspoon Guar gum."
7. If you want to make colored slime, add a specific amount of the desired color to the solution. You will need to add this exact color and amount to each of the mixtures.

Step 10: When finished making the three slimes, lay each on the counter; one at a time, determine its firmness by measuring its diameter. GALE GROUP.

8. Add 1 teaspoon of the borax solution to the guar gum solution. Stir for one minute and then let sit for at least two minutes.

9. Repeat the previous steps to make two more mixtures, replacing the ¼ teaspoon guar gum with $\frac{1}{2}$ teaspoon and $\frac{3}{4}$ teaspoon guar gum respectively. Label the two mixtures accordingly.

10. When finished making the three slimes, lay each on the counter; one at a time, determine its firmness by measuring its diameter. Note your results in a chart.

11. Hold each in your hand and describe the slime's firmness, using the "¼ guar gum" as the standard of comparison.

12. Hold one of the slimes to an edge and let it hang down. Time one minute; determine its elasticity by measuring its length, or if it breaks apart. Note your results. Repeat for two other slimes.

Summary of Results Examine the chart of your data and observations. Which amount of guar gum made the polymer the most firm? How do the physical properties of the slimes with the lowest and highest amount of guar gum compare with each other? What does measuring the diameter show? What can you conclude about the slime if it had a longer stretch than the others? What if it broke during the stretch? If you want to display the results of your slime experiment, the slime can be stored in a resealable bag. You can demonstrate the slime's firmness by having people feel it and experiment with it themselves.

Change the Variables There are many ways to vary this experiment. Here are some suggestions:

- Keep the amount of guar gum equal and vary the amount of borax.
- Keep the amount of guar gum and borax equal and vary the amount of water used.

Data chart for Experiment 2.
GALE GROUP.

	Firmness		Elasticity	
	Diameter	Description	Length	Breaks Apart
1/4 tsp. guar				
1/2 tsp. guar				
3/4 tsp. guar				

Does using more or less water give the slime added bounce?

- Place the slime in different temperature environments after you have made three mixtures that use the same measurements. Put one in the refrigerator, one at room temperature, and one in a hot-water bath.

How to Experiment Safely

Be careful when you are cutting the plastic into small pieces. Ask an adult to help cut containers that are tough. Work carefully around the boiling water. Have an adult help you remove the plastics from the boiling water.

PROJECT 3

Polymer Properties: How are the properties of hard plastics different?

Purpose/Hypothesis The plastic containers that hold liquids, foods, and numerous other everyday items are all polymers. There are many different types of plastics. One way to identify plastics is by the numbers code on the bottom of containers. The numerical code is for recycling. Because plastics have different properties, including melting points, they are sorted according to type. The recycling codes divide plastics into seven types.

Some of the plastics can keep their shape after being heated and some cannot. Plastics that are polypropylenes (PP), for example, contain crystals that prevent the polymers from softening in boiling water. These crystals are hard and rigid. Density is another property that is different among the plastic types. Plastics denser (heavier) than water will sink; plastics lighter than water will float. Alcohol is less dense than water.

In this project, you will test the properties of at least four types of plastics to better understand the different properties of polymers. You can examine if the plastics retain their shape and color after being boiled in water. You can also measure the relative density of the plastics. By testing the density of plastics in both water and alcohol, you will be able to identify how plastics that appear similar have unique properties.

Level of Difficulty Moderate.

Materials Needed

- at least 4 plastic containers with different recycling numbers, include at least one numbered 1 or 2 and at least one numbered 6 or 7

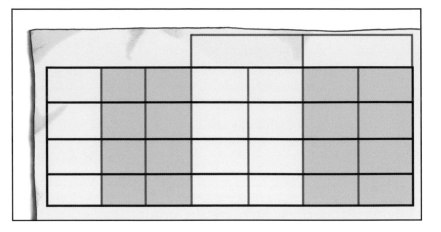

Step 1: Make a chart.
ILLUSTRATION BY TEMAH
NELSON.

- rubbing alcohol (70%)
- vinegar
- scissors
- pot
- hot plate or stove
- 4 plastic spoons
- paper towels
- tongs
- 4 small glasses

Approximate Budget $5, assuming you can use household containers that are going to be recycled.

Timetable about 1 hour.

Step 2: Cut four of the same shapes out of each plastic container. ILLUSTRATION BY TEMAH NELSON.

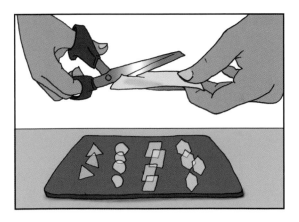

Step-by-Step Instructions

1. Make a chart similar to the illustration.
2. Decide on four different shapes, such as a triangle or diamond. Each shape should be about the size of your thumb. Cut four of the same shapes out of each plastic container. The different shapes will help you identify the plastics from one another.
3. Note the shape of each plastic.

4. Test the flexibility of each plastic by placing a plastic between your thumb and finger. Try to bend the plastic and write down the results in your chart.

Reaction to heat

1. Boil a pot of hot water. Reduce to a simmer and place one of each plastic type in the pot.
2. Allow the plastics to simmer for about five minutes.
3. Use the tongs to remove the plastics and place them on a paper towel. Note any changes in shape on the chart, such as curled edges.
4. Wait a few seconds for the plastics to cool and then try to bend each of the shapes again. Write down if the boiled plastic bends easier or harder than its corresponding plastic.

Density

1. Pour rubbing alcohol into a cup until it is about half-full. Place one of the unused plastic shapes into the liquid. Use a plastic spoon to gently press the plastic to the bottom. Remove the spoon and see if the plastic rises. Note the results on your chart.
2. Repeat this step for each of the three other types of plastics.
3. Fill another cup with water. Repeat the same steps for each of the four plastics, using new pieces of plastic. Note the results on your chart.

Summary of Results Take a look at your chart. How do the four types of plastics differ? Look at what each type of plastic container was used for and its properties. Can you draw conclusions about what types of plastics are used for long-term storage or heating. Consider how the properties of the plastic play a role in what it contains. You can also test the other types of plastic and compare your results.

Design Your Own Experiment

How to Select a Topic Relating to this Concept Polymers are everywhere. They are in your kitchen, clothes, and many disposable products that you purchase. You could examine

Step 4: Test the flexibility of each plastic by placing a plastic between your thumb and finger. ILLUSTRATION BY TEMAH NELSON.

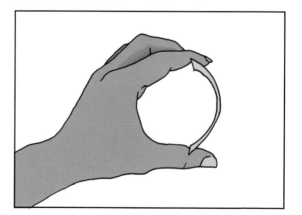

Troubleshooter's Guide

Here is a problem that may arise during this project, a possible cause, and a way to remedy the problem.

Problem: All the plastics sank in both water and alcohol.

Possible cause: You may have pressed down on the plastic too hard, causing the pieces to stick to the bottom. Repeat the density tests, pressing down each plastic slowly until it nears the bottom of the cup, and then remove the spoon. It is also possible you selected plastics that were denser than both alcohol and water. You can try the experiment again, using a different type of plastic.

Problem: The results were different when a test was repeated.

Possible cause: You have mixed up the plastics! Make sure the shapes are unique enough that you can identify each shape easily, and write down the corresponding plastic type as soon as you cut out the shape.

how polymers have changed over history or how they impact people's lives.

Check the Further Readings section and talk with your science teacher to learn more about polymers. Because polymers are so diverse, there are many different types of polymer chemists. Ask family, teachers, and friends if they know a polymer chemist you can talk with.

Steps in the Scientific Method To do an original experiment, you need to plan carefully and think things through. Otherwise, you might not be sure what question you are answering, what you are or should be measuring, or what your findings prove or disprove.

Here are the steps in designing an experiment:

- State the purpose of—and the underlying question behind—the experiment you propose to do.
- Recognize the variables involved and select one that will help you answer the question at hand.
- State your hypothesis, an educated guess about the answer to your question.
- Decide how to change the variable you selected.
- Decide how to measure your results.

Recording Data and Summarizing the Results Your data should include charts and graphs such as the one you did for these experiments. They should be clearly labeled and easy to read. You may also want to include photographs and drawings of your experimental setup and results, which will help other people visualize the steps in the experiment.

If you are preparing an exhibit, you may want to display your results, such as any experimental setup you designed. If you have completed a nonexperimental project, explain clearly what your research question was and illustrate your findings.

Related Projects You can use the many different physical and mechanical properties of polymers for further experiments and projects. For example, you could investigate the biodegradability of plastics by composting a number of materials. You could first compare the biodegradability of the six different types of polymers. You probably have several different types of plastic products (as determined by the number in the three-arrow triangle printed on a product) in your house already. You could then compare the breakdown of a specific plastic and determine how it relates to both other plastics and nonpolymer materials, such as an organic material like a food item or dead insect.

You could compare synthetic polymers' properties to synthetic non-polymer materials, such as aluminum foil or specific fabrics. To determine the specific polymer in the product you can look at the ingredients listed on the packaging or call the toll-free number. You could also look at polymers in a specific industry, such as the medical or space field, and explore how polymers have impacted the industry, everyday life, and products related to that field.

For More Information

American Chemistry Council. *plastics 101.* http://www.americanchemistry.com/s _plastics/sec_learning.asp?CID=1571&DID=5957 (accessed on February 26, 2008). This industry page has loads of basic information and news on plastics.

The Chemical Heritage Foundation. "What Do those Triangles Mean?" *Faces in the Molecular Science: Faces in Polymer.* http://www.chemheritage.org/ EducationalServices/faces/poly/readings/rec.htm (accessed on February 26, 2008). Descriptions of the recycling codes on plastic containers.

Energy Information Administration. "Recycling Plastics." *Energy Kid's Page.* http://www.eia.doe.gov/kids/energyfacts/saving/recycling/solidwaste/ plastics.html (accessed on February 27, 2008). Information on how plastics are produced, labeled, and recycled.

Polymer Science Learning Center, University of Southern Mississippi. *The MacroGalleria.* http://pslc.ws/macrogcss/maindir.html (accessed on February 26, 2008). Detailed site on all aspects of polymers, from studying them to everyday applications.

70

Potential and Kinetic Energy

Energy is involved in nearly everything we do. It is defined as the ability to do work, to set an object in motion. There are several different kinds of energy. Kinetic energy is the energy an object has when it is in motion. Vibration, forward motion, turning, and spinning are all examples of kinetic energy. Kinetic energy is directly proportional to the mass of an object. If two objects move at the same speed, and one has twice the mass of the other, the object with twice the mass will have twice the kinetic energy.

Potential energy is the energy an object has because of its position; it is energy waiting to be released. For example, a weight suspended above the ground has potential energy because it can be set in motion by gravity. Compressed or extended springs also have potential energy.

Thermal energy is the kinetic energy of atoms vibrating within matter. The faster the atoms move, the hotter the object becomes. Electrical energy is the kinetic energy resulting from the motion of electrons within any object that conducts electricity. Chemical energy is the potential energy stored in molecules. Thermal, electrical, and chemical energy are all forms of kinetic or potential energy.

The position of the boulder atop the cliff gives it potential energy. CORBIS.

What laws control energy? One of the most fundamental laws of physics is that energy cannot be created or destroyed, only transformed from one form into another. For example, if a suspended weight falls, its potential energy becomes kinetic energy. When a car burns fuel, the fuel's chemical energy is transformed into thermal energy, which in turn, is transformed into kinetic energy by the engine to make the car move.

929

WORDS TO KNOW

Chemical energy: Potential energy stored in molecules.

Control experiment: A set-up that is identical to the experiment but is not affected by the variable that affects the experimental group. Results from the control experiment are compared to results from the actual experiment.

Electrical energy: Kinetic energy resulting from the motion of electrons within any object that conducts electricity.

Energy: The ability to cause an action or to perform work.

Hypothesis: An idea in the form of a statement that can be tested by observation and/or experiment.

Kinetic energy: The energy of an object or system due to its motion.

Mass: Measure of the total amount of matter in an object.

Potential energy: The energy of an object or system due to its position.

Thermal energy: Kinetic energy caused by the movement of molecules due to temperature.

Variable: Something that can affect the results of an experiment.

Work: The result of a force moving a mass a given distance. The greater the mass or the greater the distance, the greater the work involved.

Energy can also be transferred from one object to another. Think about a game of pool. When a moving ball hits a still one, the moving ball stops and the still one begins to move. The majority of the first ball's kinetic energy has been transferred to the second ball, while a small amount has been converted to thermal energy by the collision. If you could measure the temperature on the surface of each ball, you would find there was a slight rise in temperature at the point of contact. The total amount of energy involved—kinetic and thermal—remains the same. No energy was created or destroyed by the collision.

Who wrote these laws? The person who laid the groundwork for the study of energy was English mathematician and physicist Isaac Newton (1642–1727). Newton developed the laws of motion, which describe how objects are acted upon by forces. Newton's ideas formed the basis for much of physics, in fact. He studied at Cambridge University, where he excelled in

As one ball hits another, it transfers some of its kinetic energy to that ball. PHOTO RESEARCHERS INC.

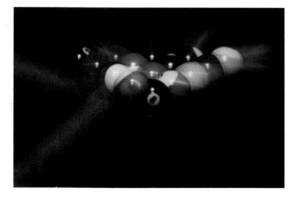

930

mathematics and developed the field of calculus while he was still a student. Newton later became a professor at Cambridge, where he built the first reflecting telescope and studied optics.

He published his most important work in 1687, the *Principia Mathematica*. This book describes Newton's three laws of motion and the law of gravitation, which are a major part of the foundation of modern science. Newton also had an interesting life. He became Master of Mint in England, where he supervised the making of money, and later became the first scientist to be knighted.

What questions do you have about energy? In the following experiments, you will have a chance to explore the topics of potential and kinetic energy. You will learn more about how these forms of energy affect us and everything we do.

EXPERIMENT 1

Measuring Energy: How does the height of an object affect its potential energy?

Purpose/Hypothesis In this experiment, you will drop a rubber ball and measure its rebound height. When you pick up the ball and raise it to a certain height, your body is performing work, and the ball is gaining potential energy as a result. When you release the ball, this potential energy changes to kinetic energy as the force of gravity causes the ball to gain speed. When the ball hits the ground, its kinetic energy changes back to potential energy as the ball comes to a stop and is compressed by the impact. A split second later, the potential energy of this compression propels the ball back into the air, giving it kinetic energy again. Finally, as the ball reaches the maximum height of its rebound, its kinetic energy is converted back into potential energy, as measured by its height above the ground.

To begin the experiment, use what you know about potential and kinetic energy to make an educated guess about the relation between the

What Are the Variables?

Variables are anything that might affect the results of an experiment. Here are the main variables in this experiment:

- the mass of the ball
- the material it is made of
- the surface on which it bounces
- the height from which it is dropped
- the force with which it is dropped
- the height to which it bounces back

In other words, the variables in this experiment are everything that might affect the rebound height of the ball. If you change more than one variable, you will not be able to tell which variable had the most effect on the rebound height.

How to Experiment Safely

In selecting your bouncing location, choose a place where you will not knock over or break anything.

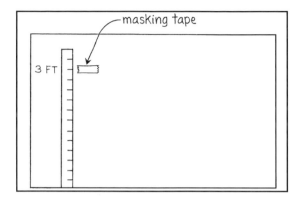

Steps 1 and 2: Measure 3 feet up a wall and mark; tape the measuring tape to the wall with the "zero" end at the floor. GALE GROUP.

Step 3: Hold the ball slightly away from the wall at the 3-foot height and simply drop it. GALE GROUP.

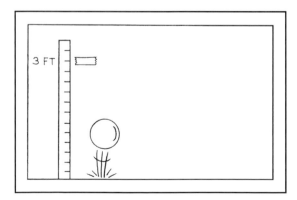

ball's initial drop height and its rebound height. This educated guess, or prediction, is your hypothesis. A hypothesis should explain these things:

- the topic of the experiment
- the variable you will change
- the variable you will measure
- what you expect to happen

A hypothesis should be brief, specific, and measurable. It must be something you can test through observation. Your experiment will prove or disprove whether your hypothesis is correct. Here is one possible hypothesis for this experiment: "The higher the height from which the ball falls, the greater its potential energy and the higher it will bounce."

In this case, the variable you will change will be the height from which you drop the ball. The variable you will measure will be the height it reaches when it bounces back. If the height of the ball's rebound increases as you increase the drop height, you will know your hypothesis is correct.

Setting up a control experiment will help you isolate one variable. Only one variable will change between the control and the experimental bounce, and that is the height from which you drop the ball. For the control, you will drop the ball from 3 feet (about 1 meter) high. For the experiment, you will change the height for each drop.

You will measure the height to which the ball bounces back each time. If the ball dropped from higher distances bounces back to higher heights, your hypothesis is correct.

Level of Difficulty Easy.

Materials Needed

- rubber ball
- flat wood or concrete floor on which to bounce the ball
- paper and pencils
- masking tape
- measuring tape, about 6 feet (2 meters) long

Trial	Height Dropped	Height Bounced
1 (control)	3 feet	
2		
3		
4		
⋮		

Recording chart for Experiment 1.
GALE GROUP.

Approximate Budget $3 for a rubber ball.

Timetable About 1 hour.

Step-by-Step Instructions

1. With your measuring tape, measure up a wall 3 feet (about 1 meter) from the floor and mark this level with a piece of masking tape. This will be your control height.

2. Tape your measuring tape to the wall with the "zero" end at the floor. You will use it to measure the heights of the bouncing ball.

3. Hold the ball slightly away from the wall at the 3-foot height and simply drop it. Do not use any force, as it will affect your results. Watch closely and use the measuring tape to determine how high the ball bounced. Repeat the drop several times and average the bounce heights. Record the height from which you dropped it and the average height to which it bounced.

4. Now drop the same ball several times from at least 12 inches (30 centimeters) higher or lower than the control level. Record its bounce heights, taking an average for each dropping height.

5. Repeat this procedure for at least five different heights, recording each height and averaging each bounce height.

Troubleshooter's Guide

Below are some problems that may occur during this experiment, possible causes, and ways to remedy the problems.

Problem: It is difficult to accurately measure the bounce height.

Possible causes:

- You are measuring the bounce against a wall that is too close to the color of the ball. Try bouncing with a ball that is significantly darker or lighter than the wall you are measuring against.

- Your measuring tape is difficult to read. Try marking off heights with chalk or masking tape so that they are easier to read.

Problem: The ball bounces so high you cannot see where the bounce ends.

Possible causes:

- The ball you are using is too rubbery. Try using a slightly less bouncy ball.

- You are exerting force when you drop the ball. Do not push down when you drop the ball. Simply let it fall from your hand.

Summary of Results Study the results on your chart. Did the drop height affect how high the ball bounced back? Was your hypothesis correct? Did the ball rebound as high as the drop height? If not, why not? Be sure to summarize what you discovered.

Change the Variables You can vary this experiment in several ways. For example, instead of changing the height, change the weight (mass) of the ball. Use a rubber ball that is much heavier and one that is much lighter, all dropped from the same height. (Change only one variable at a time.) Weigh each ball before you drop it. Use the ball from this experiment as your control. Record each bounce height again. What do you find?

You can also try using different kinds of balls, such as tennis balls or golf balls. How are they affected? What do you think makes the difference?

EXPERIMENT 2

Using Energy: Build a roller coaster

Purpose/Hypothesis Potential energy, provided by the force of gravity pulling on an object, is converted into kinetic energy as an object falls from a height. The amount of potential energy an object has is revealed by the speed with which it moves once released.

You can calculate potential energy using the formula PE = mgh, where m is mass, g is the acceleration of gravity 32.2 feet/second^2 (9.8 meters/second^2), and h is the height of the object in feet (meters). You can calculate kinetic energy using the formula KE=(0.5)mv^2, where m is mass, and v is the velocity of the object in feet/second (meters/second). The speed with which the object moves and the height to which it returns also indicate how much potential energy is being converted into kinetic energy and back to potential energy. You can explore this idea by watching a roller coaster.

In this experiment, you will build your own roller coaster and roll a marble on it to demonstrate potential and kinetic energy. Do you have an idea about how a marble will behave on a homemade roller coaster? Where will it move the fastest? Will it have enough energy from rolling down one hill to roll up the next hill?

To begin the experiment, use what you know about potential and kinetic energy to make an educated guess about how the marble will behave. This educated guess, or prediction, is your hypothesis. A hypothesis should explain these things:

- the topic of the experiment
- the variable you will change
- the variable you will measure
- what you expect to happen

A hypothesis should be brief, specific, and measurable. It must be something you can test through observation. Your experiment will prove or disprove whether your hypothesis is correct. Here is one possible hypothesis for this experiment: "The higher the first hill of the roller coaster, the higher the marble will climb on the second hill."

In this case, the variable you will change will be the height of the first hill, and the variable you will measure will be the height the marble climbs on the second hill. If the marble climbs higher on the second hill when the height of the first hill is raised, you will know your hypothesis is correct.

Only one variable will change between the control and experimental set-up, and that is the height at which the marble starts to roll. For the control, you will start your marble from a hill at 2 feet (0.6 meters) above ground. For your experiments, you will vary the heights of the first hill. You will measure the heights that the marble climbs on the second hill to compare the amount of kinetic energy produced by the potential energy of the initial drop.

Level of Difficulty Moderate.

What Are the Variables?

Variables are anything that might affect the results of an experiment. Here are the main variables in this experiment:

- the height of the first hill and the second hill
- the amount of friction between the track and the marble
- the amount of force or "push" you apply to the marble when you release it

In other words, the variables are anything that might affect the height the marble will reach on the second hill. If you change more than one variable, you will not be able to tell which variable had the most effect on the results.

A roller coaster has both potential and kinetic energy. CORBIS.

How to Experiment Safely

Choose your experiment location carefully to avoid the marble rolling into places where it cannot be retrieved. Do not release the marble from very high heights, as it could jump off the roller coaster track and hit someone.

Materials Needed

- 2 pieces of garden hose or other flexible tubing, each approximately 6 feet (1.8 meters) long
- 1 large marble
- books, bricks, or wooden blocks
- masking tape
- chair
- tape measure or ruler

Approximate Budget $20 if you need to buy a garden hose or other tubing.

Timetable Approximately 2 hours.

Step-by-Step Instructions

1. To make the roller coaster track, lay the two pieces of garden hose or tubing side by side on a flat surface and tape them together across the upper side, so the tape does not show on the lower side. Place tape about every 6 inches (15 centimeters). Flip the taped hose or tubing over so the untaped side is up. The two pieces of hose should form a channel in which the marble can roll. (You can also form the roller coaster from a single uncut length of hose by making a sharp u-bend in the middle and taping the two halves together.)

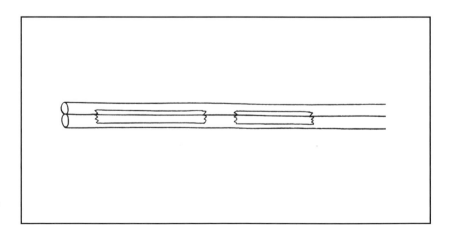

Step 1: How to assemble roller coaster track. GALE GROUP.

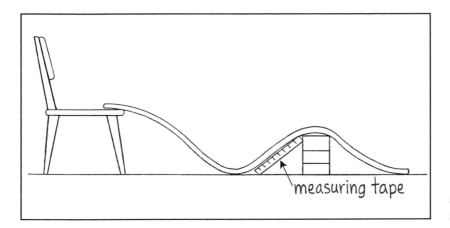

Steps 2 and 3: How to create the roller coaster. GALE GROUP.

2. Place one end of the hose track on a chair 24 inches (60 centimeters) off the ground. Let the other end fall to the ground.

3. Let the hose track follow the ground for a short distance and then place two to three bricks under the other end, creating a second hill.

4. Record the height of both hills on a data sheet (see illustration). You have created your roller coaster.

5. To make the heights easier to read, attach a tape measure or ruler vertically on the bricks that form the second hill. Be sure to put the "zero" end on the floor.

Trial	First Hill Height	Height Rolled on Hill #2
1 (control)	2 feet	
2		
3		
4		
⋮		

Step 4: Recording chart for Experiment 2. GALE GROUP.

Troubleshooter's Guide

Below are some problems that may occur during this experiment, possible causes, and ways to remedy the problem.

Problem: The marble jumped over the second hill.

Possible causes:

- Your second hill is not high enough. Use more blocks or bricks to make it higher. The height of the hill does not matter as long as you record the height the ball reaches accurately.

- Your first hill is too high. Lower it until you can release the marble and it stays on the second hill.

Problem: The marble does not stay on the hose track.

Possible cause: The marble is too large or too small for the hose. Try using a different size marble that fits well into the track.

6. Place the marble at the top of the first hill and release it. Do not push it, but simply let it go. Sight across your tape measure or ruler to determine the height the marble reaches on the second hill. You might ask a friend to help you note the highest height before the marble begins to roll back again.

7. Repeat this procedure several times and record the average height the marble reaches on the second hill.

8. Now raise the height of the first hill by adding a book or block on the chair. Record the new height of the first hill.

9. Release the marble from the higher first hill several times, taking an average of the heights it reaches on the second hill. Record the average height.

10. Repeat the procedure, raising and lowering the height of the first hill. Be sure to record each hill height and the height the marble reaches on the second hill.

Summary of Results Study the results on your chart. Compare the heights of the first hills and the heights the marble reached on the second hill. Did higher initial heights give your marble more potential energy, which created more kinetic energy to climb the second hill? Was your hypothesis correct? If you want to calculate the potential energy, use the formula described and record the number for each of your hill heights.

Change the Variables You can vary this experiment several ways. For example, remember that potential energy depends partially on the weight of the object. Try using a heavier or lighter marble. What is the effect? You can also try making the second hill steeper or more gradual. What is the effect? How high does the marble rise? Make your first hill higher and create a number of smaller hills with your hose. Can you build up enough potential energy to get your marble over more than one hill? What conditions will allow the marble to do that?

Design Your Own Experiment

How to Select a Topic Relating to this Concept If you are interested in kinetic energy, you could explore the energy in vibrations, in rotational movement, or in objects moving in straight lines or up and down. Or you could investigate the use of kinetic energy in heat or electricity.

If you are interested in potential energy, you could study the effects of springs. How does the size or flexibility of the spring affect its potential energy? How much weight can a spring move? You could study the swing of a pendulum (using a backyard swing) as its potential energy is converted to kinetic energy and back again.

Check the Further Readings section and talk with your science teacher or school or community media specialist to start gathering information on potential and kinetic energy questions that interest you. As you consider possible experiments, be sure to discuss them with your science teacher or other knowledgeable adult before trying them. Some might be dangerous.

Steps in the Scientific Method To do an original experiment, you need to plan carefully and think things through before you do it. Otherwise you might not be sure what question you are answering, what you are or should be measuring, or what your findings prove or disprove.

Here are the steps in designing an experiment:

- State the purpose of—and the underlying question behind—the experiment you propose to do.
- Recognize the variables involved, and select one that will help you answer the question at hand.
- State a testable hypothesis, an educated guess about the answer to your question.
- Decide how to change the variable you selected.
- Decide how to measure your results.

Recording Data and Summarizing the Results Your data should include charts, such as the one you did for these experiments. They should be clearly labeled and easy to read. You may also want to include photos, graphs, or drawings of your experimental setup and results. If you have done a nonexperimental project, explain clearly what your research question was and illustrate your findings.

Related Projects Besides completing experiments, you could prepare a model that demonstrates a point you are interested in with regard to kinetic and potential energy. Or you could investigate the uses of energy in industry, cooking, music, medicine, or dancing. You could explore the history of the study of energy, going all the way back to Newton and Galileo, or you could look at the future of energy, exploring nuclear and fusion energy. There are numerous possibilities.

For More Information

Bennet, Bob, Dan Keen, Alex Pang, and Frances Zweifel. *Science Fair Projects: Energy.* New York: Sterling Publications, 1998. Simple activities and ideas about science fair projects related to energy and using simple materials.

Doherty, Paul, and Don Rathjen. *The Cool Hot Rod and Other Electrifying Experiments on Energy and Matter.* New York: John Wiley & Sons, 1996. Collection of twenty-two experiments on all aspects of energy, with drawings, photos, and sidebars.

Leary, Catherine, and Michael Anthony DiSpezio. *Awesome Experiments in Force & Motion.* New York: Sterling Publications, 1998. Provides exciting ideas for kinetic energy projects.

National Energy Education Development Project. *Scientific Forms of Energy.* http://www.eia.doe.gov/kids/energyfacts/science/formsofenergy.html (accessed February 3, 2008).

Nova. *Newton's Dark Secrets.* http://www.pbs.org/wgbh/nova/newton/legacy.html (accessed February 3, 2008).

Renewable Energy

Renewable energy is energy from sources that are unlimited or replenish in a relatively short amount of time. Long before electricity, renewable energy sources powered people's daily needs. People captured the Sun's rays for warmth, burned wood to cook, and used wind to pump water. In the modern day, scientists have developed many systems to harness and transform the energy from renewable sources into energy that people can use.

Heating it up Renewable energy has become a major issue in the modern day. The main energy sources we use today come from fossil fuels. The three main fossil fuels are coal, oil, and natural gas. Fossil fuels are non-renewable. It took hundreds of thousands of years for fossil fuels to form. They are called fossil fuels because they formed from the "fossils" of plants and animals hundreds of millions years ago.

Fossil fuels all contain carbon. Burning these fuels releases the carbon, which combines with the oxygen in air to form carbon dioxide. Fossil fuels are used to power cars, planes, and produce electricity. Every year the worldwide demand for energy grows and more fossil fuels are burned.

The greenhouse effect occurs when gases such as carbon dioxide trap heat moving away from Earth. The trapped heat warms Earth's surface, leading to warmer temperatures and a shifting climate. By replacing fossil fuels with renewable energy, we can greatly reduce the emissions of greenhouse gasses.

In order for a renewable energy to replace the use of fossil fuels in modern day, the energy needs to be transformed into a form of energy that people use. That energy usually takes the form of electrical energy—electricity. Availability, cost, and the ability to capture the energy source are all issues in transforming renewable energy into usable energy.

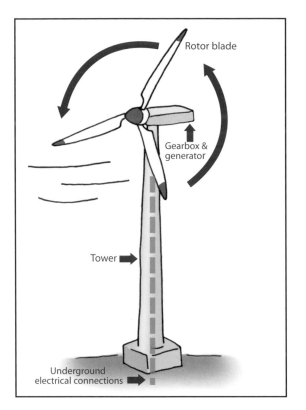

Rotor blade

Gearbox & generator

Tower

Underground electrical connections

Wind turbines capture the wind's energy. ILLUSTRATION BY TEMAH NELSON.

Where renewables come from There are many sources of renewable energy. The sources most commonly used are:

- Wind energy: Wind can be a powerful force. Wind is the result of radiation from the Sun that heats the atmosphere unevenly. The first windmills were developed thousands of years ago. The windmills were used to grind grain and pump water. By the turn of the twentieth century, people had developed small systems that generate electricity from the movement of wind. Wind turbines or blades capture the wind's energy. The turbines are placed high in the air and are spread apart, like a pinwheel. The wind turns the blades, which causes an electric generator to spin. The generator produces electricity. Groups of wind machines that produce electricity are called wind farms.

- Solar energy: Each day, the Sun provides Earth with vast amounts of energy. We use solar energy every day. Plants need the Sun's energy to live, and animals and people eat plants. The sun is used for warmth and heat. Researchers have developed several ways to capture the Sun's energy. To read more about solar energy see the Solar Energy chapter.

- Biomass: Biomass is renewable organic matter, such as trees. Plants are considered renewable because new plants can grow relatively quickly (compared to the formation of fossil fuels). When a tree is burned the energy inside the plant transforms into heat energy. People have long used wood to heat their homes. In modern day, wood is the largest biomass energy resource. To transform the plant materials are transformed into electricity by first burning them. The heat produced boils water, which produces steam. The steam turns turbines, which cause a generator to spin and the generator produces electricity. Many other sources of biomass are also used as renewable sources. Crops such as corn can produce oils. The oils can be used to fuel vehicles. Even the fumes from landfills can be used as a biomass

Glen Canyon Dam harnesses the energy from the water and converts it into electricity.
© ATLANTIDE PHOTOTRAVEL/ CORBIS.

energy source. Methane gas, produced from animal manure, is another potential source of biomass. Biomass can produce about the same amount of carbon dioxide as fossil fuels, but because plants remove carbon dioxide from the atmosphere regrowing plants can offset the carbon dioxide produced.

- Hydropower: Moving water can contain a lot of stored energy. When that energy is put to use, it is called hydropower. In the United States, hydropower is the most commonly used renewable energy source. Electricity is produced—hydroelectricity—by the force of falling water. Dams collect and move the water to create a large amount of force. The water turns the blades of a turbine, which spin a generator and produces electricity.

More renewables Another source of renewable energy that is available but not yet as commonly used is the energy deep inside Earth. This is called geothermal energy. Earth's core (center) is continuously generating heat. Thousands of feet below ground Earth's temperature is hot enough to boil water. Capturing this energy as steam spins a turbine, which in turn powers an electric generator.

In the experiments that follow, you will investigate two types of renewable energy sources: wind energy and hydropower. For experiments related to solar energy, see the Solar Energy chapter. As you conduct the

Experiment Central, 2nd edition

Renewable Energy

WORDS TO KNOW

Biomass: Organic materials that are used to produce usable energy.

Efficiency: The amount of power output divided by the amount of power input. It is a measure of how well a device converts one form of power into another.

Fuel cells: A device that uses hydrogen as the fuel to produce electricity and heat with water as a byproduct.

Generator: A device that converts mechanical energy into electrical energy,

Geothermal energy: Energy from deep within Earth.

Greenhouse effect: The warming of Earth's atmosphere due to water vapor, carbon dioxide, and other gases in the atmosphere that trap heat radiated from Earth's surface.

Hydropower: Energy produced from capturing moving water.

Hypothesis: An idea in the form of a statement that can be tested by observation and/or experiment.

Solar energy: Any form of electromagnetic radiation that is emitted by the Sun.

Turbine: A spinning device used to transform mechanical power from energy into electrical energy.

Variable: Something that can affect the results of an experiment.

What Are the Variables?

Variables are anything that might affect the results of an experiment. Here are the main variables in this experiment:

- the amount of wind
- the size of the boat
- the distance the boat travels
- the size of the sail
- the length of the mast
- the material the sail is made from

In other words, the variables in this experiment are everything that might affect the speed of the boat. If you change more than one variable at a time, you will not be able to determine which variable had the most effect on the amount of wind energy.

experiments, consider what questions about renewable energy you would like to explore further.

EXPERIMENT 1

Capturing Wind Energy: How does the material affect the amount of wind energy harnessed?

Purpose/Hypothesis People have used wind as an energy source for thousands of years. In order for wind to supply energy, the wind must be collected. One way to collect wind would be from a sail, such as on a boat. The sail creates a resistance for the wind and thus, powers the boat forward.

In this experiment you will be testing different types of materials on sailboats to determine how the material affect the amount of wind energy harnessed. You will be looking at how materials create a resistance with wind. The wind pushes on the material (the sail) and its energy moves the boat forward. The materials you will use are netting, flexible plastic, and broadcloth, which is a thick, sturdy fabric. During the experiment, you should also consider how materials need to withstand the force of the wind and not tear due to the resistance.

To begin the experiment, use what you have learned about solar energy to make a guess about how the material will affect the wind energy it captures. This educated guess, or prediction, is your hypothesis. A hypothesis should explain these things:

- the topic of the experiment
- the variable you will change
- the variable you will measure
- what you expect to happen

A hypothesis should be brief, specific, and measurable. It must be something you can test through observation. Your experiment will prove or disprove whether your hypothesis is correct. Here is one possible hypothesis for this experiment: "The boat with the sail made out of broadcloth will capture the most wind energy and so move the boat the fastest."

In this case, the variable you will change is the material the sail is made of and the variable you will measure is the speed with which the boat moves. If the wind moves the boat with the cloth the fastest, your hypothesis is correct.

Level of Difficulty Moderate.

Materials Needed

- pine wood, 6 × 3 × 1 inches (15 × 8 × 2.5 centimeters)
- 2, one-quarter inch (0.64 centimeters) dowels, both 16 inches (40 centimeters) long
- construction paper

How to Experiment Safely

Have an adult use the saw to cut the wood. Have an adult help you use the drill.

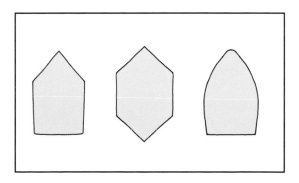

Step 1: Draw the base of the boat on wood. ILLUSTRATION BY TEMAH NELSON.

Step 5: Attach the cross bar centered on the mast and crisscross two zip ties to secure the cross bar to the mast. ILLUSTRATION BY TEMAH NELSON.

Step 9: Place the boat in a body of water. ILLUSTRATION BY TEMAH NELSON.

- netting (also called tulle), 12 inch by 12 inch (30 × 30 centimeters) piece (available at fabric stores)
- broadcloth, 12 inch by 12 inch piece (available at fabric stores)
- plastic bag, 12 inch by 12 inch piece
- 11, 3-inch (8-centimeter) zip ties
- drill with one-quarter inch bit (the bit should be the diameter of the dowels)
- hot glue gun and glue sticks
- electric fan with at least two speeds
- stop watch or watch with second hand
- small saw
- a still, wind-less day (if you are conducting the experiment outside)
- water area, at least 6 feet (1.8 meters) in length (a bathtub works well)

Approximate Budget $15.

Timetable About 40 minutes for setup; 30 minutes to complete and record results.

Step-by-Step Instructions

1. Draw the base of the boat on wood. (See illustration).
2. Have an adult cut out the boat base with a saw.
3. Drill a small and shallow hole in the center of the boat. Do not drill all the way through the wood. This hole is for inserting the mast.
4. Use hot glue to insert and hold the one piece of doweling in the hole. This is the boat's mast.
5. After the glue has dried, attach the cross bar centered on the mast about 3 inches (7.6 centimeters) from the bottom of where the mast and boat meet. Crisscross two zip ties to secure the cross bar to the mast. Trim the cross bar to leave 6 inches (15 centimeters) on each side of the mast.

6. Make a pattern for a sail out of construction paper, using a 12-inch (30-centimeter) triangle.

7. Use the pattern to cut a sail out of each of the three types of material: the netting, broadcloth, and plastic.

8. Attach one of the sails to the boat using zip ties on all three corners (at the mast and cross bar ends).

9. Place the boat in a body of water. If you are using a bathtub place the boat on one end. If you are using a natural body of water, mark a place where you are setting the boat and note a spot about 6 feet (1.8 meters) away.

10. Aim the fan at the boat and turn it on the low speed. If the boat does not move across the water with the low speed, turn the fan on the higher speed.

11. Use the stopwatch to time how long it takes for the boat to cross the body of water (or reach a set mark if the boat is on a long stream or other natural body of water). Record the time. Repeat the test for two more trials.

12. Repeat Steps 8–10, attaching the two remaining sails of different materials each time.

Troubleshooter's Guide

Below are some problems that may arise during this experiment, some possible causes, and ways to remedy the problems.

Problem: The mast keeps falling down.

Possible causes:

1. The hole may be too large or too shallow. The dowel should fit snugly in the hole. If it is loose, try using a smaller drill bit. If the dowel fits snugly, try drilling the hole slightly deeper into the wood, without drilling through the wood. Repeat the tests.

Problem: The boat tips over in the water.

Possible cause:

1. The sails may be too large for the boat. Try making the sails 2 inches (5 centimeters) smaller and repeat.

Possible cause: The wind from the fan may be too strong.

1. If you are conducting the experiment outside, make sure it is not a windy day. Use the lowest setting on the fan and move the fan farther away from the boat.

Summary of Results After you average the three trials for each of the materials, analyze your data to determine if the type of material affected the amount of wind that the sail collected. Was there one material that gathered more wind energy than others? Is it possible to gather too much wind? Consider if some materials might be better for certain strengths of wind. Write a paragraph summarizing your results. You may want to include pictures or drawings.

Change the Variables You can vary this experiment by changing the shape of the sail to determine if certain shapes capture greater amounts of wind. How does a square shape capture wind energy, for example? You can test

What Are the Variables?

Variables are anything that might affect the results of the experiment. Here are the main variables in this experiment:

- the amount of pressure
- the number of spoons
- the size of the spoons
- the size of the water wheel
- the construction of the water wheel
- the distance of the water wheel from the water energy source

In other words, the variables in this experiment are everything that might affect the movement of the water wheel. If you change more than one variable, you will not be able to tell which variable had the most effect on the water energy.

Steps 1: 3 and 4: Insert spoons about an 1 to 1.5 inches apart. In the same slot, insert the straw or stirrer. ILLUSTRATION BY TEMAH NELSON.

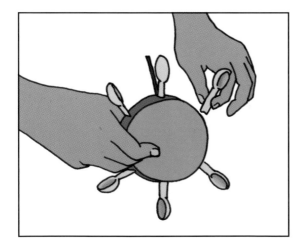

different sizes as well as shapes. You can also try varying the wind speed to explore how the material can withstand greater amounts of wind energy. In order to increase accuracy of results, complete three time trials of each sail type and average the results?

EXPERIMENT 2

Hydropower: How does water pressure affect water energy?

Purpose/Hypothesis Water is a source of energy that has existed for thousands of years. Ancient cultures used water to move ships and grind grain. In the modern day, hydropower is a major source of electricity. An important aspect of hydropower is the pressure caused by the movement and also, the weight of the water. The more stored water in a set area, the more water there is to push downwards. The downward pressure of the water can create a lot of force. In hydropower, the moving water is harnessed and used to produce usable energy.

In this experiment you will look at how the pressure of stored water affects the amount of energy the water produces. The water will exit onto a water wheel. You can measure how the force of moving water affects the amount of energy harnessed by counting the revolutions of a water wheel.

To begin your experiment, use what you know about hydropower and renewable energy to make an educated guess about water pressure and energy. This educated guess, or prediction, is your hypothesis. A hypothesis should explain these things:

- the topic of the experiment
- the variable you will change
- the variable you will measure
- what you expect to happen

A hypothesis should be brief, specific, and measurable. It must be something you can test through observation. Your experiment will prove or disprove whether your hypothesis is correct. Here is one possible hypothesis for this experiment: "An increase in stored water increases the energy harnessed in water, which will make the wheel spin faster."

In this case, the variable you will change is the amount of stored water. If the water wheel makes more revolutions with the greater amount of water you will know your hypothesis is correct.

Level of Difficulty Moderate.

Materials Needed

- 2 gallon or larger container (an extra large liquid laundry detergent container works well)
- 5 or more gallons of water
- swim noodle with a hollow center
- 6 plastic spoons
- utility knife
- stop watch or clock with second hand
- 12 inch piece of dowel
- pitcher
- permanent marker
- colored straw or coffee stirrer
- 2 to 3 helpers

Approximate Budget $10.

Timetable Approximately 90 minutes.

Step-By-Step Instructions 1.) Create the water wheel

1. Have an adult cut off a 2 inch (5 centimeters) section of the swim noodle. This will be the center of your water wheel.
2. Break off the handles of the spoons.

How to Experiment Safely

Have an adult assist you in using the knife.

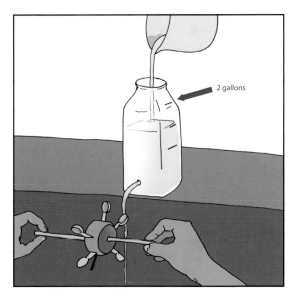

Step 2:6 Pull the plug and pour water into the container at a steady rate to maintain the water at the 1 gallon mark.
ILLUSTRATION BY TEMAH NELSON.

2 gallons

3. Make a slit in the noodle and insert a spoon. Continue around the circle, placing spoons about an 1 to 1.5 inches (2.5–3.8 centimeters) apart. Five to six spoons should fit around the circle. All spoons should be facing the same way.

4. In the same slot as one of the spoons, insert the straw or stirrer.

2.) Force of water energy

1. Mark three lines on the container at 1, 1.5, and 2 gallons.

2. Poke a hole in the side of the container with a pencil, 1 inches (2.5 centimeters) up from the base; it should be on the narrowest side. Place a pencil in the hole to plug the hole until you are ready to start the trials.

3. Slide the water wheel on the dowel.

4. Hold the dowel and wheel below the container and out approximately 6 inches (15 centimeters). You will need to allow some water to come out of the hole to determine the best point to hold the wheel. The best point is where the water wheel moves free and consistently. Once this is determined, tape the wheel in place so it is consistent for all trials.

5. Fill the container to the 1 gallon mark.

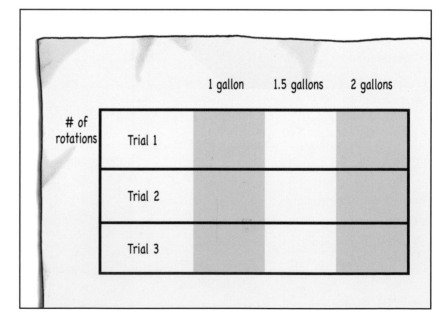

Step 2:8 Record the results.
ILLUSTRATION BY TEMAH NELSON.

6. Have a helper ready with a pitcher of water. Once the plug is pulled, the helper will need to pour water into the container at a steady rate to maintain the water at the 1 gallon mark. This will keep the water pressure steady.

7. Pull the plug on the water and time for one minute.

8. Use the colored straw or stirrer to count the number of revolutions the wheel makes in one minute with one gallon of water. Record the results.

9. Conduct two more trials at this level of water and note the revolutions for each trial.

10. Repeat Steps 6–9, filling the container first to the 1.5 gallon mark and then to 2 gallons. For each amount of water, conduct three trials and note the results.

Troubleshooter's Guide

In any experiment, problems can occur. Sometimes, experiments that do not work perfectly can turn out to be helpful. Here is one problem you may encounter, some possible causes, and ways to fix the problem.

Problem: The wheel is not moving freely.

Possible cause: The spoons may be facing the wrong way. Turn the spoons so they are facing the opposite way If the wheel is still not moving freely, you may want to purchase a pinwheel and try the experiment again.

Summary of Results After the experiment is finished, average the number of revolutions for each amount of water. Analyze your data table to determine the affect of water pressure on energy. Does more pressure result in more harnessed energy?

Change the Variables You can change several variables in this experiment. Try moving a toy boat or another object rather than the water wheel. You can also change the shape or size of the water wheel. Does temperature affect the water energy?

Design Your Own Experiment

How to Select a Topic Relating to this Concept Consider all the different types of renewable energy. Think about what aspect of renewable energy you are interested in, such as ways to use this energy or how a certain renewable is generated into electricity. You might want to investigate whether pollution is changing the effects of renewable energy on our world. You may want to look around where you live or go to school to see if any homes, schools, or businesses use renewable energy sources.

Check the Further Readings section and talk with your science teacher or community media specialist to start gathering information on renewable energy questions that interest you.

Steps in the Scientific Method To conduct an original experiment, you need to plan carefully and think things through. Otherwise you might not be sure which question you are answering, what you are or should be measuring, and what your findings prove or disprove.

Here are the steps in designing an experiment:

- State the purpose of—and the underlying question behind—the experiment you propose to do.
- Recognize the variables involved, and select one that will help you answer the question at hand.
- State a testable hypothesis, an educated guess about the answer to your question.
- Decide how to change the variable you selected.
- Decide how to measure your results.

Recording Data and Summarizing the Results Every good experiment should be documented so that other people can understand the procedures and results. Make diagrams, charts, and graphs of any information that is useful. You might also want to include small scale models related to your renewable energy experiment or project. Your experiment, whether it proves or disproves your hypothesis, is information that others can learn from.

Related Projects Renewable energy sources are all around us. What types of renewable energy have you used or would you like to use? You can design and build small generators, powered by a renewable energy source. You can also conduct a project in energy efficiency in your home or school. Can you shift any part of the energy system into a renewable energy source? Compare carbon emissions both before and after the change. How does cost play a role in selecting renewable energy sources?

For More Information

Asimov, Issac. *The Sun and Its Secrets.* Milwaukee, WI: Gareth Stevens Publishing, 1994. Discusses the Sun's origins, content, and historical facts.

Energy Information Administration. "Renewable Energy." *Energy Kid's Page.* http://www.eia.doe.gov/kids/energyfacts/sources/renewable/renewable.html (accessed July 24, 2008). Answers to basic questions about renewable energy types and sources.

"The Energy Story." *Energy Quest.* http://www.energyquest.ca.gov/story/chapter17.html (accessed on April 13, 2008). Information and projects related to renewable energy.

"Renewable. Energy." *Energy Kid's Page.* http://www.eia.doe.gov/kids/energyfacts/sources/renewable/renewable.html (accessed on April 13, 2008). Basic information on different forms.

"Solar Energy Animation." *Ocean Motion.* http://oceanmotion.org/html/resources/solar.htm (accessed on March 18, 2008). Information demonstrates how the intensity of the energy from the sun varies with location and time.

Suzuki, David and Kathy Vanderlinden. *Eco-Fun.* Vancouver: BC: Greystone Books, 2001. Project and experiments related to the environment.

U.S. Department of Energy. *Kids Saving Energy.* http://www.eere.energy.gov/kids/ (accessed on April 13, 2008). Information on renewable energy sources and energy-saving tips.

72

Rivers

The Carson begins in California, rushing northward from the headwaters on Sonora Peak in the Sierra Nevada Mountains, then rambling through gorges and alpine meadows. After leaving California, its next destination is the desert plain of Nevada. The Carson is a river, a main course of water into which many smaller bodies of water flow. The longest river in North America is the Mississippi. At 2,280 miles (3670 kilometers), it's the tenth longest on Earth. The Nile River, the world champion in length, winds 4,145 miles (6670 kilometers) from the equator to the Mediterranean Sea.

First things first The source of a river's waters, in fact, all the waters of the world, is the hydrologic cycle, which circulates and distributes the fresh water on Earth. To examine this cycle, we might begin with the sea. The Sun warms the ocean water, causing some of the surface water to evaporate and rise into the air as water vapor. Upon meeting cooler air above, this water vapor condenses and forms rain droplets, or it freezes into ice crystals. The droplets or crystals eventually fall again as precipitation: rain, snow, or hail. Some precipitation falls back into the sea, while some falls on land where it sinks into the ground, or runs into rivers, lakes, ponds, and streams.

French scientist Claude Perrault was one of the first to describe the hydrologic or water cycle. In 1674, he measured the precipitation that fell into the upper Seine River's basin and compared it with the estimated amount of water flowing into the Seine from streams and smaller rivers. The precipitation added about six times as much water as the streams. This was a significant discovery because previously scientists had thought that all rivers were fed by underground springs,

The Niagara River and its falls have carved out a 100-foot (30-meter) deep plunge pool.
PHOTO RESEARCHERS INC.

955

The Nile River plays an important part in the hydrologic cycle. PETER ARNOLD INC.

Mapping out the journey Rivers begin in mountains as several streams. These streams are formed from runoff consisting of rain, melted snow, sleet, and hail, as well as underground water that rises to the surface. Smaller streams gather into larger streams until they form a river. The river makes its home in a channel, a shallow trench carved into the ground from the pressure, volume, and movement of the water.

The journey of a river is rarely straight. Wide, shallow rivers with pebbly islands in the middle are called braided rivers. The islands split the river into many streams, which then come together again, just like braided hair. Lowland rivers that twist and turn before flowing to the sea are called meandering rivers. The term originated from the Latin word *maeander*. For example, the Menderes River in Turkey is famous for its windy course. Scotland's Deveron River meanders 26 miles (42 kilometers) back and forth across the land, but its actual straight-line length is only 6.5 miles (10.5 kilometers).

The power of water Where does a river's energy come from? The elevation of the land triggers its push, even in areas where the slope is gentle. The speed and volume of a river descending a steep slope can reshape Earth's surface, picking up soil and rocky debris and then dropping it when the water slows down and loses some of its energy. Rivers have gouged out canyons, built mud and stone landforms, and sculpted solid rock into pillars and arches.

An example of how powerful a river's force can be is the Niagra River, which runs through Canada and the United States. As it courses downslope on its 35-mile (56-kilometer) trail, the water pounds everything along its way. The cliff that creates its falls is a ridge made of dolomite, a very tough limestone. The river has worn down the ridge's overlying rock, creating a lower area that focuses the fall of the water.

In the following two experiments, you will explore ways that water changes the shape of our environment. The experiments will help you

WORDS TO KNOW

Braided rivers: Wide, shallow rivers with multiple channels and pebbly islands in the middle.

Channel: A shallow trench carved into the ground by the pressure and movement of a river.

Control experiment: A set-up that is identical to the experiment but is not affected by the variable that will be changed during the experiment.

Deposition: Dropping of sediments that occurs when a river loses its energy of motion.

Glacier: A large mass of ice formed from snow that has packed together and which moves slowly down a slope under its own weight.

Hydrologic cycle: Continual movement of water from the atmosphere to Earth's surface through precipitation and back to the atmosphere through evaporation and transpiration.

Hypothesis: An idea in the form of a statement that can be tested by observation and/or experiment.

Meandering river: A lowland river that twists and turns along its route to the sea.

Moraine: Mass of boulders, stones, and other rock debris carried along and deposited by a glacier.

River: A main course of water into which many other smaller bodies of water flow.

Sediment: Sand, silt, clay, rock, gravel, mud, or other matter that has been transported by flowing water.

Variable: Something that can affect the results of an experiment.

---

appreciate how rivers and streams have influenced the shape of your own community.

EXPERIMENT 1

Weathering Erosion in Glaciers: How does a river make a trench?

Purpose/Hypothesis In this experiment you will investigate the effects that glaciers, rivers of ice, have on the landscape, such as forming trenches and moraines, arc-shaped ridges of rocky debris. Before you begin, make an educated guess about the outcome of this experiment based on your knowledge of glaciers. This educated guess, or prediction, is your hypothesis. A hypothesis should explain these things:

- the topic of the experiment
- the variable you will change
- the variable you will measure
- what you expect to happen

What Are the Variables?

Variables are anything that might affect the results of an experiment. Here are the main variables in this experiment:

- size of the ice flow
- size of pieces of sediment
- temperature surrounding ice flow
- duration of the experiment

In other words, the variables in this experiment are everything that might affect the sediment erosion. If you change more than one variable, you will not be able to tell which variable had the most effect on erosion.

A hypothesis should be brief, specific, and measurable. It must be something you can test through observation. Your experiment will prove or disprove whether your hypothesis is correct. Here is one possible hypothesis for this experiment: "Ice flow causes sediment erosion."

In this case, the variable you will change is the presence of an ice flow, and the variable you will measure is the movement of soil in the ice flow's path. You expect the ice flow to cause erosion.

As a control experiment, you will set up one tray of sand with no ice flow in it. That way, you can determine whether the sand moves even with no ice flow. If the sand moves under the ice flow, but not in the control tray, your hypothesis will be supported.

Level of Difficulty Moderate.

Materials Needed

- 10 pounds (4.5 kilograms) play sand for sandboxes
- 24-inch (60-centimeter) square of window screening
- two 8 × 24-inch (20 × 61-centimeter) plastic trays (Liners for window boxes are ideal.)
- water
- freezer
- ruler
- bucket

Step 1: Screening over the bucket. GALE GROUP.

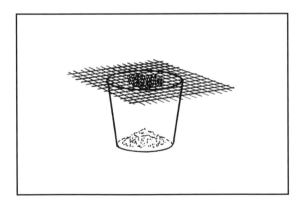

Approximate Budget $15.

Timetable 30 minutes to set up; 5 minutes a day to add water over a 30-day period.

Step-by-Step Instructions

1. Place the screening over the bucket and sift the sand by pouring it through the screen. Save any sand that remains on the screen. Discard any sand that goes through the screen.

2. Pour the sand that remained on the screen into both plastic trays.

3. Using the side of the ruler, smooth the surface of the sand in the trays and measure the depth of the sand. Make sure the sand is the same depth in both trays.

4. Using your finger, make a well in the sand at one end of both plastic trays.

5. Place the trays inside the freezer and prop up the ends with the well about 1 inch (2.5 centimeters).

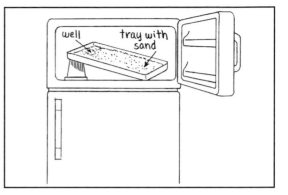

Step 5: Place the trays inside the freezer and prop up the ends with the well about 1 inch. GALE GROUP.

6. Pour 0.25 cup (60 milliliters) of water into the well of one tray (the experimental tray) and close the door. The control tray will have no water—and thus no ice. Add another 0.25 cup (60 milliliters) of water to the experimental tray daily for 30 days.

7. After 30 days, record the length of the ice flow that formed in the experimental tray.

8. Carefully remove both trays from the freezer.

9. Allow the ice flow to melt six to 12 hours.

10. Diagram the pattern the ice caused in the sand; describe the sand pattern in the control tray.

11. Measure the depth of the sand in the trench and at the end of the ice flow in the experimental tray. Measure the sand depth at both ends of the control tray. Record your findings.

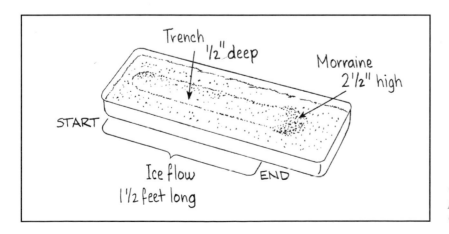

Steps 10 and 11: Tray showing pattern left by ice flow. GALE GROUP.

Troubleshooter's Guide

Here is a problem that may arise during this experiment, some possible causes, and ways to remedy the problem.

Problem: After 10 days, there is no ice accumulation near the well in the experimental tray. All the water flows quickly through the sand to the bottom of the tray.

Possible causes:

1. The angle is too steep. Lower both trays to a very gentle slope.
2. The sand is too coarse. Try a finer mesh screen and use smaller grains of sand.

What Are the Variables?

Variables are anything that might affect the results of an experiment. Here are the main variables in this experiment:

- the kind of soil being used (size and composition)
- the flowrate of water used
- the slope of the landscape
- the duration of the water flow

In other words, the variables in this experiment are everything that might affect the stream pattern. If you change more than one variable, you will not be able to tell which variable had the most effect on the pattern.

How to Experiment Safely

Handle the bricks carefully to prevent injury.

Summary of Results Organize your data on a chart that shows the sand levels in both trays at the beginning and the end of the experiment. Compare your end results. Did the ice flow move sediment? Did erosion take place in the control tray? Write a paragraph summarizing what you found.

Change the Variables You can change the variables in this experiment by using different soils. You might try top soil or a more rocky soil. Also, you can change the angle of the slope and see how the depth of the trench is affected. Gravity plays a large role in soil movement. The steeper the slope, the greater the pull of gravity.

EXPERIMENT 2
Stream Flow: Does the stream meander?

Purpose/Hypothesis Rivers and streams can carve patterns into Earth's surface. This experiment will simulate the force that water can have in an environment. Will a water travel in a straight path down a slope? Before you begin, make an educated guess about the outcome of this experiment based on your knowledge of stream patterns. This educated guess, or prediction, is your hypothesis. A hypothesis should explain these things:

- the topic of the experiment
- the variable you will change
- the variable you will measure
- what you expect to happen

A hypothesis should be brief, specific, and measurable. It must be something you can test through observation. Your experiment will prove or disprove whether your hypothesis is correct. Here is one possible hypothesis for this experiment: "A gentle flow of water across a downward sloping landscape will create a meandering stream path, while a more forceful flow will create a straighter path."

In this case, the variable you will change is the velocity of the water flow, and the variable you will measure is the resulting stream pattern. You expect the stream to meander for low flows and be straighter for higher flows.

Level of Difficulty Easy.

Materials Needed

- flat outdoor area
- hose and water supply
- 24-inch (61-centimeter) long shallow pan, such as a plant tray
- 5 pounds (2.2 kilograms) sand for a sandbox
- 5 pounds (2.2 kilograms) gravel
- 2 bricks or wooden blocks for support

Approximate Budget $8 for sand and gravel.

Timetable 45 minutes.

Step-by-Step Instructions

1. Pour equal amounts of gravel and sand into the tray and mix well. Make the surface level and smooth from one end to the other.
2. Lift one end approximately 6 inches (15 centimeters) high and place a brick underneath. Place the other brick in front of the lower end to keep it from sliding.
3. Place the end of the hose at the high end of the box.
4. Turn the hose on for two minutes, allowing a very soft flow of water to run over the sand.
5. After two minutes, turn off the water and diagram the pattern of water.
6. Turn the water on again for two more minutes; then turn it off and diagram the pattern again.

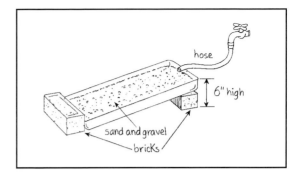

Steps 1 to 3: Set-up of sand and gravel tray. GALE GROUP.

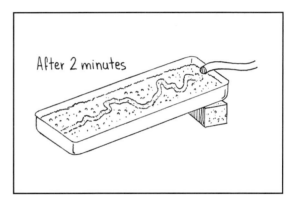

Step 5: Diagram the pattern of water flow after 2 minutes. GALE GROUP.

Step 6: Diagram the pattern of water flow after 4 minutes. GALE GROUP.

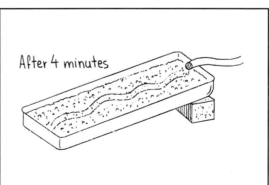

Troubleshooter's Guide

Here is a problem that may arise during this experiment, a possible cause, and a way to remedy the problem.

Problem: The sand or gravel did not move or show a pattern in the first two minutes.

Possible cause: Not enough water was applied. Allow the water to flow longer, until a stream bank begins to form.

7. Smooth the surface of the sand and gravel and repeat Steps 4 through 6 with a higher water flow rate.

Summary of Results Study your diagrams and the tray of sand. Which size particle of sand or gravel moved the most? As the stream flowed longer, how were the patterns affected? Did your stream begin to meander at the lower flow-rate and go straighter at the higher flowrate? Write a paragraph summarizing your results and explaining them.

Change the Variables To vary this experiment, experiment with the angle of the slope or the size of the particles in the streambed.

EXPERIMENT 3

River Flow: How does the steepness and rate of water flow affect river erosion?

Purpose/Hypothesis Rivers are found in many elevations and they flow at varying rates. Water racing down a steep incline will erode materials in a different way than water slowly moving down a shallow incline. The rate at which the water flows also plays a role in erosion.

In this experiment, you will make a mini-river and place sediment on the bottom of it. By varying the rivers steepness and water rate, one at a time, you can measure how each factor affects erosion.

Before you begin, make an educated guess about the outcome of this experiment based on your knowledge of rivers and erosion. This educated guess, or prediction, is your hypothesis. A hypothesis should explain these things:

- the topic of the experiment
- the variable you will change
- the variable you will measure
- what you expect to happen

A hypothesis should be brief, specific, and measurable. It must be something you can test through observation. Your experiment will prove or disprove whether your hypothesis is correct. Here is one possible hypothesis for this experiment: "The steepest river with the highest rate of water flow will cause the most erosion, while the shallowest river with the lowest water rate will cause the least erosion."

In this case, the variables you will change is the river steepness and water rate, one at a time, and the variable you will measure is the remaining sediment.

Level of Diffculty Moderate.

Materials Needed

- 24 cups of dirt
- 2 strips of wood, between 6 to 8 feet long (1×2 inches or 2×4 inches)
- measuring cup
- container that holds 4 cups
- protractor
- 2 funnels, with one spout width about 50% wider than the other (you could make a funnel by rolling and taping a plastic, such as a pastry sheet)
- tape measure
- Duct tape
- plastic tarp, shower curtain, or garbage bags
- marker
- 2 to 4 helpers
- an outside area

Approximate Budget $10.

Timetable about 1 hour and 30 minutes.

Step-by-Step Instructions
To Make the "River:"

1. Tape one side of the plastic to one strip of wood. See illustration.
2. Tape the second side of the plastic to the other strip of wood.

What Are the Variables?

Variables are anything that might affect the results of an experiment. Here are the main variables in this experiment:

- elevation of the river
- width of the river source
- amount of water
- type of sediment
- placement of sediment
- amount of sediment

In other words, the variables in this experiment are everything that might affect the sediment erosion. If you change more than one variable, you will not be able to tell which variable had the most effect on erosion.

Step 1: Tape one side of the plastic to one strip of wood.
ILLUSTRATION BY TEMAH NELSON.

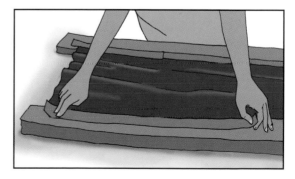

How to Experiment Safely

This experiment poses no safety hazards but it can get messy.

3. Roll the wood over the plastic several times, if needed. This will create your river. You will be able to adjust the width of the river by rolling the plastic in or out.

4. Have two people on each side hold the boards firmly. Your river bed should be at least 10 inches wide. It should have a little slack in it. Make sure you maintain the same width throughout each test.

5. Mark a pour point at the top of the river. This will be the point where the water flow will begin for each trial.

6. Use tape or a marker to mark off a two to three foot section of the river about 3 feet from the bottom. This will be where you will spread the sediment each trial.

To test for erosion:

7. Lift the top of the river to 18 inches and hold it tight. Use the protractor to measure the angle of elevation at the end of the river (where the river meets the ground).

8. Spread out 4 cups of dirt or sand between the marked points.

9. Pour 4 cups of water into a container.

Steps 10 and 11: Using the narrow funnel, pour the container of water into the funnel at the pour point down the river. Observe the erosion pattern. ILLUSTRATION BY TEMAH NELSON.

10. Using the narrow funnel, pour the container of water into the funnel at the pour point down the river.

11. Observe the erosion pattern. You may want to sketch the pattern.

12. Use your measuring cup to measure the amount of dirt left in the river. Try to measure all the remaining sediment.

13. Record your results on a table similar to the illustration.

14. Starting with a clean river, lift the top of the river to 24 inches. Repeat Steps 2–7, using fresh dirt. Note the angle of elevation with the protractor.

15. Lift the top of the river to 36 inches (91 centimeters), and repeat Steps 2–7. Again, use fresh dirt and measure the angle of elevation.

16. Repeat the test at the three incline heights, using the wider funnel, thus increasing the rate of water flow. Match the angle of elevation for each incline.

River	Smallest incline angle		Medium incline angle		Greatest incline angle	
	Narrow Funnel	Wide Funnel	Narrow Funnel	Wide Funnel	Narrow Funnel	Wide Funnel
Angle						
Height						
Length a constant						
Initial sediment						
Final sediment						

Mark the results in a chart.
ILLUSTRATION BY TEMAH NELSON.

Summary of Results Analyze your data to determine how the incline angle affects the erosion process. How would erosion differ in a mountain river versus a plains river? Does the steepness changes in a river disturb the water flow and thus, change the water path at different points? Does the angle of the river or the amount of water flow have more of an impact on erosion?

Change the Variables There are several ways you can change the variables in this experiment. You can add natural debris to the sediment, such as leaves or twigs. Determine if natural debris positively or negatively impacts erosion. You can also add small pebbles and stones. The length of the river may also plays a factor in river erosion. Try changing the length to a shorter and longer river.

Design Your Own Experiment

How to Select a Topic Relating to this Concept Rivers of water have carved Earth's landscape, whether flowing in streams and rivers or creeping slowly as glaciers. You can try other experiments relating to rivers, involving topics such as water velocity and turbidity (amount of mud in the water) or

Troubleshooter's Guide

Here is a problem that may arise during this experiment, a possible cause, and a way to remedy the problem.

Problem: Water is leaking from the "river."

Possible cause: The plastic is not taped well enough. Be sure to tape the back of the bags (or other material) with Duct tape so that there are no holes.

Problem: All the dirt keeps washing away.

Possible cause: If all dirt is washing off the river, decrease your heights of elevation and try the experiment again.

Problem: The river keeps moving during the trials.

Possible cause: If it is too difficult to hold the river width tight, try using a detached playground slide or piece of guttering for the sides of the river. You could also build a smaller river.

a river's rates of erosion, deposition, and weathering. You might also investigate underground rivers or cave-forming rivers.

Check the Further Readings section and talk with your science teacher or school or community media specialist to start gathering information on river questions that interest you.

Steps in the Scientific Method To do an original experiment, you need to plan carefully and think things through. Otherwise, you might not be sure what question you are answering, what you are or should be measuring, or what your findings prove or disprove.

Here are the steps in designing an experiment:

- State the purpose of—and the underlying question behind—the experiment you propose to do.

- Recognize the variables involved, and select one that will help you answer the question at hand.

- State a testable hypothesis, an educated guess about the answer to your question.

- Decide how to change the variable you selected.

- Decide how to measure your results.

Recording Data and Summarizing the Results It is important that your data be kept organized in graphs or charts. When you finish your experiment, you must summarize the data and record your results. Reflect on the original question you wanted to answer. Write a paragraph explaining what happened and why so others can learn from your research.

Related Projects To develop an experiment on this topic, think about a question that you want answered. Where does the water flow the fastest? What is the largest size rock that can be carried by a river? Where does the water come from and go to? Investigate ways to measure and analyze rivers in order to answer your questions.

The Maruia River on South Island, New Zealand, is a meandering river. CORBIS-BETTMANN.

For More Information

BBC. "Rivers and Water Management." *Schools. Science: Geography.* http://www.bbc.co.uk/schools/gcsebitesize/geography/riverswater/riverprocessesrev2.shtml (accessed on March 15, 2008). Basic information on river erosions.

Knapp, Brian. *River.* Danbury, CT: Grolier Educational Corp., 1993. Offers facts about rivers, including how they work and rivers of the world. Includes simple experiments.

Pringle, Lawrence. *Rivers and Lakes.* New York: Time-Life Books, 1985. Explains how rivers change the landscape and how their energy is harnessed. Good chapter about organisms and wildlife that depend on rivers for their survival.

U.S. Geological Survey. "Earth's Water." *Water Science for Schools.* http://ga.water.usgs.gov/edu/mearth.html (accessed on March 12, 2008). Information and illustrations about the properties of water.

73

Rocks and Minerals

According to archaeologists (scientists who study the past remains of human activities), the Copper, Bronze, and Iron Ages were named for the main minerals that were being used in tools during those time periods, which spanned 10,000 B.C.E. to 2,000 B.C.E. Minerals are natural, nonliving solids—tiny particles arranged in definite patterns. Rocks are solid mixtures of minerals. If you look at a rock with a magnifying lens, you can often see the distinct grains of several different minerals.

Earth is a living machine At the end of the eighteenth century, James Hutton (1726–1797), a Scottish doctor, met once a week in Edinburgh to talk with other visionary men about new ideas. The Industrial Revolution was just beginning, and the men he met included James Watt, inventor of the steam engine, and Joseph Black, the chemist who discovered carbon dioxide. Hutton was interested in the rock and soil of his homeland and discussed his theories with this group.

Certain cliffs overlooking the North Sea, called Siccar Point, particularly fascinated Hutton. The upper part of the cliffs is red sandstone in horizontal layers, while the lower half is a dark rock tilted almost vertically. He knew the cliffs did not just magically appear in this form. After years of study, Hutton concluded that Earth was like a living machine, driven by heat within. He theorized that over thousands of centuries, the heated material within Earth's core erupted and formed deposits on the ocean bottom. Over time, these deposits rose to form new land. Then rains eroded them, sending some of the soil and rock particles back into the oceans. It was part of a continual cycle of creation and destruction.

In 1788, Hutton presented his ideas to the Royal Society of Edinburgh. He was not entirely correct, but his theory was accepted at the time and represented the beginning of modern geology, the science of rocks, volcanoes, earthquakes, and the history of Earth.

James Hutton (right) founded modern geology by studying rocks such as those at Siccar Point in Scotland. LIBRARY OF CONGRESS.

Shake, rattle, and roll Earth's very hot, solid inner core is the machine that Hutton envisioned. Earth's inner core is surrounded by an outer core, a hot layer of liquid metal. After that comes a layer called the mantle, which produces the liquid rock of volcanoes. Earth's crust is the top layer, the one on which we live.

Huge, moving blocks of rock called plates make up Earth's crust. Their fit is similar to the pieces of a cracked eggshell. The boundaries where the pieces meet are called seismic belts. Cracks along these belts allow heat from the upper mantle to escape. Within seismic belts, movement, heat, and eruptions combine to form various minerals, each kind with a specific crystal form. Some valuable minerals are located by mining near seismic belts.

Classifying this old rock Rocks vary enormously because of the way they are formed. Geologists, scientists who study rocks, classify them into three categories: igneous, sedimentary, and metamorphic rocks. Igneous (pronounced IG-knee-us) rocks are formed when rock material cools from a hot, liquid state called magma. Magma is a thick substance like melted glass. When it reaches Earth's surface, usually through volcanic eruptions, it is called lava.

The molten lava from this Hawaiian volcano is a form of rock that shot up from the depths of Earth's mantle. PHOTO RESEARCHERS INC.

Sedimentary rocks are formed from particles that have broken away from other rocks and have been washed down and deposited on the bottoms of lakes or oceans. These particles may become mixed with fragments of dead plants or seashells. Over millions of years, these deposits may get buried under other rocks and soil. The pressure of tons of earth above the particles packs them together in layers and hardens them into rock.

Metamorphic (pronounced meta-MORE-fic) rocks are formed from sedimentary and igneous rock that become deeply buried in Earth. They are not formed from melting. Instead, the combination of intense heat and pressure changes them into different minerals. Metamorphic, in fact, means "changed in shape."

When you think about it, Earth really is a living machine that forms the rocks and minerals that serve as the foundation of our daily lives. In the two projects that follow, you will examine rocks and minerals closely to learn more about them.

Mountains may include rocks of many types. PHOTO RESEARCHERS INC.

PROJECT 1

Mineral Testing: What kind of mineral is it?

Purpose/Hypothesis In this project, you will determine the characteristics of mineral samples, such as hardness, luster, and color. Each mineral has specific characteristics, or properties, that distinguish it from other minerals and can help you identify it.

Level of Difficulty Moderate/difficult.

Materials Needed

- white ceramic tile
- hammer
- magnifying lens

WORDS TO KNOW

Cleavage: The tendency of a mineral to split along certain planes.

Crust: The hard, outer shell of Earth that floats upon the softer, denser mantle.

Fracture: A mineral's tendency to break into curved, rough, or jagged surfaces.

Geology: The study of the origin, history and structure of Earth.

Igneous rock: Rock formed from the cooling and hardening of magma.

Inner core: Very dense, solid center of Earth.

Lava: Molten rock that occurs at the surface of Earth, usually through volcanic eruptions.

Luster: A glow of reflected light; a sheen.

Mantle: Thick, dense layer of rock that underlies Earth's crust and overlies the core.

Metamorphic rock: Rock formed by transformation of pre-existing rock through changes in temperature and pressure.

Mineral: An inorganic substance found in nature with a definite chemical composition and structure. Most have a crystal form.

Outer core: A liquid core that surrounds Earth's solid inner core; made mostly of iron.

Plates: Large regions of Earth's surface, composed of the crust and uppermost mantle, which move about, forming many of Earth's major geologic surface features.

Rock: Naturally occurring solid mixture of minerals.

Sedimentary rock: Rock formed from the compressed and solidified layers of organic or inorganic matter.

Seismic belt: Boundaries where Earth's plates meet.

Streak: The color of the dust left when a mineral is rubbed across a rough surface.

- glass plate or cup (used, since you will be scratching it as part of the experiment)
- penny
- 4 samples of unpolished minerals (gathered outdoors or purchased at a store; avoid polished samples because they lose some of their natural properties)
- 4 index cards
- goggles

Approximate Budget Less than $10 for a tile, minerals, and a magnifying lens.

Timetable 20 minutes.

Step-by-Step Instructions

1. Prepare an index card, as illustrated, to record data for each of your samples.

2. Number each sample and write the same number on an index card.

3. Determine and record the color or colors of each sample.

4. Check the streak. The streak of a mineral is the color of the dust left when the mineral is rubbed across a rough surface. Using the underside of the ceramic tile, firmly rub the mineral across the tile. Record the color of any residue left on the tile.

5. Examine the luster or shine of the mineral. If the mineral is shiny gold, silver, or grey, it is considered metallic. If it is not shiny, it is considered nonmetallic. Describe the luster of each mineral (metallic or nonmetallic) on its card.

6. Determine how each mineral breaks apart when struck. Cleavage is a mineral's tendency to break in along smooth, flat planes. Fracture is a mineral's tendency to break into curved, rough, or jagged surfaces.

> **How to Experiment Safely**
>
> Wear goggles at all times when testing minerals. Mineral fragments and dust can irritate your eyes.

Step 1: Index card set-up. GALE GROUP.

Mineral name: _____

Characteristics: _____

Color: _____ Luster: _____

Streak: _____   Cleavage:

(Draw fragment)

Hardness: _____

Special properties: _____

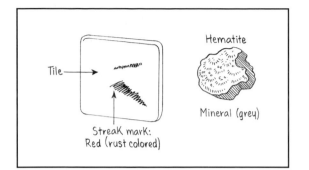

Step 4: Using the underside of the ceramic tile, firmly rub the mineral across the tile. GALE GROUP.

Wearing your goggles, strike the mineral with a hammer and break it. Using the magnifying lens, observe how many flat surfaces exist on the broken pieces. Draw your findings on the data card.

7. Check each mineral's hardness, using the Moh's Hardness Scale. The scale ranges from 1 (softest mineral, such as talc) to 10 (hardest mineral, such as a diamond). To determine the hardness of each mineral, see what it scratches. For instance, if the mineral scratches glass, it registers a 5.5–5.6 on the Moh's Hardness Scale; if it scratches a penny, but does not scratch glass, it registers 3.5–5.5 on the Scale; if it scratches a fingernail, but does not scratch a penny or glass, it registers 2.5–3.5 on the Scale; if it does not scratch a fingernail, penny, or glass, it registers 1.0–2.5 on the Scale.

8. Some minerals have special properties, such as being magnetic or dissolving in water. Some have a different smell, taste funny, react with acid, or glow under ultraviolet light. If you notice any special properties for each mineral, record them on its card.

Summary of Results Compare your results. What colors were your samples? Did the color of the streaks surprise you because they were different from the mineral? Could you tell if the samples were metallic or nonmetallic? How did the samples compare in hardness? If you wish, use a mineral identification guide and the properties you identified to

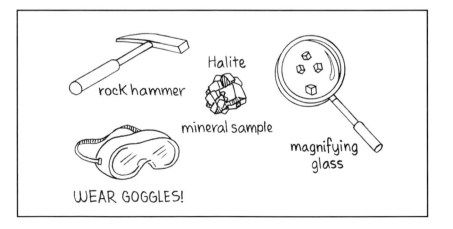

Step 6: Determine how each mineral breaks apart when struck. Wear your goggles! GALE GROUP.

determine the name of each sample. Set up a display of your samples and their data cards.

PROJECT 2

Rock Classification: Is it igneous, sedimentary, or metamorphic?

Purpose/Hypothesis This project will give you the basic knowledge needed to classify igneous, sedimentary, and metamorphic rocks.

Level of Difficulty Moderate.

Materials Needed

- hammer
- 12 rock samples of different colors, sizes, and textures
- flat, hard surface—old table or board
- egg carton
- permanent marking pen
- goggles
- magnifying lens

Approximate Budget $0. If possible, gather rock samples outdoors and borrow a hammer and goggles. Other materials should be available in the average household.

Timetable 1 hour.

Step-by-Step Instructions

1. Using the hammer outside on the table or board, carefully crack each rock sample to expose a fresh surface.
2. Place a sample of each rock into the egg carton wells.
3. Use the marking pen to label each sample with a number from 1 to 12.
4. Construct a data sheet to log all observations (see illustration).

> **How to Experiment Safely**
>
> Wear goggles at all times and use the hammer outside, away from others.

Step 1: Carefully crack each rock sample with the hammer to expose a fresh surface. GALE GROUP.

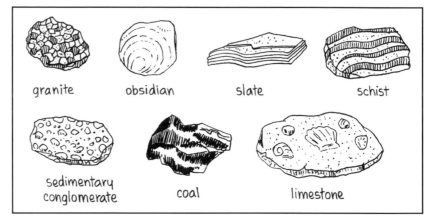

5. Using a magnifying lens, examine each rock. Look for characteristics such as:

    a. Igneous rocks (formed from cooled, liquid rock): Contain large or small crystals; appears glassy with seashell pattern when cracked.

    b. Metamorphic rocks (derived from pre-existing rock that was changed by heat and pressure): Layers that appear wavy.

    c. Sedimentary rocks (formed from pre-existing rock fragments or seashells or dead plants or animals): Include fossils—preserved

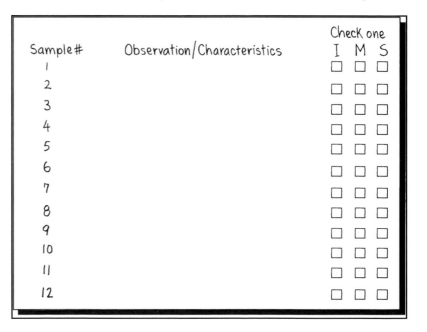

plant or animal remains; contains pebbles, sand, silt, or clay particles; contains carbon or coal; contains layers.

Summary of Results Examine your data sheet. Based on the visible properties, place each rock in one of the three categories. Remember, you must see some evidence to justify your conclusion. For example, sample 3 in the illustration, fossilized limestone, has sand grains as well as small sea shell fragments, so it must be sedimentary rock.

Modify the Project To further your understanding of rocks and make this project more challenging, you can experiment with how rocks break down. We know that wind, rain, rivers and rock slides can change the shapes of rocks. Rocks are also broken apart by repeated freezing and thawing. As the water in a rock freezes it expands, producing cracks in the rock. Over time these cracks will push the minerals apart and the rock will separate Into pieces. What type of rock is more likely to crack due to freezing and thawing?

In Project 2, you classified rocks into three categories, igneous, sedimentary and metamorphic. Using what you know about the characteristics of each type of rock, make a prediction about which type is more likely to break apart after freezing and thawing. Place your igneous, sedimentary and metamorphic rocks in separate plastic containers. Cover the rocks with water and place all the containers in the freezer. When the water has frozen remove container from the freezer and allow the water to melt. Look closely at the rocks do you see any cracks? Repeat this process of freezing and thawing four to six times.

Was your hypothesis right? Which type of rock has changed the most? Record your data and consider what would happen if you soaked the rocks overnight in the water before freezing. Would this make a difference in your results and

Troubleshooter's Guide

Here are some problems that may arise during this experiment, some possible causes, and ways to remedy the problems.

Problem: You cannot see any visible characteristics in some of the samples.

Possible cause: Some samples may be too small. A larger sample may be needed. For example, layers in metamorphic rock may be hard to see in a small sample.

Problem: A sample seems to possess properties of two groups, such as metamorphic layers and sand grains.

Possible cause: Since metamorphic rock is derived from other types of rocks, a sample may possess properties from other categories.

As the water in a rock freezes it expands, producing cracks in the rock. ILLUSTRATION BY TEMAH NELSON.

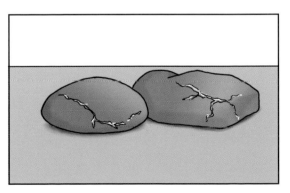

if so why? Consider that some rocks may absorb more water than others and therefore may have a higher water content upon freezing.

Design Your Own Experiment

How to Select a Topic Relating to this Concept Rocks and minerals are present in your daily life, from the rocks in the cement of our sidewalks to the minerals in bath powder. Choose a type of rock or mineral to study. Minerals used in household cleaning and rocks used in industry are just two leads you can investigate.

Check the Further Readings section and talk with your science teacher or school or community media specialist to gather information on rock and mineral questions that interest you. As you consider possible experiments, be sure to discuss them with a knowledgeable adult before trying them.

Steps in the Scientific Method To do an original experiment, you need to plan carefully and think things through. Otherwise, you might not be sure what question you are answering, what you are or should be measuring, or what your findings prove or disprove.

Here are the steps in designing an experiment:

- State the purpose of—and the underlying question behind—the experiment you propose to do.
- Recognize the variables involved, and select one that will help you answer the question at hand.
- State a testable hypothesis, an educated guess about the answer to your question.
- Decide how to change the variable you selected.
- Decide how to measure your results.

Recording Data and Summarizing the Results Make drawings, graphs, and charts to display your information for others. You might also draw conclusions about your findings. Which minerals seem to be the most common in your region? Why might that be?

Related Projects If you are interested in rocks and minerals and want to discover more of their uses in your daily life, you might investigate how rocks are used to prevent erosion or what consistency is the best for plaster, whose main ingredient is minerals. The possibilities are almost as endless as our supply of rocks and minerals.

For More Information

Barrow, Lloyd H. *Adventures with Rocks and Minerals.* Hillside, NJ: Enslow Publishing, 1991. Describes geological experiments. Chapters include what causes minerals to break and what freezing does to rocks.

Cox, Shirley. *Earth Science.* Vero Beach, FL: Rourke Publications, Inc., 1992. Chapters include how to choose geology projects.

GMB Services. *RocksForKids.* http://www.rocksforkids.com/ (accessed February 7, 2008). Information on rock formation, identification, and collection.

Parker, Steve. *The Earth and How It Works.* North Bellmore, NY: Marshall Cavendish, 1993. Outlines a variety of projects and experiments that examine Earth's composition.

U.S. Geological Survey. *Rocks and Minerals Site Contents.* http://wrgis.wr.usgs.gov/parks/rxmin/index.html (accessed February 7, 2008). Provides information on rocks and minerals.

Rotation and Orbits

Earth, like all the planets in our solar system, is in constant motion. All of the planets revolve or orbit around the Sun. An orbit is when one object in the universe goes round another one without touching it. For Earth, it takes about 365 days to complete one orbit around the Sun. Without Earth's rotation and orbit, the world would be a far different place. The rotation gives Earth its night and day. That allows the many life forms on Earth to remain at a comfortable temperature, warming during the sunlight hours and cooling down at the night. It affects the direction of wind and the ocean's daily tides. The orbit and tilt of rotation also give Earth its four seasons.

All the planets in the solar system also rotate, or spin, as they orbit the Sun. On average, Earth rotates once every 24 hours—or more precisely, 23 hours, 56 minutes, 4.091 seconds. The complete rotation of an object with respect to the stars is called a sidereal (pronounced sy-DEER-ee-awl) day.

Renaissance rules Today's knowledge of planets' rotations and orbits evolved during the sixteenth and seventeenth centuries in what is known as the Renaissance age. Scientists at that time were building telescopes and were able to observe how celestial objects behaved in detail for the first time. In 1543 Polish astronomer Nicolaus Copernicus (1473–1543) published his theory that Earth spins on its axis once daily and revolves around the sun annually. The widespread belief at that time was that the Sun and other planets revolved around Earth. Copernicus' theory caused great controversy and most people did not accept it.

Some scientists did believe Copernicus however, including German astronomer Johannes Kepler (1571–1630). In the early 1600s Kepler worked out three laws that applied to planetary motion. One of the laws stated that Earth orbits the Sun in an elliptical path. With this knowledge, astronomers could predict the movement of other planets through observations and mathematical calculations.

Each planet revolves as it orbits the Sun. GALE GROUP.

All of the planets in the solar system revolve, or orbit, around the Sun; the planets also rotate, or spin, as they orbit the Sun. GALE GROUP.

*Earth time		Period of revolution*	Period of rotation
	Mercury	88 days	59 days
	Venus	225 days	243 days
	Earth	365 days	24 hours
	Mars	687 days	25 hours
	Jupiter	12 years	10 hours
	Saturn	29 years	10 hours
	Uranus	84 years	18 hours
	Neptune	165 years	18 hours
	Pluto	248 years	6.4 days

Around and around There are many orbits in the solar system. Planets and other objects orbit around the Sun. Moons orbit around their planets. The main reason why objects orbit around another object is due to gravity. Gravity is the force pulling all matter together.

In the seventeenth century, English scientist Isaac Newton (1642–1727) realized the revolutionary idea of gravity when he was just twenty-three years old. Newton explained that the force of gravitation makes every pair of bodies attract and applies to all objects in the universe. This gravitational force relates to why objects fall to Earth as well as the motion of the moon and the planets in orbit. (For further information on gravity, see the Force chapter.)

The pull of gravity is stronger from heavier objects, and so lighter objects orbit the heavier one. The Sun is the heaviest object in the solar system. It is about a thousand times heavier than the largest planet, Jupiter, and more than 300,000 times heavier than Earth. The gravity of the Sun keeps Earth and all the planets in their orbits. The gravity of Earth pulls our Moon into its orbit around Earth.

Why we spin All the planets in the solar system rotate on their axis. A planet's axis is an imaginary line drawn through its center from the North to South Pole. The Earth's axis is tilted at a 23.45° angle from vertical. Other planets rotate at different angles. Except for Venus and Uranus, all planets rotate in the same direction that they orbit the Sun—from west to east.

Earth's continuous rotation began as the planet was formed, an estimated 4.6 billion years ago. The solar system formed from clouds of dust and gases that were spinning around the Sun. When these materials collapsed together they formed a larger and larger object that eventually formed a planet. Since these materials were already spinning, they began to spin faster as they collapsed inwards. This phenomenon is similar to an ice skater spinning. When the ice skater brings his or her arms closer to the body, he or she will spin faster.

Astronomers theorize that a large object collided with the newly formed planet, setting Earth spinning at a faster rate. The collision also may have tilted Earth's axis to its 23.45° angle. The seasons are caused by this angle of rotation. Since the axis is tilted, different parts of the planet are oriented towards the Sun at different times of the year. For example when Earth is at a certain place in its orbit, the northern hemisphere (the half of the planet north of the equator, including the United States) is tilted toward the Sun. During this portion of Earth's orbit, the northern hemisphere experiences the summer season. Six months later Earth is on the opposite side of the Sun. The northern hemisphere is tilted away from the Sun and experiences the winter season.

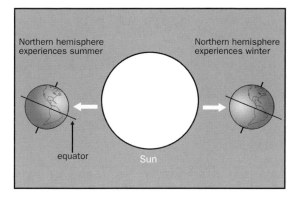

The tilt of the Earth on its axis, and its rotation, causes the four seasons. GALE GROUP.

The Earth spins continuously because there is no force in space to make it stop. One of the laws of motion states that a force is required to slow or stop a moving object. For example, when you roll a ball along the ground it will eventually stop due to the friction with the ground and the force of the air pushing against the ball. For Earth rotating on its axis, there is no force to counteract the rotation. That means it does not require any energy to keep it rotating.

Rotation's moving effects Earth's daily tides are caused both by gravity and our planet's spinning movements. Both the Sun and Moon produce a gravitational pull on Earth. Yet because the Moon is closer to Earth than the Sun, it has about double the gravitational force as that of the Sun, which means it has about double the influence on the tides.

As the Moon revolves around Earth, the earth and Moon are revolving together, like one unit, around a common point located within Earth. This point is called the center of gravity or the center of mass. At this center of gravity, the gravitational forces of Earth and the Moon pull out on each other equally. As the two objects rotate as one system, everything in and on Earth experiences centrifugal force. (While

Centrifugal force is caused by an object's tendency to keep moving in a straight line. This outward-pull effect occurs in all rotating objects. GALE GROUP.

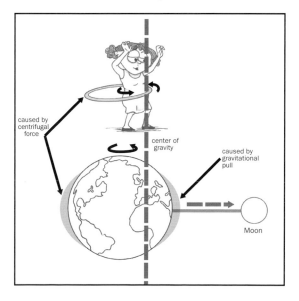

Leaves fall from the trees in autumn as a prelude to the coming winter season. FIELD MARK PUBLICATIONS.

centrifugal force actually acts on all matter, only the water is free to move about.)

Centrifugal force is actually not a force, but the absence of a force. A force is a push or pull. Centrifugal force is caused by an object's tendency to keep moving in a straight line. This outward-pull effect occurs in all rotating objects. For example, when a car turns sharply the passenger will seem to be pushed to the outside of the curve. The centrifugal force that the rider is experiencing is not due to an actual push: The passenger's body is trying to keep moving forward in the same direction. Centrifugal force causes Earth's water to be pulled away from the center of the spin.

On the side of Earth closest to the Moon, the Moon's gravity is strong enough to overcome the centrifugal force. The total or net gravitational force is in the direction of the Moon and causes a bulge or tide that is pulled towards the Moon. (For further information on tides, see the Ocean chapter.)

On the side of Earth opposite the Moon, the Moon's gravity is not strong enough to overcome the centrifugal force. The net gravitational force is away from Earth, causing a second bulge or tide to occur on the opposite side of the Moon. At any one time there are two bulges of water of roughly equal size, one towards and one away from the Moon. Low tides are created in areas about halfway between these two high-tide bulges when the water withdraws.

Curving around Another effect caused by Earth's rotation causes large moving bodies on or above Earth's surface to curve instead of moving in a straight path. Called the Coriolis force, this bending movement is named after French mathematician Gustave-Gaspard Coriolis. In 1835, he explained mathematically that this phenomenon is due to the object's course relative to the rotation of Earth.

The direction the object will curve depends on whether it is located north or south of the equator. In the northern hemisphere an object will turn to the right of its direction of movement; in the southern hemisphere, to the left. At the equator moving objects do not turn at all.

The circumference or distance around Earth at the equator is larger than it is at the poles. Since the whole Earth rotates once every 24 hours, the surface of the earth at the equator moves faster than it does at the poles. People living at the equator might not feel it, but they are rotating at a rate of about 1,000 miles per hour (1,609 kilometers per hour). As the equator moves more quickly to the east than other points on Earth, objects traveling away from the equator are deflected to the east.

The Coriolis force is a relatively weak one for most objects and is not noticeable. In large objects that move over a length of time, the Coriolis force can have a significant effect. For example, winds naturally move in ways that equalizes their warmth. Warm winds located at the equator move towards cold air at the poles; cold air at the poles moves toward the equator. The Coriolis force causes these winds to follow a curved path as they move.

What Are the Variables?

Variables are anything that might affect the results of an experiment. Here are the main variables in this experiment:

- the length of the pendulum's cord
- the amount of time the pendulum swings
- wind

In other words, the variables in this experiment are everything that might affect the pendulum's swing. If you change more than one variable at the same time, you will not be able to tell which variable had the most effect on the pendulum's swing.

EXPERIMENT 1

Foucault Pendulum: How can a pendulum demonstrate the rotation of Earth?

Purpose/Hypothesis In 1851, French physicist Jean-Bernard-Leon Foucault (1819–1868) proved that Earth rotates on its axis through a demonstration with a pendulum. A pendulum consists of a free-swinging cord set at a fixed point with a weight hanging from it. A pendulum swings at a constant rate and direction if there is no force moving against it.

Foucault hung a pendulum from a high ceiling and noted that the path of the pendulum's swing slowing changed its direction of swing. Since there was no force acting on the pendulum, he concluded that Earth had to be rotating beneath it.

The rotation of the Earth causes the Coriolis force. GALE GROUP.

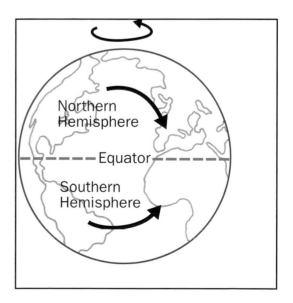

The first picture of Earth and Moon in a single frame, taken September 18, 1977, by Voyager 1. THE NATIONAL AERONAUTICS AND SPACE ADMINISTRATION.

In this experiment you will make a simple Foucault pendulum. When a pendulum is moving freely in air, the air resistance causes the pendulum to slow down and eventually stop. A heavy weight and tall pendulum will reduce the effect of friction. (Foucault's original pendulum consisted of a 62-pound (28-kilogram) iron ball suspended on a 220-foot (67-meter) steel wire.)

You will use a bag of sand as the pendulum's weight, and then note how the sand moves as it trickles from the bag. To observe results from the pendulum it should swing for at least 30 to 60 minutes. After that time, note the apparent change in the direction in which the pendulum is swinging.

To begin this experiment, make an educated guess about the outcome of the experiment based on your knowledge of Earth's rotation. This educated guess, or prediction, is your hypothesis. A hypothesis should explain these things:

- the topic of the experiment
- the variable you will change
- the variable you will measure
- what you expect to happen

A hypothesis should be brief, specific, and measurable. It must be something you can test through further investigation. Your experiment will prove or disprove whether your hypothesis is correct. Here is one possible hypothesis for this experiment: "The lines of sand falling from the Foucault pendulum will shift slightly over time as Earth is continuously rotating."

In this experiment, the variable you will change is time. The variable you will measure will be the appearance of the pendulum's swing.

Level of Difficulty Moderate to Difficult (because of the difficulty in keeping the swing straight).

Materials Needed

- 13 feet (4 meters) of nylon cord or strong string
- cloth or canvas sack

Axis: An imaginary straight line around which an object, like a planet, spins or turns. Earth's axis is a line that goes through the North and South Poles.

Centrifugal force: The apparent force pushing a rotating body away from the center of rotation.

Circumference: The distance around a circle.

Control experiment: A setup that is identical to the experiment, but is not affected by the variable that acts on the experimental group.

Coriolis force: A force that makes a moving object appear to travel in a curved path over the surface of a spinning body.

Gravity: Force of attraction between objects, the strength of which depends on the mass of each object and the distance between them.

Hypothesis: An idea in the form of a statement that can be tested by observation and/or experiment.

Orbit: The path followed by a body (such as a planet) in its travel around another body (such as the Sun).

Rotate: To turn around on an axis or center.

Sidereal day: The system of time to measure a day based on the motion of the stars.

Variable: Something that can affect the results of an experiment.

- ladder at least 12 to 15 feet (3.5 to 4.5 meters) high, high swing set, or other tall stable outdoor structure
- fine, dry sand (available at hardware stores or greenhouses)
- calm, nonwindy day
- large garbage bag
- watch or timer
- tape
- sharp nail
- chair

Approximate Budget $8.

Timetable 75 minutes.

Step-by-Step Instructions

1. Fill the sack with sand. Make sure there are no leaks in the bag by holding it over a clean surface and moving it gently.
2. Tie the open end of the sack together with the cord or string, and stand on a chair to hang the bag from the top of the ladder or other stand. You may need an adult's help with this.

How to Experiment Safely

Make sure the pendulum stand you are using is securely attached to the ground and will not tip over. Be careful when handling the sharp nail. Also, be careful when you are attaching the string to the tall structure. Ask an adult to either help you balance or attach the string for you.

3. Use the nail to punch a small hole in the bottom of the sand bag. The hole should be slightly larger than the tip of a pen, to allow the sand to fall out slowly. Hold the bag up to make sure that sand drops out at a visible rate. When it is flowing properly, seal the hole with a piece of tape.

4. Lay out the garbage bag on the ground under and around the pendulum.

5. Make sure the bag of sand hangs straight down and is not tilted. If it is, adjust either the sack or the cord.

6. Keep the cord tight and pull the bag straight back about 4 feet (1.2 meters) high. Remove the tape and carefully set the pendulum in motion. Make sure you swing in a straight line and do not have an elliptical swing.

7. Over the next 45 to 60 minutes, carefully give the cord an extra swing when it slows down. Try to keep the pendulum swinging for 60 minutes. Make sure you simply push the swing in the direction it is moving and do not shift the cord at all. This experiment may take more than one attempt.

Summary of Results Draw the pattern of the sand. Explain the results, including how the Coriolis force influences the direction of the sand lines. For example, a Foucault pendulum set in motion in the northern hemisphere traces out a line that is always shifted toward the right.

How many degrees the pendulum shifts depends on where it is geographically located or its latitude. Latitude identifies the north-to-south position of a point on Earth The equator is 0° latitude; the north and south poles are each 90° latitude. At the equator the pendulum would not shift at all. At either of the poles the pendulum's swing would complete a circle in about 24 hours. You can figure out the rate of rotation where you live by finding your latitude and figuring out the following equation through longhand or a

Step 6: Carefully release the sack so that the pendulum moves in a straight line.
GALE GROUP.

calculator. Mathematically, the pendulum's rate of shift is equal to the rate of rotation of Earth multiplied by the sine of the number of degrees of latitude: n = 360 degrees x sine (latitude), where n equals the number of degrees of rotation. The sine of latitude represents the angular distance of a place from the equator.

Change the Variables By increasing the time you keep the pendulum swinging, the more the sand lines will shift and the better you will be able to observe Earth's rotation. You can attempt to find an even taller structure from which to hang your pendulum. Keeping the pendulum swinging manually is challenging because of any inadvertent shifting of the swing's direction. One way to increase the swing time of a Foucault pendulum is to build a mechanical device that automatically pushes the cord back and forth. There are several such designs available. See the Further Readings section, talk to your teacher, or research the topic independently.

Troubleshooter's Guide

Below are some problems that may arise during this experiment, some possible causes, and some ways to remedy the problem.

Problem: The bag is moving in a circular, elliptical path.

Possible cause: You may not have pushed the bag in a straight line for the first push or any subsequent pushes. Try practicing a straight-line push with the tape on the bag, and then repeat the experiment.

Problem: There was no shift in the lines of sand.

Possible cause: You may have set the cord slightly off-kilter during one of your pushes, or the pendulum may not have swung long enough. Try practicing a straight-line push with the tape on the bag, and then repeat the experiment, making sure to keep the pendulum swinging for at least 60 minutes.

EXPERIMENT 2

Spinning Effects: How does the speed of a rotating object affect the way centrifugal force can overcome gravity?

Purpose/Hypothesis The term centrifugal force comes from the Latin meaning "center-fleeing" or "away from the center," which explains the outward movement of an object experiencing centrifugal force. Centrifugal force can overcome the effects of gravity. One of the factors that affect centrifugal force depends on the speed of rotation or an object's velocity. The greater the speed of the object, the greater the force.

In this experiment you will observe centrifugal force occurring with different velocities, and see how each overcomes the effects of gravity. You will measure the outward pull of water in a small container that is revolving. The faster you spin the container, the higher its velocity. You will spin the container at two different speeds, each for the same length of time.

Before you begin, make an educated guess about the outcome of this experiment based on your knowledge of centrifugal force and gravity.

What Are the Variables?

Variables are anything that might affect the results of an experiment. Here are the main variables in this experiment:

- length of string
- speed of rotation
- shape of container
- mass of spinning object

In other words, the variables in this experiment are everything that might affect the way the water moves. If you change more than one variable at the same time, you will not be able to tell which variable had the most effect on centrifugal force.

This educated guess, or prediction, is your hypothesis. A hypothesis should explain these things:

- the topic of the experiment
- the variable you will change
- the variable you will measure
- what you expect to happen

A hypothesis should be brief, specific, and measurable. It must be something you can test through further investigation. Your experiment will prove or disprove whether your hypothesis is correct. Here is one possible hypothesis for this experiment: "At higher speeds, the water will be pushed further outwards."

In this case, the variable you will change is the velocity of a spinning object. The variable you will measure is the distance the water was pushed outwards.

Conducting a control experiment will help you isolate each variable and measure the changes in the dependent variable. Only one variable will change between the control and the experimental trials. Your control experiment will use no centrifugal force and, thus, will only have the effects of gravity. At the end of the experiment you can compare your observations from the control with the experimental trials.

Level of Difficulty Easy.

Materials Needed

- 5 feet (1.5 meters) of string
- shallow Styrofoam or thin plastic cup
- single hole puncher
- clear area outside
- tape measure
- small cloth rag
- water
- watch with second hand
- partner

Step 5: Swing the container overhead. GALE GROUP.

Approximate Budget $5.

Timetable 20 minutes.

Step-by-Step Instructions

1. Punch two holes on opposite sides of the plastic cup and thread the string through the holes.
2. Punch holes all around the sides of the container.
3. Stand in an open area outside and use an object to mark where you are standing.
4. Wet the rag with water until it is dripping wet, and place it in the cup. This is the control. Wait a few seconds and note your observations of what happens to the water.
5. Wet the rag again and replace it the container. Slowly swing the container in an arc until you get a slow circular motion over your head.
6. Have your partner time you and count the number of complete revolutions you make in 10 seconds.
7. Increase the speed of the revolutions and again count the number of revolutions you make in 10 seconds.
8. Find the mid-point of where the water landed in the circle for the first set of revolutions. Measure from that point to the mark where you were standing.
9. Repeat the measurement at the midpoint of where the water landed for the first higher-speed revolutions.

Summary of Results Construct a chart with your results and graph the data. Examine how the outward force of the water changes with the velocity of the spinning object. How does gravity affect the control experiment? The experimental setups? What does the velocity of the revolving container illustrate about the speed of rotation and planets?

How to Experiment Safely

Be careful that your partner or anyone else is not too close when you are swinging the cup. You may get wet so wear the appropriate clothes.

Troubleshooter's Guide

Below is a problem that may arise during this experiment, a possible cause, and a way to remedy the problem.

Problem: The water stopped coming out of the container before the revolutions stopped.

Possible cause: The rag may not have been wet enough. Try pouring a little water in the container to a point below where the holes start. Dump the rag in water, place it in the container, and repeat the experiment.

Change the Variables To change the variables in this experiment you can alter the weight of the revolving object. Fill up a container with different amounts of water and weigh each object before you start spinning. You can also change the spinning object to a solid material, such as a marble or a rock. Another variable that you can change is the length of the string.

Design Your Own Experiment

How to Select a Topic Relating to this Concept The movements of celestial objects have fascinated people long before there were any astronomical gadgets. For projects related to rotation and orbits, you can think about how the movements of the Sun and Moon have an effect on Earth. You can also visit a local planetarium to view how objects in our solar system move. Check the Further Readings section and talk with your science teacher to learn more about rotations and orbits of celestial objects. Remember that if you conduct a project where you observe celestial objects, never look directly at the Sun to avoid damage to your eyes.

Steps in the Scientific Method To conduct an original experiment, you need to plan carefully and think things through. Otherwise, you might not be sure what question you are answering, what you

At any one time there are two bulges of water (or high tide) of roughly equal size, one towards and one away from the Moon. Low tides are created in areas about halfway between these two high-tide bulges. Here, boats docked near the shore are beached during low tide.
© NIK WHEELER/CORBIS.

are or should be measuring, or what your findings prove or disprove.

Here are the steps in designing an experiment:

- State the purpose of—and the underlying question behind—the experiment you propose to do.
- Recognize the variables involved and select one that will help you answer the question at hand.
- State your hypothesis, an educated guess about the answer to your question.
- Decide how to change the variable you selected.
- Decide how to measure your results.

Recording Data and Summarizing the Results Your data should include charts and drawings such as the one you did for the experiments in this chapter. They should be clearly labeled and easy to read. You may also want to include photographs and drawings of the experimental setup, models of any celestial setup, and the results, which will help other people visualize the experiment.

If you are preparing an exhibit, you may want to display your results, such as any experimental setup you designed. If you have completed a nonexperimental project, explain clearly what your research question was and illustrate your findings.

Related Projects There are multiple projects related to the orbits and rotations of celestial bodies. You can focus on the Moon's orbit through the sky, recording its phases throughout a month and its effect on Earth. There are certain celestial bodies that are held together by mutual gravitational attraction, such as the Earth and the Moon. You can examine other planet-moon systems, determine the point at which the bodies orbit around, and map out the orbit of each body. Another factor relating to orbits is the relationship between the time it takes a planet to complete one orbit and its distance from the Sun. You can explore how mass and distance affect a celestial body's orbit.

Another project could be to focus on the basic shapes of planetary orbits. Each planet has its own unique orbital path; some are close to circular and others are far more elliptical. You can map out the paths of the orbits on paper or construct a model. To further explore tides, you could examine how the Sun impacts tides and map the high and low tides in your area. Ocean tides are not exactly twelve hours apart. Another possible project is to explore what causes the time between tides, look up tidal information in a certain area, and then predict the high and low tides for the next month. Scientists have found that a planet's rotation affects its shape. You can explore this principle on Earth and other celestial bodies. For a research project, you can look at the many people and discoveries that led to the understanding that Earth orbits and rotates around the Sun.

For More Information

Arnett, Bill. *The Eight Planets.* http://www.nineplanets.org (accessed on February 16, 2008). Overview of the history, mythology, and science of the planets, moons and other objects in our solar system.

"Coriolis Force." *Department of Atmospheric Sciences at the University of Illinois at Urbana-Champaign.* http://ww2010.atmos.uiuc.edu/(Gh)/guides/mtr/fw/crls.rxml (accessed on February 16, 2008). Brief explanation of the Coriolis force with a video.

Curious about Astronomy. http://curious.astro.cornell.edu/index.php (accessed on February 17, 2008). Clear answers to many astronomy questions and the chance to ask questions.

Groleau, Rick. "What Causes the Tides?" *PBS: Nova.* http://www.pbs.org/wgbh/nova/venice/tide_nf.html (accessed on February 17, 2008). PBS's *Nova* site illustrates the centrifugal force that causes tides.

NASA Observatorium. http://observe.arc.nasa.gov/nasa/space/centrifugal/centrifugal_index.html (accessed on February 16, 2008). Detailed explanation of centrifugal force.

National Aeronautics and Space Administration. *The Space Place.* http://spaceplace.jpl.nasa.gov/en/kids/ (accessed on February 16, 2008). Answers to space-related questions, activities, and clear space science explanations.

Scagell, Robin. *Space Explained: A Beginner's Guide to the Universe.* New York: Henry Holt & Company, 1996. Look at how the universe was created; includes lots of illustrations.

Simon, Seymour. *Our Solar System.* New York: William Morrow & Co., 1992. Simple description of the origins, characteristics, and future of the solar system, with lots of illustrations.

75

Salinity

What gives ocean water its salty taste? The answer lies in its salinity, the total salt content of the water. Saline (salty) substances are present in all water, even rain water, but sodium and chlorine are the two most abundant saline substances dissolved in ocean water.

Get out the yardstick In 1872, the H.M.S. *Challenger* began its worldwide ocean expedition from Portsmouth, England. On board were 240 sailors and scientists, including four naturalists and their support team. Originally built as a warship, the ship was converted into a floating scientific lab by the British government to study the biology of the sea, as well as the chemical and physical properties of the water. Between 1872 and 1876, the ship sailed 68,890 miles (110,908 kilometers) and made 492 stops. Nearly 5,000 new species, including giant worms and deep-sea shrimp almost as big as lobsters, were brought on board and identified.

Samples of seawater were also collected and analyzed for their chemical composition. The main substances present included bicarbonates and sulfates, as well as salts such as calcium, magnesium, potassium, sodium, and chloride. Sodium and chloride were the most abundant. While the samples showed that different salinity measurements existed, the average salinity of all the samples was about 3.5%, or 35 pounds (kilograms) of salt per 1,000 pounds (kilograms) of seawater. Scientists today still use this average salinity figure, and the *Challenger*'s salinity samples are still the only worldwide set of analyzed seawater. In fact, this voyage helped launch modern oceanography. John Murray, one of naturalists onboard, later supervised the publication of 50 volumes of *Challenger Reports* based on the expedition's discoveries.

In 1872, the crew of the H.M.S. Challenger were the first to measure ocean salinity. NORTH WIND PICTURE ARCHIVE.

WORDS TO KNOW

Buoyancy: The upward force exerted on an object placed in a liquid.

Calibration: To standardize or adjust a measuring instrument so its measurements are correct.

Density: The mass of a substance compared to its volume.

Density ball: A ball with the fixed standard of 1.0 gram per milliliter, which is the exact density of pure water.

Hydrometer: An instrument that determines the specific gravity of a liquid.

Hypothesis: An idea in the form of a statement that can be tested by observation and/or experiment.

Nansen bottles: Self-closing containers with thermometers that draw in water at different depths.

Oceanography: The study of the chemistry of the oceans, as well as their currents, marine life, and the ocean bed.

Salinity: The amount of salts dissolved in water.

Specific gravity: The ratio of the density of a substance to the density of pure water.

Standard: A base for comparison.

Variable: Something that can affect the results of an experiment.

Where did the salt come from? Millions of years ago, one ocean covered Earth. This vast ocean was just barely salty. Over time, land formed, and rain washed salt and minerals from the land into the ocean. Salt also came from rocks and sediments on the ocean floor, and from undersea volcanic activity that literally erupted salts into the water. All these accumulated salts made ocean water heavier, that is, gave it a greater density than fresh water.

The Red Sea has a salinity level of 27 percent. PETER ARNOLD INC.

The discoveries made on the *Challenger* gave us an average salinity for oceans, but this number can vary quite a bit. For example, the Baltic Sea near Sweden has a salinity content of 1%; while the Red Sea near Egypt has a salinity content of 27%. Salinity increases through evaporation, which begins as the surface water of the ocean is warmed by the Sun. The heated water becomes water vapor and rises into the atmosphere, leaving the salt behind.

Generally, waters in climates with strong sunlight and high temperatures, such as the region around the Red Sea, tend to have a higher salinity level because the surface water there evaporates at a faster rate. In the Baltic Sea region, rain, fresh water from adjoining rivers, and melting ice keep the salinity level low. The colder weather there also reduces the evaporation rate.

Getting the evidence Two instruments used to analyze ocean water are hydrometers, which measure seawater density, and Nansen bottles. Nansen bottles are more sophisticated versions of those collection bottles used on the H.M.S. *Challenger.* The bottles are self-closing containers with thermometers; they can draw in water at different depths. Through their use, scientists have learned that the sea has different layers of water with specific salinity levels and temperatures.

In the two experiments that follow, you will learn more about salinity by measuring it in different ways.

What Are the Variables?

Variables are anything that might affect the results of an experiment. Here are the main variables in this experiment:

- the amount of water in the sample
- the amount of salt in the water
- the temperature of the water
- the accuracy of the hydrometer measurements

In other words, the variables in this experiment are everything that might affect the specific gravity of the water. If you change more than one variable at a time, you will not be able to determine which variable had the most effect on the specific gravity.

EXPERIMENT 1

Making a Hydrometer: How can salinity be measured?

Purpose/Hypothesis In this experiment, you will create a scientific instrument called a hydrometer. A hydrometer is used to measure the specific gravity of water, comparing the density of one water sample to that of pure water. Pure water has a density of 1.000 grams/milliliter. If any salts or chemicals are added, they will dissolve and their added mass will increase the density of the water. This will increase the specific gravity. The greater the specific gravity, the greater the salinity.

A hydrometer works on the Archimedes Principle of buoyancy, which states that a liquid exerts an upward buoyant force on an object equal to the amount of liquid displaced by the object. Thus if an object floats partially submerged in water, the downward weight of the object must be counterbalanced by the upward buoyant force, which is equal to the weight of the water displaced. Otherwise, the object would sink to the bottom.

If you add salt to the water, the downward weight of the object will displace less water because the water is now denser—that is, it has more

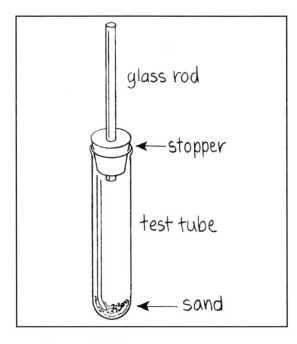

Steps 1 and 2: Making a hydrometer. GALE GROUP.

mass for a given volume. As a result, the object will float higher in the water, with less of it submerged. If you place measurement graduations along the surface of the object where the water touches, you have created a hydrometer. The hydrometer measurements can then be equated to the specific gravity, and in turn to the amount of salt in the water, or salinity.

To begin the experiment, use what you have learned about salinity to make a guess about what will happen to the specific gravity of water when salt is added. This educated guess is your hypothesis. A hypothesis should explain these things:

- the topic of the experiment
- the variable you will change
- the variable you will measure
- what you expect to happen

A hypothesis should be brief, specific, and measurable. It must be something you can test through observation. Your experiment will prove or disprove whether your hypothesis is correct. Here is one possible hypothesis for this experiment: "The more salt in the water, the higher its specific gravity."

In this case, the variable you will change is the amount of salt in the water, and the variable you will measure is the water's specific gravity. If the specific gravity increases with an increase in salt, your hypothesis is correct.

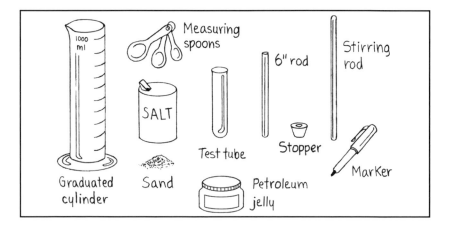

Materials for Experiment 1. GALE GROUP.

Level of Difficulty Moderate/difficult because accurate measurements and adjustments are required.

Materials Needed

- one 1-quart (1-liter) graduated cylinder filled with distilled water at room temperature
- one 5-inch (12.7-centimeter) test tube
- one 6-inch (15.2-centimeter) glass rod
- 1 rubber test tube stopper with a single hole that fits the glass rod
- 2 tablespoons (30 milliliters) sand
- 1 to 3 cups (250 to 750 milliliters) table salt
- small amount of petroleum jelly
- fine tip permanent marker
- measuring spoons
- stirring rod

Approximate Budget $0 to $10. Ideally, you can borrow most of the materials from school. Ask your science teacher for help.

Timetable About 1 hour.

Step-by-Step Instructions

1. Place a small dab of petroleum jelly on the end of the glass rod. Push the glass rod through the stopper until it reaches the bottom of the stopper.
2. Place a pinch or two of sand into the test tube and place the stopper into it. You have made a hydrometer.
3. Place the test tube hydrometer into the graduated cylinder of distilled water.
4. Add or remove some of the sand from the test tube until the hydrometer floats vertically in the water with approximately 1 inch (2.5 centimeters) of the glass rod above the water.

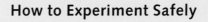

How to Experiment Safely

Be sure to handle glass carefully.

Steps 3 to 8: Hydrometer in graduated cylinder of distilled water with different water levels marked. GALE GROUP.

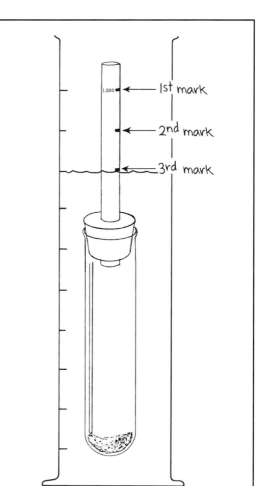

Troubleshooter's Guide

Below is a problem that may arise during this experiment, a possible cause, and a way to remedy the problem.

Problem: The test tube does not float vertically in the water.

Possible cause: There is not enough weight in the bottom of the tube to keep it upright. Use more sand or substitute a denser material instead of sand, such as small roller bearings.

5. Use the marker to write 1.000 on the glass rod at the level of the surface of the water.

6. Remove the hydrometer from the water and stir in 3 tablespoons of salt. This is equivalent to about 3.5 ounces (100 grams) of salt. Stir until all of the salt is dissolved.

7. Place the hydrometer in the water and mark the new water level. It should be lower on the rod because the water is denser and the hydrometer is now floating slightly higher. The increased water density, compared to the density of pure water, means the salty water has a higher specific gravity.

8. Add another 3 tablespoons of salt and mark the water level again. The hydrometer should float even higher in the water as the density (and specific gravity) of the water increases.

Summary of Results Study the marks on your hydrometer. Do they support your hypothesis? Did the specific gravity increase each time you added more salt to the water? What does this tell you about the salinity of the water? Write a paragraph describing and explaining your results.

Change the Variables You can change the variables in this experiment in several ways. For example, you can chill the water by placing it in a refrigerator to determine the effect of water temperature on salinity. You could also use a different kind of salt—for example, potassium chloride instead of sodium chloride.

EXPERIMENT 2

Density Ball: How to make a standard for measuring density

Purpose/Hypothesis This experiment is designed to create a standard. A standard is an object or instrument that has a fixed value. In this experiment, you will create a standard for measuring the density of a solution, called a density ball. A density ball has the fixed standard of 1.0 gram/milliliter, which is the exact density of pure water. You will then determine if your standard can accurately indicate if a water sample's density is greater than or equal to pure water.

This experiment is similar to Experiment #1, except here you will determine density by watching whether the density ball standard is suspended or floats.

To begin the experiment, use what you know about the density of pure water to make an educated guess about how a density ball will work. This educated guess, or prediction, is your hypothesis. A hypothesis should explain these things:

- the topic of the experiment
- the variable you will change
- the variable you will measure
- what you expect to happen

A hypothesis should be brief, specific, and measurable. It must be something you can test through observation. Your experiment will prove or disprove whether your hypothesis is correct. Here is one possible hypothesis for this experiment: "By creating a standard for the density of pure water, you will be able to determine whether a solution has a density greater than or equal to 1.0 gram/milliliter."

In this case, the variable you will change is the amount of salt in the water, and the variable you will measure is how your density ball reacts to changes in density. If your density ball accurately predicts whether a water sample is greater than or equal to the density of pure water, you will know your hypothesis is correct.

What are the Variables? Variables are anything that might affect the results of an experiment. Here are the main variables in this experiment:

- the amount of water in the sample
- the amount of salt in the water
- the temperature of the water
- the behavior of the density ball

In other words, the variables in this experiment are everything that might affect the density reading indicated by the density ball. If you change more than one variable, you will not be

> ## How to Experiment Safely
>
> Be sure to handle glass safely.

Materials for Experiment 2.
GALE GROUP.

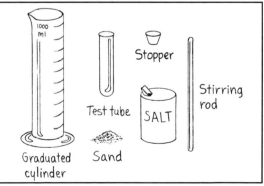

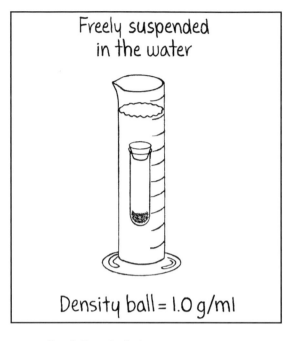

Freely suspended
in the water

Density ball = 1.0 g/ml

Step 4: Test tube freely suspended in water. GALE GROUP.

Step 4: What to do if test tube sinks to bottom or floats to surface. GALE GROUP.

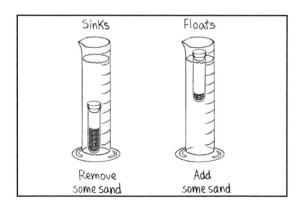

Sinks Floats

Remove some sand Add some sand

able to determine which variable had the most effect on the density reading.

Level of Difficulty Moderate, because delicate adjustments are required for this experiment.

Materials Needed

- one 1-quart (1-liter) graduated cylinder filled with distilled water at room temperature
- one 5-inch (12.7-centimeter) test tube
- 1 rubber test tube stopper without a hole
- 2 tablespoons (30 milliliters) sand
- 1 to 2 cups (250 to 500 milliliters) salt
- measuring spoons
- stirring rod

Approximate Budget $0 to $10. See if you can borrow the lab materials from your science teacher. You probably have salt and perhaps sand at home.

Timetable 30 minutes.

Step-by-Step Instructions

1. Place a pinch or two of sand in the test tube.
2. Place the stopper in the opening of the test tube securely. This is your density ball.
3. Place the test tube into the graduated cylinder of distilled water.
4. Wait 15 to 20 seconds and note where the test tube is positioned. If it is suspended freely in the water without floating to the surface or sinking to the bottom, it has the same density as water at room temperature: 1.0 gram/milliliter. If the test tube sinks to the bottom, remove some sand and try again. If it floats to the surface, add some sand.

5. Remove the test tube and stir 3 table-spoons—about 3.5 ounces (100grams)—of salt into the water.

6. Place the test tube back into the water and note its position. (It should float now because the added salt makes the water denser than the ball.)

Summary of Results Did your density ball indicate the density of the water and support your hypothesis? Write a paragraph explaining what you have learned during this experiment. How did your density ball behave in different solutions? What does this tell you about the solutions?

Change the Variables You can change the variables and conduct other similar experiments. For example, try your 1.0 grams/milliliter standard density ball in another liquid, such as corn oil or vinegar, to determine if those liquids are more or less dense than pure water. How is the density of these liquids affected if you add salt?

Troubleshooter's Guide

Below are some problems that may arise during this experiment, some possible causes, and ways to remedy the problems.

Problem: The test tube sinks and rests on the bottom.

Possible cause: The test tube is too heavy. Remove a pinch of sand from it and try again.

Problem: The test tube floats at the surface.

Possible cause: The test tube is not heavy enough. Add a pinch more sand and try again.

Design Your Own Experiment

How to Select a Topic Relating to this Concept If you are interested in salinity or its effects, there are many fascinating experiments you can explore. For example, how is salt used in the human body? Why does salt cause metal corrosion? How do marine animals adapt to their environment? These are all possible questions you can explore.

Check the Further Readings section and talk with your science teacher or school or community media specialist to start gathering information on salinity questions that interest you. As you consider possible experiments, be sure to discuss them with your science teacher or another knowledgeable adult before trying them. Some of the materials or procedures might be dangerous.

Steps in the Scientific Method To do an original experiment, you need to plan carefully and think things through. Otherwise, you might not be sure what question you are answering, what you are or should be measuring, or what your findings prove or disprove.

Here are the steps in designing an experiment:

- State the purpose of—and the underlying question behind—the experiment you propose to do.
- Recognize the variables involved, and select one that will help you answer the question at hand.
- State a testable hypothesis, an educated guess about the answer to your question.
- Decide how to change the variable you selected.
- Decide how to measure your results.

Recording Data and Summarizing the Results Your data should include charts that are labeled and easy to read. You may also want to include photos, graphs, and drawings of your set-up and results. When working with salinity, you may be able to set up your experiment as a demonstration model. Do not forget to share what you have learned about salinity.

Related Projects You might do an experiment on how salinity affects plants. Another possibility is to find the corrosion rate on metals exposed to salts. You may also want to explore the use of salts in chemistry and manufacturing. Be sure to talk with your teacher before starting a project.

For More Information

"Deep Ocean Creatures." *Extreme Science.* http://www.extremescience.com/DeepestFish.htm (accessed on March 14, 2008.) Nice pictures and facts on deep ocean creatures.

Lambert, David. *The Kingfisher Young People's Book of Oceans.* New York: Kingfisher, 1997. Includes nine ocean topics with related subjects. Describes how the oceans formed and the composition of seawater.

"Ocean Water: Salinity." *Office of Naval Research.* http://http://www.onr.navy.mil/Focus/ocean/water/salinity1.htm (accessed on March 14, 2008). Brief explanation and animation of the tides.

Rothaus, Don P. *Oceans.* Chanhassen, MN: The Child's World Inc., 1997. Describes the characteristics of the world's oceans including the chemistry of seawater.

76

Scientific Method

When you encounter a problem, how do you solve it? Do you consider what you already know about the problem, think of a possible answer, and then see if your answer is correct? If so, you are using the scientific method. The scientific method is a way of carefully collecting evidence about a question or problem, using that evidence to form a possible answer, and then testing the answer to see if it is accurate.

You can use this method as a tool for solving problems in science class and in many other areas of your life. For example, it could help you figure out why your pencils keep disappearing, how to wrap your sandwich so it does not dry out by lunchtime, or why your dog no longer likes his favorite food.

What are the steps in the scientific method? The scientific method has six steps, described below. They will help you solve all kinds of problems, in and out of school.

Step 1: State a problem or ask a question.
Step 2: Gather background information.
Step 3: Form a hypothesis.
Step 4: Design and perform an experiment.
Step 5: Draw a conclusion.
Step 6: Report the results.

Step 1: State a problem or ask a question. To begin using the scientific method, think about the world around you. You may see something that makes you curious, such your sandwich drying out by lunchtime on some days but not on others. You might see an unexplained light in the sky. You might hear a statement that you are not sure is true. For example, a friend might tell you that wearing glasses makes your eyes become weaker.

Put your curiosity into the form of a problem or question, such as these:

- Why does my sandwich dry out some days but not others?
- What is that light in the sky?

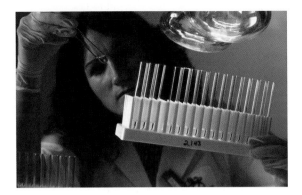

You do not have to be a scientist to use the scientific method. PHOTO RESEARCHERS INC.

- Does wearing glasses make your eyes weaker?

Step 2: Gather background information. Read more about the problem or question. Observe it closely.

Step 3: Form a hypothesis. Now use what you know about the situation to think of a possible answer for your question. This answer, or guess, is your hypothesis. A hypothesis is an idea in the form of a statement that can be tested by observations and/or experiment. You will use what you already know about the situation to form a hypothesis. Here are possible hypotheses to answer the questions above:

- Plastic bags that seal keep more moisture in bread than waxed paper or plastic bags without seals do.
- That light in the sky is an airplane.
- Wearing glasses does not make your eyes become weaker.

All of these hypothesis are testable: You can make observations, do research, or set up experiments to determine whether each hypothesis is correct. Here are some examples of hypotheses that are vague and untestable:

- Sandwiches taste better when you seal them in plastic bags. *How can you measure "taste better?"*
- The light in the sky might be a reflection or something. *How can you measure "might be" or "something?"*
- Wearing glasses might make your eyes weaker, if you wear them long enough. *How long is "long enough?"*

The ancient Greeks often hypothesized about the causes of natural events. However, they assumed they could figure out the correct explanations just by thinking about the situation long enough. They usually did not experiment to find out whether their explanations were accurate. Aristotle, a famous Greek philosopher, developed theories that led to many discoveries, but his theories were based mostly on reasoning, not experimentation. For example, he hypothesized that the flies that he found on rotting fruit just appeared out of the air. He did not experiment to find out whether his hypothesis was true.

Step 4: Design and perform an experiment. In this step, you go beyond the ancient Greeks: you prove or disprove your hypothesis. You might be

Hypotheses: Is the light in the sky just an airplane—or something else? PHOTO RESEARCHERS INC.

able to establish whether your hypothesis is accurate by research, such as checking the local airport to see if an airplane flew over your house at a certain time last night. Or you might gather expert opinions about how wearing glasses affects people's eyesight. For the sandwich problem, the best approach is an experiment.

An experiment is a controlled observation. The experimenter carefully changes one condition at a time, such as the type of sandwich wrapping, and observes what happens. In most experiments, a control experiment is set up with the same conditions as the actual experiment. The conditions remain the same in the control experiment but are changed in the actual experiment, one condition at a time. If something happens only in the actual experiment and not in the control, it is clear that it was caused by changing a condition in the actual experiment. The control experiment for our sandwiches might be leaving a slice of bread unwrapped to see what happens to it and comparing it to those in various wrappings.

Conditions that change during an experiment and affect the results are called variables. The variables in our sample experiment include the type of bread, how fresh it is, the size of the piece of bread being wrapped, any fillings used with the bread, the length of time the bread is wrapped, the temperature of the wrapped bread during the experiment, and the type of sandwich wrapping. Only one variable is changed at a time during

Is your sandwich still fresh at lunchtime? KELLY A. QUIN.

the experiment. The variable being changed is called the independent variable, which in our experiment is the type of sandwich wrapping.

What might happen if we change two variables at a time, such as wrapping wheat bread with waxed paper and putting rye bread in a sealed plastic bag? If the rye bread is fresher than the wheat bread at the end of the experiment, we cannot be sure which variable is the cause—the type of bread or the type of wrapping.

The condition that changes during an experiment is called the dependent variable. In our example, the dependent variable is the amount of moisture in the bread. Results of experiments must be measurable, so we need a way to measure this moisture. We decide to weigh each slice of bread before and after the experiment. The difference in the weight would be the amount of moisture that evaporated.

Experiments must also be repeatable. We must write down our procedure and follow it carefully, so that someone else could carry out the same procedure and see if the same results occur.

Step 5: Draw a conclusion. The next step in the scientific method is to graph or chart our results, analyze them, and determine whether our hypothesis was correct. For some experiments, we might have quite a bit of data to analyze. For our sample experiment, we compare the loss in weight of each bread slice after the wrapping is removed. What is our conclusion? Did our results support our hypothesis?

Even if the results did not support our hypothesis, we have learned something just by asking the question and doing the experiment. Often there is no "right" answer when we use the scientific method. Instead, we simply gather more information about the problem, which is valuable in itself.

Step 6: Report the results. Reporting our results allows other scientists to build on our work—and to repeat our experiment to see if they get the same results. Without the sharing of results, little scientific progress would be made. Scientists publish their findings in scientific journals as a way of sharing what they have learned.

In the two experiments that follow, you will use information you gather to identify mystery powders, and you will use the scientific

WORDS TO KNOW

Control experiment: A set-up that is identical to the experiment but is not affected by the variable that affects the experimental group.

Dependent variable: The variable in an experiment whose value depends on the value of another variable in the experiment.

Experiment: A controlled observation.

Hypothesis: An idea phrased in the form of a statement that can be tested by observation and/or experiment.

Independent variable: The variable in an experiment that determines the final result of the experiment.

Scientific method: Collecting evidence and arriving at a conclusion under carefully controlled conditions.

Variable: Something that can change the results of an experiment.

method to prove or disprove Aristotle's hypothesis that fruit flies appear out of thin air.

EXPERIMENT 1

Using the Scientific Method: What are the mystery powders?

Purpose/Hypothesis In this experiment, you will begin with three mystery powders and ask yourself, "What are these powders?" Then you will gather information from a chart that shows how three kinds of powder react when mixed with water, iodine, and vinegar. Next, you will hypothesize the identity of each mystery powder. Then you will test how each powder reacts with water, iodine, and vinegar. You will compare your results with the chart and draw a conclusion about the identity of each powder. Then you will know whether your hypothesis was correct.

A hypothesis should explain these things:

- the topic of the experiment
- the variable you will change
- the variable you will measure
- what you expect to happen

A hypothesis should be brief, specific, and measurable. It must be something you can test through observation. Your experiment will prove or disprove whether your hypothesis is correct.

Level of Difficulty Easy/moderate.

What Are the Variables?

Variables are anything that might affect the results of an experiment. Here are the main variables in this experiment:

- the purity of the sample of each powder
- the amount of water, iodine, and vinegar that is added to each powder
- the accuracy of your observations

In other words, the variables in this experiment are everything that might affect how each powder reacts to the water, iodine, and vinegar.

Materials Needed

- 3 ounces (85 grams) of baking soda in its original container
- 3 ounces (85 grams) of cornstarch in its original container
- 3 ounces (85 grams) of flour in its original container
- 6 small labels
- 6 small dishes
- 3 spoons
- water
- iodine (the kind used to prevent infections)
- vinegar
- eye dropper
- black paper
- magnifying lens
- goggles or other eye protection

Approximate Budget Up to $10; most materials available in the average household.

Timetable Approximately 30 minutes.

Step-by-Step Instructions

1. Turn three of the small dishes upside down and attach a label to each bottom that says *baking soda, cornstarch,* or *flour.*
2. Turn the three dishes right side up.
3. Put about 3 ounces (85 g) of the powder on the label (baking soda, cornstarch, or flour) into each dish. Make sure the amounts are equal. After the dishes are filled, you should no longer be able to read the labels on the bottom.
4. Move the dishes around until you no longer know which powder is which. (You might ask another person to do this while you wait in another room.)
5. Add a label to the side of each dish that says *A, B,* or *C.*
6. Gather information by studying Table 1 (see illustration). Notice how each powder looks or feels and how it reacts with water, iodine, and vinegar. Iodine will turn a powder black if the powder

contains starch. Vinegar, an acid, will make a powder bubble or fizz if the powder is a base. The acid and base react with each other to produce carbon dioxide.

7. Create a table similar to the one illustrated above. You will fill in the table as you test each powder.

8. Pour a small amount of Powder A on the black paper, and carefully observe it with the magnifying lens. Repeat with Powders B and C. Do you notice any slight variations in color or any other differences? Add your observations to Table 2.

9. Feel each powder, rinsing your hands after touching each one. Record your observations on Table 2.

10. Based on your observations, make a hypothesis about the identities of Powders A, B, and C. Remember that a hypothesis is a clear, testable statement of your educated guess about the identity of the unknown powders. Here is a possible hypothesis: "Powder A is baking soda. Powder B is flour. Powder C is cornstarch."

11. Fill an empty dish with about 2 ounces (60 ml) of water. Add about $\frac{1}{2}$ ounce (14 grams) of Powder A and stir with a spoon. Notice whether the powder dissolves in the water and the water

How to Experiment Safely

Wear goggles to prevent the iodine, vinegar, or any of the powders from getting in your eyes. *Never* taste substances you are using in an experiment.

Table 1
Characteristics of Three Powders

Powder	Appearance or feel	Reaction with water	Reaction with iodine	Reaction with vinegar
baking soda	powdery	slowly dissolves	none	bubbles or fizzes
cornstarch	silky smooth	turns cloudy	turns black	none
flour	gritty	turns cloudy	turns black	none

Step 6: Table 1, Characteristics of Three Powders GALE GROUP.

remains clear, or whether the powder does not dissolve and the water becomes cloudy. Record your observations in Table 2.

12. Throw away the powder sample you just tested. Rinse and dry the spoon and small dish. Use the same spoon and dish each time you test Powder A.

13. Repeat Steps 11 and 12 with Powder B and Powder C, using the other two dishes. Record your observations.

14. Place about $\frac{1}{2}$ ounce (14 grams) of Powder A into its empty dish.

15. Use the eye dropper to add 1 to 2 drops of iodine to Powder A. Observe what happens and record the results in your table. If Powder A contains starch, the iodine will turn it black or purple.

16. Repeat Steps 14 and 15 with Powder B and Powder C. When you are finished, rinse out the eye dropper. Record what you observed in Table 2.

17. Repeat Steps 14 and 15 with each of the powders, adding 1–2 drops of vinegar this time. Add your observations to Table 2. If the powder is a base, the acidic vinegar will mix with it and form fizzling carbon dioxide gas.

Summary of Results Compare the results in Table 2 with the characteristics in Table 1. Can you use your test results to establish the identity of

Table 2 Chart of Reactions				
Powder	Appearance or feel	Reaction with water	Reaction with iodine	Reaction with vinegar
A				
B				
C				

Step 7: Create a Chart of Reactions for Experiment 1.
GALE GROUP.

each powder? Then pick up each dish of powder and read the label on the bottom. Were you correct? Write a paragraph summarizing your findings and explaining whether they support your hypothesis.

Change the Variables You can vary this experiment in these ways:

- Use other powders, such as salt, granulated sugar, or powdered sugar.

- Set up the experiment for someone else, perhaps a younger student, and see if he or she can identify a mystery powder you have selected.

- With an adult's help, place a sample of baking soda, cornstarch, and flour, separately, on a square of aluminum foil and heat the sample with a candle. Notice which powders melt and which turn black. Use this information to help identify mystery powders.

- Mix each powder with a little water and test it with red and blue litmus (pH) paper. If the powder is acidic, blue litmus paper will turn red. If the powder is basic, red litmus paper will turn blue. If the paper does not change color, the powder is neutral. This test provides one more characteristic to help identify the powders.

EXPERIMENT 2

Using the Scientific Method: Do fruit flies appear out of thin air?

Purpose/Hypothesis In this experiment, you will test Aristotle's assumption that fruit flies are created spontaneously—from nothing. You will determine whether the flies are present in all air and can appear anywhere or whether they are attracted from other places by rotting fruit.

Troubleshooter's Guide

Below is a common problem that may arise during this experiment, a possible cause, and a way to remedy the problem.

Problem: All of the powders reacted the same in the tests.

Possible cause: Your samples might have become contaminated if the spoon, dish, and eye dropper were not cleaned before each test. This contamination will affect your test results. Try the experiment again, being careful to keep your equipment clean.

Step 15: Add 1 to 2 drops of iodine to Powder A. GALE GROUP.

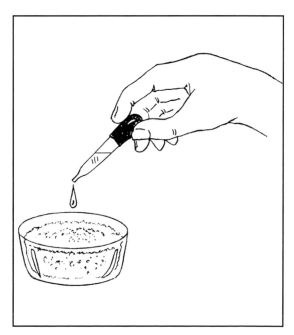

What Are the Variables?

Variables are anything that might affect the results of an experiment. Here are the main variables in this experiment:

- the ripeness of the banana slices (this variable will be controlled by taking all the slices from the same banana)
- the temperature of the air around both sets of banana slices (flies are more active in warm temperatures)
- whether the container with the experimental slices is tightly sealed
- the opportunity for flies to be attracted to the fruit (in a sealed, air-conditioned room, flies are unlikely to be near enough to be attracted to the bananas)

The independent variable, the one you will change, is whether the bananas are in a sealed container or exposed to the air around them. The dependent variable, the one you will measure, is the presence or absence of fruit flies.

First, form a hypothesis about the outcome of this experiment based on your understanding of fruit flies and bananas, the fruit you will use in this experiment.

A hypothesis should explain these things:

- the topic of the experiment
- the variable you will change
- the variable you will measure
- what you expect to happen

A hypothesis should be brief, specific, and measurable. It must be something you can test through observation. Your experiment will prove or disprove whether your hypothesis is correct. Here is a possible hypothesis for this experiment, one that Aristotle thought was true: "Fruit flies will appear on bananas even if they are kept in a covered container."

In your experiment, you will place several slices of a ripe banana in a covered container. As a control experiment, you will leave several other slices of the same banana exposed to the air. If flies appear on both the covered and the exposed banana slices, you will know that your hypothesis is correct.

Level of Difficulty Easy/moderate.

Materials Needed

- 1 very ripe banana, unpeeled, with no obvious rotten spots
- clear container that can be completely sealed
- small, shallow bowl
- table knife
- magnifying lens
- water for cleaning the banana
- a warm, shaded area outside (or a warm area inside that is near a window or door)

Approximate Budget $0 to $5; materials should be available in the average household.

Timetable 15 minutes to set up; five minutes to record observations each day for a week to 10 days.

Step-by-Step Instructions

1. Gently rinse the unpeeled banana to clean off any fly eggs that might already be on it.
2. Peel the banana, and use the table knife to cut it into about ten slices.
3. Put half of the slices in the clear container and seal it tightly.
4. Put the rest of the slices in the uncovered, shallow dish.
5. Place the sealed container and the shallow dish in a warm, shady spot, outside if possible.
6. Starting the next day, use the magnifying lens to check for fruit flies. Record your observations in Table 3 each day for seven to 10 days, or until flies appear.

Summary of Results Study the data on your table and decide whether your hypothesis was correct. Did flies appear in the sealed container? Did they appear on the slices in the shallow dish? Write a paragraph summarizing your findings and explaining whether they support your hypothesis. If your hypothesis was not supported, what did you learn?

Change the Variables Here are some ways you can vary this experiment:

- Use a different kind of fruit or try raw meat, such as hamburger.
- Put both containers in a warmer or a cooler place to see how that affects the results of the experiment.
- Put a banana that has obvious rotten areas on it inside a sealed container to see if flies appear from eggs already on the banana.

How to Experiment Safely

Ask permission before beginning this experiment, as it is likely to attract flies. Handle the table knife with caution.

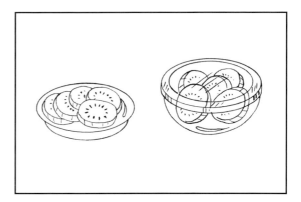

Steps 3 and 4: Place some slices in a covered container, and more in an uncovered container. GALE GROUP.

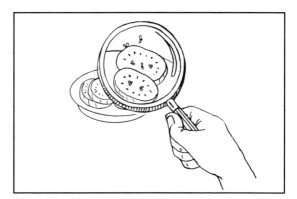

Step 6: Observe containers for the presence of fruit flies. GALE GROUP.

Troubleshooter's Guide

Below are some problems that may arise during this experiment, some possible causes, and ways to remedy the problems.

Problem: Flies appeared on the slices in the sealed container.

Possible cause: The banana must have already contained fly eggs. Try the experiment again, choosing a banana that is not so ripe and rinsing it thoroughly before you start.

Problem: No flies appeared anywhere.

Possible cause: The area around your experiment is just too clean! Try placing both containers outside, if the weather is warm, or inside in a place that is well traveled. Both containers must be exposed to the same environment.

Modify the Experiment You can often change the level of difficulty of an experiment by adding to or simplifying it. Sometimes, this involves altering your hypothesis. Whenever you modify an experiment, make sure that you still isolate only one variable at a time.

You could add another part to this experiment, for example, by testing the theory of spontaneous generation among different items. Are there certain items that attract organisms more than others? It may help you understand why the theory of spontaneous generation was believed for so long. Test a series of items, preferably outside in a warm environment. You can test food items, such as an apple or soda, along with other items, such as a plastic cup. Make sure each item is clean. For each item, your control will be the same clean item sealed in a clear container.

Make a note of your results in a chart, noting the food item and any organisms that appear. You could also try to isolate what part of the item attracted the organisms. For example, if ants began hovering around a cookie, you can isolate the different items in the cookie (sugar, flour, milk) and see which of the items attracts the ants again.

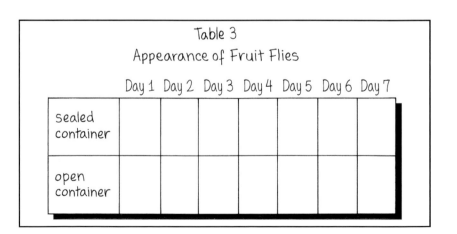

	Day 1	Day 2	Day 3	Day 4	Day 5	Day 6	Day 7
sealed container							
open container							

Table 3
Appearance of Fruit Flies

Table 3 for Experiment 2. GALE GROUP.

Design Your Own Experiment

How to Select a Topic Relating to this Concept You can explore many questions using the scientific method. What has always intrigued you? For example, you could use this method to see which brand of a product gets the best results, which studying techniques help you or others learn more, or how long microwave popcorn should cook in order to pop all the kernels and burn none.

Check the Further Readings section and talk with your science teacher or school or community media specialist to start gathering information on questions that interest you. As you consider possible experiments, be sure to discuss them with your science teacher or another knowledgeable adult before trying them. Some materials or procedures are dangerous to use.

Steps in the Scientific Method To do an original experiment, you need to plan carefully and think things through. Otherwise, you might not be sure which question you are answering, what you are or should be measuring, or what your findings prove or disprove.

Here are the steps in designing an experiment:

- State the purpose of—and the underlying question behind—the experiment you propose to do.
- Recognize the variables involved, and select one that will help you answer the question at hand.
- State a testable hypothesis, an educated guess about the answer to your question.
- Decide how to change the variable you selected.
- Decide how to measure your results.

Recording Data and Summarizing the Results In your unknown powder and fruit fly experiments, your raw data might include tables, drawings, or photographs of the changes you observed. If you display your experiment, make clear the question you are trying to answer, the variable you changed, the variable you measured, the results, and your conclusions. Explain what materials you used, how long each step took, and other basic information.

Related Projects You can undertake a variety of projects related to the scientific method. For example, you might find out how much sunlight a day produces the fastest growing seedlings, which kind of software is the easiest to learn how to use, or how to speed up the life cycle of a fruit fly. Many, many of the questions that occur to you can be answered using the scientific method!

For More Information

Gardner, Robert. *Science Projects about Chemistry.* Hillside, NJ: Enslow Publishers, 1994. Describes many science projects, including separating and identifying substances and detecting unknown solids.

VanCleave, Janice. *A+ Projects in Chemistry.* New York: Wiley, 1993. Outlines many experiments and includes information about the scientific method.

Seashells

Shells are familiar sights in nature. In general, a shell is a hard protective covering that encloses a variety of animals and fruits. Eggshells protect unborn birds. Plants produce seeds that have coverings to keep their fruit and seeds safe. Coconuts and peanuts are example of shelled foods. Insects have an exoskeleton, a hard outer covering, which protects their bodies.

Seashells are the shells, or protective coverings, of marine animals. Shells from the sea come in all sizes, shapes, and colors and house a variety of animals. To understand seashells, we need to look at the animals that made them.

Who has shells? Animals such as birds, fish, reptiles, and mammals have internal skeletons or backbones that provide structure and support to protect the animal. There are also animals that have a hard outer covering or shell to protect their soft bodies from predators. Snails, crabs, and lobsters are animals with an outer shell. These animals are called invertebrates and they have an exoskeleton (or external skeleton), like many insects. Most invertebrates do not have an internal skeleton or backbone. Exceptions to this include tortoises and turtles, who have both an internal skeleton (backbone) and an outer shell.

The largest group of shelled creatures is the mollusks. Mollusk means "soft-bodied." There are approximately 75,000 species of mollusks, which include the snail, oyster, and octopus. These animals have evolved over time to live in many different environments. The snail, for example, is a mollusk that lives in the ocean, freshwaters, and on land. (Slugs are similar to snails except they do not carry a shell.) Most mollusks have shells with the exception of the octopus, squid, and slug.

Mollusks can be grouped into many categories depending upon the characteristics of the animal. Some of the more common categories are the gastropod and bivalve. Gastropod comes from the Greek words "foot" and "stomach." Snails are gastropods and in their spiral shaped

One type of mollusk is the invasive zebra mussels, a bivalve mussel. AP PHOTO/ U.S. DEPARTMENT OF AGRICULTURE.

Some of the more common categories of mollusks are the gastropod and bivalve. ILLUSTRATION BY TEMAH NELSON.

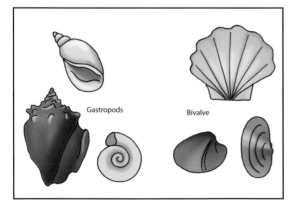

Gastropods

Bivalve

shell they use their foot (the fleshy part of their body that protrudes from the shell) to propel themselves forward. Bivalve uses the prefix "bi," which means two, because bivalve organisms have a two-part shell. The two shells in a bivalve connect to cover the animal. Common bivalves are the clam, oyster, and scallop shells.

Another group of animals that have a hard shell-like outer covering is the crustaceans. Crustaceans are invertebrates. They have a segmented body with a hard exoskeleton. Some common crustaceans are crabs, lobsters, crayfish, and shrimp.

How shells are made The shells of gastropods and bivalves are made of calcium carbonate. Mollusks take in calcium that they find in their environment from food and the water they live in to create their shell. When baby mollusks hatch from their eggs, they have a tiny shell that grows with them. They use a part of their body called the mantle (soft tissue that is located between the shell and its inner organs) to continually produce layers of calcium carbonate crystals to their shell. Adding calcium carbonate enlarges and strengthens the shell.

Each species of mollusk forms a shell with a unique shape and color. However, within a particular species there are differences in shells due to the environment, food, and climate. For example, color differences among shells can be due to the diet of the animal that lives inside it and the water quality of its environment.

The shells of crustaceans are made out of a substance called chitin. When lobsters, crabs, and other crustaceans hatch from eggs, they are born with a hard layer of skin that serves as an exoskeleton. A chitin exoskeleton is strong yet flexible, allowing the animals to move their legs and claws. Crustacean shells are segmented to cover the entire body but also allow for movement, much like a suit of armor. As the crustacean grows, it sheds the old skin and grows a new one. This shedding process is called molting. An adult lobster will molt his skin yearly. During this molting time a crustacean is vulnerable to

WORDS TO KNOW

Bivalve: Bivalves are characterized by shells that are divided into two parts or valves that completely enclose the mollusk like the clam or scallop.

Calcium carbonate: A substance that is secreted by a mollusk to create the shell it lives in.

Chitin: Substance that makes up the exoskeleton of crustaceans.

Camouflage: Markings or coloring that help hide an animal by making it blend into the surrounding environment..

Crustacean: A type of arthropod characterized by hard and thick skin, and having shells that are jointed. This group includes the lobster, crab, and crayfish.

Exoskeleton: A hard outer covering on animals, which provide protection and structure.

Gastropod: The largest group of mollusks; characterized by a single shell that is often coiled in a spiral. Snails are gastropods.

Hypothesis: An idea in the form of a statement that can be tested by observation and/or experiment.

Internal skeleton: An animal that has a backbone.

Invertebrate: An animal that lacks a backbone or internal skeleton.

Mantle: Soft tissue that is located between the shell and an animal's inner organs. The mantle produces the calcium carbonate substance that create the shell of the animal.

Mollusk: An invertebrate animal usually enclosed in a shell, the largest group of shelled animals.

Molting: A process by which an animal sheds its skin or shell.

Shell: A hard outer covering that protects an animal that lives inside.

Variable: Something that can affect the results of an experiment.

---

predators as its outer shell is not yet hardened. In order to protect itself, the crustacean will often hide until its shell is hard.

Shells for survival Shells provide many ways that help the soft bodied animals inside them survive. The hard exterior shell is an obvious protection from a predator but the shape of the shell is also useful to the mollusk. Some shell shapes are designed to make it easy to burrow into the sand to hide. There are bivalves with deep ridges in the shell that helps the shell anchor itself to the bottom of their environment. Other shells grow long spiny spikes that collect seaweed and help to hide the animal.

Shells are often used as camouflage. They often blend into their environment appearing the same color as sand or rocks. The cowry shell is a brightly colored shiny shell whose animal is also brightly colored but with a different pattern. When threatened by a predator the animal will retreat into its shell, thus confusing the predator.

What Are the Variables?

Variables are anything that might affect the results of an experiment. Here are the main variables in this experiment:

- the type of shell
- the force with which the wood is dropped
- the height of the wood block

In other words, the variables in this experiment are everything that might affect the amount of water the plant draws in or out of its cells. If you change more than one variable, you will not be able to tell which variable affected the shell breaking.

In this case, the variable you will change is the type of shell. The variable you will measure is which shell breaks first.

Shells are vital to the existence of the animals that live inside them. In the experiment and project to follow, you will test the strength of two different shells and classify various seashells. The activities will highlight the characteristics unique to shells, and help you think of your own experiments relating to seashells.

EXPERIMENT 1

Shell Strength: Which shell is stronger: a clam shell or lobster shell?

Purpose/Hypothesis A strong shell offers an animal protection from other animals and the environment. Clam shells and lobster shells are composed of two different types of materials. A clam shell is primarily made of calcium carbonate. A lobster shell is made of chitin, a type of carbohydrate, along with protein. A clam shell is formed over time by the mollusk that lives inside it and the lobster shell is repeatedly replaced as the lobster grows. The clam shell is hard and rigid and can become thick. The lobster shell is a segmented hard skin-like covering with some flexibility at the joints. Given the properties of these two shells, what shell do you think is stronger?

In this experiment, you will test the strength of both shells by dropping a weight onto the shells from various heights. The weight will be a block of wood, and you will create a pulley system to repeatedly and evenly drop the wood. The shell that remains intact the longest from the weight dropping is the stronger shell.

Before you begin, make an educated guess about the outcome of this experiment based on your knowledge of shells and material strength. This educated guess, or prediction, is your

A lobster is a crustacean. ©
BROWNIE HARRIS/CORBIS.

hypothesis. A hypothesis should explain these things:

- the topic of the experiment
- the variable you will change
- the variable you will measure
- what you expect to happen

A hypothesis should be brief, specific, and measurable. It must be something you can test through further investigation. Your experiment will prove or disprove whether your hypothesis is correct. Here is one possible hypothesis for this experiment: "The wooden block will cause the clam shell to break first as it is more rigid than the lobster shell."

Level of Difficulty Moderate/difficult (due to the materials and building the pulley system).

Materials Needed

- lobster shell tail, fresh with lobster meat extracted (available from fish markets, who may give you the tail shell for free) When purchasing lobster try to have the store steam it. If this is not possible then you will need an adult to help you steam or boil the lobster and remove the meat prior to the experiment.
- clam shell, approximately 2–3 inches (5–7.5 centimeters) in width (use found shells or available from online stores)
- 4 pieces of wood, about 28 inches (71 centimeters) long, 2 inches (5 centimeters) wide, and 1 inch (2.54 centimeters) in depth
- 1 piece of wood, 18 inches long, 1 inch wide, and 1 inch in depth
- block of wood, about 7 inches (18 centimeters) long, 3 inches (7.5 centimeters) wide, and 1 inch in depth
- 1-inch pulley (available at hardware stores)
- string, about 6 feet (1.8 meters)
- 1 screw hook
- marker
- 1 foot (0.3 meters) of thin wire
- 2 nails

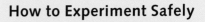

Building the pulley.
ILLUSTRATION BY TEMAH NELSON.

	Gastropod	Bivalve	Other
Size			
Color			
Weight			
Geography			

Use the chart to track your findings. ILLUSTRATION BY TEMAH NELSON.

- hammer
- pliers (to cut and secure wire)

Approximate Budget $20–30 (use found shells and scrap wood if possible).

Timetable Approximately 45 minutes.

Step-by-Step Instructions 1.) Building the pulley:

1. Use the four long pieces of wood (28 x 2 x 1) to build two pieces shaped like the letter "A." For each wood "A." shape, cross the ends of two pieces of wood over each other and secure them together with a nail.

2. Take the length of wood measuring 18 x 1 x 1 and place it across the two "A." frames at the top. Secure both ends of this piece of wood onto the "A." frames using wire and pliers. You should now have a frame that will stand by itself on a table.

3. Attach the pulley to the middle of the frame at the top with another piece of wire.

4. Take the block of wood and attach the screw hook in the middle of the width of the block. The block should hang down lengthwise.

5. Take the string and pull it through the top of the pulley. On one end tie a knot with a loop in it.

6. Attach the block with the screw hook onto this loop. You should now have a block of wood attached to a string that runs through the pulley.

Step 2:1: Mark a line on the string at the point you want to stop. ILLUSTRATION BY TEMAH NELSON.

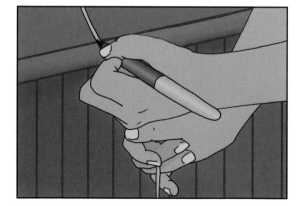

2.) Testing for strength:

1. Place a clam shell directly under the block of wood. Pull the string against the edge of your work table to raise the block of wood about a third of the way up from the bottom of the pulley. Mark a line on the string at the point you want to stop. The exact height does not matter as you have the mark so that it is repeatable.

2. Release the string to let the wood drop. Note the results.

3. Repeat this step with the lobster shell, pulling the string to the same mark to drop it from the same height.

4. If neither shell is broken, place the clam shell under the block of wood again. Pull the string against the edge of your work table to raises the block of wood about two thirds of the way up from the bottom of the pulley. Mark a line on the string.

5. Release the string to let the wood drop. Note the results.

6. Repeat this step with the lobster shell, pulling the string to the same mark to drop it from the same height.

7. If neither shell is broken, drop the block from a higher point on both shells. Repeat the same process of dropping the wood block, pulling the string against the edge of the table to raise the block of wood about two thirds of the way up.

8. If the shells are still intact, raise the block to the top of the pulley. Continue dropping the block, counting each drop, until each shell breaks. Note the number of times it took to break.

Troubleshooter's Guide

Here are some of the problems that may arise during this experiment, some possible causes, and ways to remedy the problems.

Problem: The clam shell did not break.

Possible cause: The clam shell could be too large and thick, try a smaller shell. The height of the block when dropped was too low, try a higher height. Change the position of the shell, make sure that it is directly under the wooden block.

Problem: The lobster shell breaks too easily.

Possible cause: The lobster was too dry. Use the lobster shell within 24 hours of when the meat is removed.

Summary of Results What were your results? Was your hypothesis correct? Consider how the strength of a shell can help an animal survive. Do you think there could be a negative side to having a strong shell? Write a paragraph of your findings. You may want to chart your results.

PROJECT 2

Classifying Seashells

Purpose/Hypothesis In this project, you will gather found and/or purchased seashells and classify them given what you already know about seashells. When scientists classify a group of animals, rocks, or in this case seashells, they are looking for similarities in the animals that

Step 2:2 Release the string to let the wood drop. ILLUSTRATION BY TEMAH NELSON.

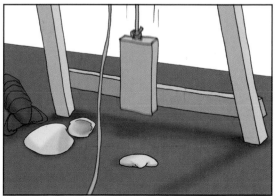

live in the shell or in the shell itself. Classification is important because it means that there is a universal system for identifying or naming something. You will group the shells into categories: gastropod, bivalve, crustacean, and echinoderms. You will then classify each of the groups into its characteristics. If you come across a shell that is difficult to classify, conduct some research about the shell and determine where it belongs.

Level of Difficulty Easy/moderate

Materials Needed

- 30–50 shells, found and/or purchased, try to find shells of all shapes and sizes (available from online seashell sellers or from your own collection).
- poster board
- containers: glass canning jars and shoe boxes work well
- gram scale (optional)
- tape measure(optional)

Approximate Budget $15 for purchasing shells; $0 if use found shells.

Timetable one to two hours to sort through and organize shells by characteristic. Consider this project as an ongoing hobby that you can continue as you find and collect new shells.

Step-by-Step Instructions

1. Find a large space, table or area on the floor and spread out all the shells.
2. Organize the shells by shape. Determine if the shell falls into one of the four categories below: gastropod, bivalve, crustacean, or echinoderm

   - Gastropod: Cone-like or spiral shell.
   - Bivalve: Two shells that are identical and hinged together to form a complete covering for the animal that lived inside.
   - Crustacean: Hard outer covering that is segmented with flexible joints.
   - Echinoderm: Spiny or spiky outer covering of animal like a sea urchin or live sand dollar. Star fish are unique in that they have five distinct arms, like a star.

3. Put aside any shells that do not fit into the four categories.

4. Separate each of the groups into smaller groups of the animals that lived inside the shells, such as snails, clams, scallops, and crabs.

5. There are many ways you can further classify the shells in each group. You can group them by:

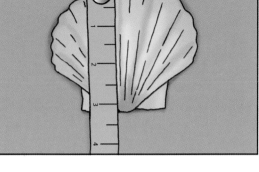

Step 5: Use a tape measure to determine the length of the shells. ILLUSTRATION BY TEMAH NELSON.

   • Size: Use a tape measure to determine the length of the shells; for the volume you can measure the amount of water each shell holds.
   • Color: If there is more then one color, categorize by the main color or you can group by patterns.
   • Weight: Weigh each on a gram scale.
   • Geography: Separate the general location of where the shell was found, such as in the Northeast or Southeast of the United States.

6. You can display your shells by gluing them to paper and writing the name of the shell or type of shell under it. You can also group them by type into containers: jars or boxes.

Summary of Results Examine the physical characteristics of the shells in each groups. Do some shells have ridges, for example, and others do not? Choose how to display each category of shells, on a poster board or in containers. Consider what each characteristics tells about the group of shells. Write what you know about each type of shell. Researchers still have many questions about seashell characteristics. You can look to see if your questions are some of the same questions scientists are exploring.

Design Your Own Experiment

How to Select a Topic Relating to this Concept Seashells are products of their environment. Consider why and how different environments yield different shells. Water temperature and acidity, types of shoreline: sandy vs. rocky are just some of the factors that can affect a shell's development.

Check the Further Readings section and talk with your science teacher or school or community media specialist to start gathering information on seashells and questions that interest you.

Steps in the Scientific Method To do an original experiment, you need to plan carefully and think things through. Otherwise, you might not be sure what question you are answering, what you are or should be measuring, or what your findings prove or disprove.

Here are the steps in designing an experiment:

- State the purpose of—and the underlying question behind—the experiment you propose to do.
- Recognize the variables involved, and select one that will help you answer the question at hand.
- State a testable hypothesis, an educated guess about the answer to your question.
- Decide how to change the variable you selected.
- Decide how to measure your results.

Recording Data and Summarizing the Results It is important to document as much information as possible about your experiment. Part of your presentation should be visual, using charts and graphs. Remember, whether or not your experiment is successful, your conclusions and experiences can benefit others.

Related Projects Seashell formation and characteristics encompass animals, the environment, geography, and other sciences. There are many experiments and projects you can do to get more information about seashells. For instance, scientists are finding that some scallop shells have ridges that can determine the age of the shell and the environment the shell lived in, such as water temperature. Also, you could consider how shells differ by geography and why. Do warmer waters produce more or fewer shells, or different colored shells? You can also explore how increased carbon dioxide in the atmosphere could affect the acidity of the oceans and its resulting effect on seashells.

For More Information

Arthur, Alex. *Shell*. New York: Alfred A. Knopf, 1989. Provides a good overview of different types of shells focusing on aspects of camouflage and collection

"Conchologists of America, Inc." *COA Kid's*. http://www.conchologistsofamerica.org/kids/inicial/default.asp (accessed May 23, 2008). Facts, games, and activities on shells.

Dance, S. Peter. *The World's Shells*. New York: McGraw Hill Book Company, 1976. A guide for collectors of the world's shells.

National Geographic. *Science and Space.* http://science.nationalgeographic.com/science/earth (accessed May 23, 2008). Provides up to date articles on the oceans and seashells

San Diego Natural History Museum. "Frequently Asked Questions about Marine Invertebrates." *Marine Invertebrates.* http://www.sdnhm.org/research/marine-inverts/marifaq.html (accessed May 23, 2008). Answers to basic questions about seashells and collecting shells.

78

Separation and Identification

Most natural and manufactured materials are mixtures, not pure substances. In a mixture, each of the substances has its own chemical properties. Salt water, gravel, and cookies are a few examples of mixtures. People can use physical means to separate mixtures into their component parts. Separating mixtures is important because it allows people to identify the substances that make up the mixture.

Separating the components in a substance is usually one of the first steps in identifying its components. All mixtures can be separated and identified by the distinguishing chemical or physical properties of the components. The separation technique chosen depends on the type of mixture and its characteristics. After a mixture is separated, one or all of its components can be identified. Researchers can match the properties of the unknown substance to those properties of a known substance. Appearance and the way the unknown substance reacts with other substances are ways to identify a substance.

Separation and identification techniques are used for all types of different purposes. If there are pollutants in the water, scientists first separate and identify the pollutants to clean the water. Forensic scientists, people who work in criminal investigations, use the techniques to identify evidence, such as fabrics or blood. Research scientists will separate unknown biological samples to identify the molecules in the sample. In blood tests doctors may need to identify and then separate iron or another component out of the blood.

Mixing it up Anything a person can combine is a mixture. Mixtures with varying compositions are called heterogeneous, meaning that they have different appearance and properties at different points in the mixture. For example, a mixture of oil and water is a heterogeneous mixture. The two substances form layers because of their different chemical properties, and one part of the mixture will have a higher concentration

When mixed together, oil and water form a heterogeneous mixture. Here, a layer of olive oil floats atop a layer of water. © KELLY A. QUIN.

Doctors often need to separate and identify components in patients' blood—for example, iron—in order make a diagnosis. © TOM AND DEE ANN MCCARTHY/CORBIS.

of oil, while another part of the mixture will have a higher concentration of water.

Solutions are a type of mixture in which all the substances are evenly distributed, or homogeneous. A solution has the same appearance and properties throughout the entire mixture. When sugar is mixed into a cup of hot tea, for example, the sugar molecules dissolve and are spread evenly throughout the cup. The sugar-tea mixture is a solution. The sugar molecules are called the solute molecules. The substance it dissolved in, the tea water, is called the solvent.

Separating by size Size is one method used to separate many simple mixtures. If the parts of a heterogeneous mixture are large enough, the mixture can be separated by hand or by a sieve. A sieve has holes in it that are small enough for some of the solid substance or substances to pass through and the larger particles will remain above the holes. Soil, for example, is sifted through a sieve to separate out the chunks of rock and gravel from the fine soil particles.

Filtration is a commonly used separation technique similar to a sieve except it separates undissolved solid particles from a liquid. In filtration, a mixture passes through a filter, a material with spaces in it that holds back the particles. Filters are used frequently to clean water, make coffee, and purify air.

Other simple separation techniques include settling and evaporation. Settling is when the larger, heavier components will sink or settle to form distinct layers. When muddy water sits for a period of time, for example, the dirt will sink to the bottom. In evaporation, the liquid is heated until it becomes a gas and leaves behind the solid particles.

Separating by speed One widely used method that scientists use to identify the parts in a solution is known as chromatography. Chromatography is a technique that separates components based on the rate each moves over a specific material. Each component has properties that determine its movement. Chromatography has many uses. It is commonly used in laboratories to isolate new compounds, analyze differences between environmental samples, and identify drugs from urine or blood samples.

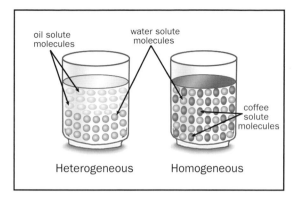

In chromatography, a gas or liquid mixture travels over an unmoving substance. The unmoving substance chosen depends on the type of mixture. Paper chromatography is one of several types of chromatography that are all based on the same principles. In paper chromatography the unmoving substance is paper. The components in the mixture move at different rates over the paper based on their attraction to the paper. Some large-sized components may stick to the paper and hobble along; other small-sized components may glide over the paper and travel quickly. For example, to separate the colors in a dye, the dye is made into a preparation. A spot of the dye preparation is placed on the end of a piece of chromatography paper. Different colors that make up the dye then travel at varying rates along the paper.

Paper chromatography is one of the most basic types of chromatography. Other types include gas chromatography and liquid chromatography. Gas chromatography has a gaseous mixture while liquid chromatography uses liquids. Each is used in many ways including detecting explosive materials, analyzing fibers and blood, and testing water for pollutants.

What is it? Over the years scientists have gathered and compiled the many properties of individual substances. To identify an unknown substance in a mixture, scientists try to match the properties of the unknown substance to those of known substances. While there are numerous properties used in identification, there are some routine techniques that test for common properties.

A substance's shape and color is one of the first pieces of evidence scientists note. Its solubility or its ability to dissolve in another substance is another first step in identification. Because water is a common and known substance, it is the standard for many tests. A substance that dissolves in water is called soluble in water, and one that does not is called insoluble in water. Another common method used to identify a liquid is to determine its pH, or the measure of its acidity. The pH scale goes from 0 to 14. The lower the pH, the more acidic the solution. For example, lemons are acidic and so would have a lower pH than soaps, which are basic. At the midway point, where the pH is 7, the substance is neutral. Water is an example of a neutral substance.

In a homogenous mixture, solute molecules are evenly distributed; in a heterogeneous mixture, molecules are unevenly distributed and can be visually distinguished from one another. GALE GROUP.

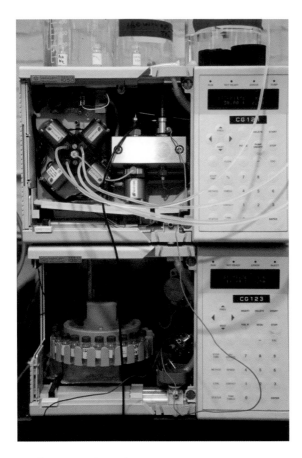

A chromatography machine is commonly used in laboratories to isolate new compounds, analyze differences between environmental samples, and identify drugs from urine or blood samples. CUSTOM MEDICAL STOCK PHOTO

The effect of heating a substance can also provide several pieces of information. The temperature where a solid substance turns into a liquid is called its melting point. The temperature where a liquid turns into a gas is called its boiling point. Different substances also give off unique colors when placed in a flame. Potassium, for example, gives off a violet flame when heated in a flame; sodium emits a yellow-colored flame.

In the following two experiments, you will use separation and identification techniques to identify a mixture.

EXPERIMENT 1

Chromatography: Can you identify a pen from the way its colors separate?

Purpose/Hypothesis Chromatography is a common technique used to identify substances, from drugs in blood samples to a type of pen used in a crime. The word chromatography comes from the Greek word *chromato*, which means color.

In this experiment, you will use paper chromatography to separate the colors out of four different types of black ink. The color black is a mixture of several colors. Different types of pens mix together varying amounts of colored inks to produce black ink. Once the colors are separated you will have a partner select one of the black pens as

A pH scale ranges from 0 to 14 and is used to determine a solution's acidity. With 7 being neutral, a pH of 0 is the highest acid value and a pH of 14 is the highest base value. GALE GROUP.

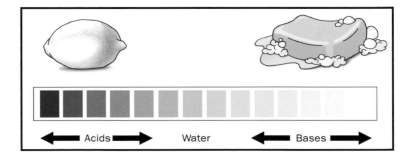

WORDS TO KNOW

Boiling point: The temperature at which a substance changes from a liquid to a gas or vapor.

Chromatography: A method for separating mixtures into their component parts (into their "ingredients") by flowing the mixture over another substance and noting the differences in attraction between the substance and each component of the mixture.

Control experiment: A setup that is identical to the experiment, but is not affected by the variable that acts on the experimental group.

Filtration: The mechanical separation of a liquid from the undissolved particles floating in it.

Heterogeneous: Different throughout.

Homogenous: The same throughout.

Hypothesis: An idea in the form of a statement that can be tested by observation and/or experiment.

Insoluble: A substance that cannot be dissolved in some other substance.

Melting point: The temperature at which a substance changes from a solid to a liquid.

Mixture: A combination of two or more substances that are not chemically combined with each other and that can exist in any proportion.

pH: A measure of a solution's acidity. The pH scale ranges from 0 (most acidic) to 14 (least acidic), with 7 representing a neutral solution, such as pure water.

Solubility: The tendency of a substance to dissolve in some other substance.

Solute: The substance that is dissolved to make a solution and exists in the least amount in a solution; for example, sugar in sugar water.

Solution: A mixture of two or more substances that appears to be uniform throughout except on a molecular level.

Soluble: A substance that can be dissolved in some other substance.

Solvent: The major component of a solution or the liquid in which some other component is dissolved; for example, water in sugar water.

Variable: Something that can affect the results of an experiment.

---

the unknown. You will then identify the unknown pen based on the pattern of the colors.

Paper chromatography identifies the parts of a mixture by first treating the paper with a solvent, a liquid that can dissolve other substances, and then observing how those substances travel different distances over the paper. How far each substance travels depends on the attraction it has for the paper.

Before you begin, make an educated guess about the outcome of this experiment based on your knowledge of chromatography and separation. This educated guess, or prediction, is your hypothesis. A hypothesis should explain these things:

What Are the Variables?

Variables are anything that might affect the results of an experiment. Here are the main variables in this experiment:

- type of paper
- time allowed for separation
- concentration of alcohol and water
- type of ink used in the pens

In other words, the variables in this experiment are everything that might affect the ink colors moving over the paper. If you change more than one variable at the same time, you will not be able to tell which variable had the most effect on color separation.

- the topic of the experiment
- the variable you will change
- the variable you will measure
- what you expect to happen

A hypothesis should be brief, specific, and measurable. It must be something you can test through further investigation. Your experiment will prove or disprove whether your hypothesis is correct. Here is one possible hypothesis for this experiment: "Different colors will separate out from each other by traveling different distances on the stationary phase. The pattern of the separated colors can then be used for identification."

In this case, the variable you will change is the type of black ink. The variable you will measure is the pattern of how the ink's colors separate.

Conducting a control experiment will help you isolate each variable and measure the changes in the dependent variable. Only one variable will change between the control and the experimental trials. Your control experiment will use an ink of one color, either red or blue.

Level of Difficulty Moderate to Difficult.

Materials Needed

Step 8: Experiment 1 setup. Make sure the ink dots are not submerged in the liquid. GALE GROUP.

- 4 paper coffee filters
- pencil

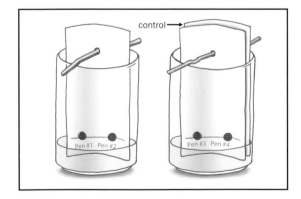

- 4 different kinds of black pens, permanent ink
- red or blue pen (control)
- 91% isopropyl alcohol
- water
- ruler
- measuring cups
- 2 small glasses about 4 inches (10 centimeters) tall
- 3 paperclips
- scissors
- marking pen

Approximate Budget $10.

Timetable 2 hours.

Step-by-Step Instructions

1. Cut the coffee filter paper into four strips measuring 2 inches by 4 inches (5 centimeters by 10 centimeters). One paper will hold the control ink, one the unknown ink, one the two black inks, and one the other two black inks.

2. Assign each of the four black pens a number, 1 through 4.

3. On each strip of paper, draw a line about 0.75 inches (2 centimeters) from the end of the paper with a pencil (NOT a pen). This end will be the bottom of the strip.

4. To separate the four unknown pen inks: Take two of the strips of filter paper. On the pencil line, about 0.5 inches (1.3 centimeters) in from the edge of the paper, make a large dot with Pen 1. The dot should be about the size of an eraser on a pencil. On the same pencil line on the opposite edge of the paper make a dot with Pen 2. Use the pencil to label each dot below the line (between the line and the bottom of the strip) with the pen number. (For example, the dot made with pen number 1 should be labeled "1.") On a fresh strip of filter paper, repeat this process for Pen 3 and Pen 4.

5. To separate the control ink: On the pencil line in the middle of a fresh strip of paper, make a large dot with the control ink. The control is a single color ink of red or blue. Label the dot "Control."

6. Stir together ¼ cup (60 milliliters) of the alcohol with ¼ cup (60 milliliters) of water. Pour this mixture into each of the two glasses so that the liquid sits below the 2-centimeter line. It should be about halfway to the line.

7. Straighten the two paperclips. Push one paperclip carefully through the top (the end without the dots) of two labeled

Step 14: Different types of pens mix together varying amounts of colored inks to produce black ink. Measure from the top of every new color to the pencil line to determine how far the separate colors traveled up the strip GALE GROUP.

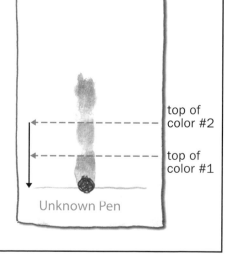

top of color #2

top of color #1

Unknown Pen

Troubleshooter's Guide

Below are some problems that may arise during this experiment, some possible causes, and some ways to remedy the problem.

Problem: The spot disappeared off of the paper.

Possible cause: The liquid level is too high and is over the line. The ink dot could have dissolved into the liquid. Repeat the experiment with less liquid in the glass, making sure the dots are not submerged in the liquid.

Problem: The ink spot does not spread.

Possible cause: The ink is not soluble in the liquid. Repeat the experiment using a different type of ink.

Problem: The black ink did not separate into its different components.

Possible cause: The paper may not be able to separate all the components. Repeat the experiment using a filter paper of a finer grade or of a different weave. You can also purchase chromatography paper from a lab supply house.

Problem: The unknown ink did not match any of the inks already separated.

Possible cause: There may have been a problem during the experiment for any of the reasons above, or you may have changed more than one variable, which is the unknown pen. Check that the mixture preparation was given the same amount of time to move up the paper. Make sure the paper was the same. If you prepared a different mixture preparation, that could also have altered the results. Repeat the experiment, making sure that all the other variables are equal.

strips of paper, and push the second paperclip through the top of the third strip of paper.

8. Rest each straightened paper clip across the top of one glass, with the bottom of the paper strips hanging down into the liquid. There will be two strips of paper in one glass and a third strip of paper in the second glass. The ink dots should be close to the surface of the liquid, but NOT submerged in it.

9. Wait 30 minutes.

10. While you are waiting, turn away and have a partner select one of the four pens tested. This will be the "Unknown" ink.

11. To separate the unknown ink: On the pencil line in the middle of a fresh strip of paper make a large dot with the unknown pen. Label the dot "Unknown." Push a straightened paperclip carefully through the top.

12. Remove the first three strips of paper after the 30 minutes, and rest the paperclip holding the "Unknown" pen along the top of one of the glasses. This strip should also sit in the liquid 30 minutes.

13. Allow the first three strips of paper to dry (about 30 minutes). When the unknown ink has been submerged for 30 minutes, remove and let dry.

14. For each of the known inks, measure from the top of every new color to the pencil line to determine how far the separate colors traveled up the strip. Write your results in a table, noting the description and measurement for the four pens.

15. Repeat the measurements for the separated colors of the unknown ink. Identify the unknown pen by comparing its measurements and pattern to the four black pens.

Summary of Results Examine the results of the table compared to that of the unknown pen. How closely does the unknown pen match the pattern of one of the inks? Scribble a few lines with each of the black pens and label the scribble with the associated pen number. Compare each of the pen's patterns with its associated color black. Can you see a difference between the shades of each black pen? Look at the color of each black pen again and re-examine the table. Evaluate whether the black inks that appear more similar also have a greater likeness in their patterns.

Change the Variables Changing some of the variables may lead to interesting results. Try changing the type of paper you are using to a coffee filter paper or a finer grade of white paper. You could also change the mobile phase. Try using water without adding alcohol or alcohol without adding water. Mix the two in different amounts and record what your results. You can also change the color and types of pen you use.

EXPERIMENT 2

Identifying a Mixture: How can determining basic properties of a substance allow you to identify the substances in a mixture?

Purpose/Hypothesis Because the components in a mixture keep their own chemical properties, scientists can identify the substances in a mixture by knowing the properties of its components. In order to identify a substance, its components are isolated and tested.

In this experiment, you will determine different properties of several substances that are similar in appearance. You will then have a partner create a mixture with two of the substances. Using the properties of the substances that you determined, you will identify the composition of the mixture.

The substances you will use are three household items: flour, sugar, and baking soda. The properties you will determine for each substance are its appearance, solubility in water, solubility in vinegar, and pH.

To determine pH you will use red cabbage. The chemicals that give red cabbage its red/purplish color also can act as a pH indicator. The red cabbage pH indicator does not determine an exact pH number, but it can distinguish between acid (pH of 0 to 6), neutral (pH near 7), and base (pH of 8 to 14). When the juice of red cabbage is added to an acid, such as vinegar or lemon juice, it will become pink to red; when it is added to a

What Are the Variables?

Variables are anything that might affect the results of an experiment. Here are the main variables in this experiment:

- the substance
- the solvent
- the quantity of each component in the mixture
- the temperature of the solvent
- the pH indicator

In other words, variables in this experiment are anything that might affect the identification of the components in the mixture. If you change more than one variable, you will not be able to tell which variable impacted the determination of the substance's properties and, thus, the mixture's composition.

base, it will turn blue or green. If the solution turns purple, it indicates that the substance is neutral, neither an acid nor a base.

To begin this experiment make an educated guess about what you think will occur based on your knowledge of mixtures. This educated guess, or prediction, is your hypothesis. A hypothesis should explain these things:

- the topic of the experiment
- the variable you will change
- the variable you will measure
- what you expect to happen

A hypothesis should be brief, specific, and measurable. It must be something you can test through further investigation. Your experiment will prove or disprove whether your hypothesis is correct. Here is one possible hypothesis for this experiment: "A mixture can be identified by determining the properties of the individual substances in the mixture."

In this experiment the variable you will change will be the substances that might possibly make up the mixture. The variable you will measure will be the mixture's properties.

Level of Difficulty Moderate.

Materials Needed

- clear plastic cups (at least six, as many as twenty)
- water
- vinegar
- white flour (about a cup)
- white sugar (about a cup)
- baking soda (about a cup)
- measuring spoons
- measuring cups
- mixing spoons
- red cabbage
- sealable sandwich bag
- knife

- measuring cups
- marking pen

Approximate Budget $12.

Timetable 2 hours.

Step-by-Step Instructions

1. Prepare a chart with four columns down and four rows across. Label the columns with the headings of "Flour," "Sugar," "Baking Soda," and "Unknown." Label the rows: "Appearance," "Soluble with water," "Soluble with vinegar," and "Acid/Base/Neutral."

2. Label one clear plastic cup "Flour," a second "Sugar," and a third "Baking Soda." The cups may be reused throughout the experiment by rinsing them thoroughly with water and drying.

3. Put 1 teaspoon of each of the three substances in the appropriate plastic cup.

4. Record the color and description of the substance's appearance on the chart (for example, powder, grainy, etc.)

	Flour	Sugar	Baking Soda	Unknown
Appearance				
Soluble with Water				
Soluble with Vinegar				
Acid, Base, or Neutral				

Step 1: Prepare a chart to record the results of Experiment 2. GALE GROUP.

5. Add ¼ cup (about 60 milliliters) of water to each of the cups and stir vigorously for 30 to 60 seconds. Allow the mixtures to stand for 15 minutes, then record whether each substance is soluble in water. If the solvent is clear it is soluble; if the solvent is cloudy and most of the substance remains at the bottom of the cup, it is insoluble.

6. In a clean cup, repeat Step 4 and Step 5, using vinegar in place of water.

7. Prepare a pH indicator: Chop red cabbage into small pieces and measure ½ cup of the pieces. Put the pieces into a sealable sandwich bag. Add ½ cup (about 120 milliliters) of very warm water to the cabbage. Close the bag and mix gently by squeezing. Let the water and cabbage sit for five minutes, mixing occasionally. Pour the purple water into a separate plastic cup.

8. In a clean cup, add 1 teaspoon of each of the substances into the appropriate cup.

9. Place 2 teaspoons (10 milliliters) of the purple pH indicator into each of the three cups and stir. Note whether the substance is an acid (solution turns pink to red), a base (solution turns blue or green), or neutral (solution remains purple).

10. Turn away and have a partner mix two of the three substances together, using 2 tablespoons of each of the substances into a clean cup. Have your partner write down the two substances he or she selected.

11. Follow the procedures in Steps 4 through 9 to test the mixture for the properties defined in the chart. (You can use the same pH indicator made in Step 7.) For example, after recording the appearance of the mixture, add vinegar and stir the mixture to determine if it is soluble in water, and so on. Remove 1 teaspoon of the mixture each time you test for a specific property.

Summary of Results Use the data you have collected for each property to identify which of the substances made up the unknown mixture. When you have reached a conclusion check with your partner. How did each of the properties enable you to narrow down the identification of

Step 5: Stir completely before you note if the mixture is soluble or not soluble GALE GROUP.

the mixture? Hypothesize how a mixture of another two substances would have reacted. Record your results and list the steps you took to identify your mixture.

Change the Variables There are numerous ways you can change the variables in this experiment. You can use different food substances that have the same powdery appearance as the ones given. Cream of tartar, powdered sugar, and cornstarch are some examples. You can change the look of the materials completely and use any substances that appear similar. You can also examine how other liquids react with these substances. Make sure you change only one variable at a time for each test, and keep careful records of your results.

Design Your Own Experiment

How to Select a Topic Relating to this Concept Separation techniques and identification are used in many professions for a variety of reasons. Wherever there is a mixture, there is some way to separate it.

Check the Further Readings section and talk with your science teacher to learn more about separation and identification. You can examine the *CRC Handbook of Chemistry and Physics,* listed in Further Readings, which provides detailed tables of chemicals' behaviors and characteristics. Using this book as a guide could provide ideas on how to separate and identify substances. If you construct a project that uses heat or flames, make sure you have adult supervision.

Steps in the Scientific Method To conduct an original experiment, you need to plan carefully and think things through. Otherwise, you might not be sure what question you are answering, what you are or should be measuring, or what your findings prove or disprove.

Troubleshooter's Guide

Below are some problems that may arise during this experiment, some possible causes, and some ways to remedy the problem.

Problem: Some of the substance will not dissolve.

Possible cause: The mixture may need to be stirred further, or more solvent should be added to the substance. Repeat the test, stirring the solution thoroughly.

Problem: The solvent has turned a slight color.

Possible cause: The substance you are using may not be pure and some small part of the substance may be soluble in the solvent. Make sure you are using pure white flour and white sugar, and repeat the test.

Possible cause: You may not have rinsed the cups thoroughly. Repeat the test, washing the cup again or using a fresh plastic cup.

Here are the steps in designing an experiment:

- State the purpose of—and the underlying question behind—the experiment you propose to do.
- Recognize the variables involved and select one that will help you answer the question at hand.
- State your hypothesis, an educated guess about the answer to your question.
- Decide how to change the variable you selected.
- Decide how to measure your results.

Recording Data and Summarizing the Results Your data should include charts and graphs such as the one you did for these experiments. They should be clearly labeled and easy to read. You may also want to include photographs and drawings of your experimental setup and results, which will help other people visualize the steps in the experiment.

If you are preparing an exhibit, you may want to display your results, such as any experimental setup you designed. For any unknown substance you may want to have a sample out so that people can note the characteristics of the substance. If you have completed a nonexperimental project, explain clearly what your research question was and illustrate your findings.

Related Projects Separation and identification is a broad topic that can branch out to many projects. You can use paper chromatography to analyze the makeup of other liquid mixtures, such as candy or the pigments in vegetables. To identify the makeup of solid substances, you can examine rocks and minerals. Rocks are made of minerals and minerals each have specific properties. Certain minerals will dissolve in an acid like vinegar, for example, and others will not.

You can also explore how different fields of study use separation and identification techniques, and what techniques they use. You can select one profession to focus and conduct an experiment related to that area of study. Or you can research the many techniques and uses used by a range of professions. For example, the biotechnology field performs separation techniques on many biological substances to identify the molecules. Astronomers use separation and identification techniques to analyze any chunks of rocks or other materials that have landed on Earth from space. Examples of other professions you can explore include art conservators, archaeologists, and food scientists.

For More Information

BBC. "Mixtures."Mixtures. *Schools. Science: Chemistry.* http://www.bbc.co.uk/schools/ks3bitesize/science/chemistry/elements_com_mix_6.shtml (accessed on February 18, 2008). Basic information on the chemistry of mixtures.

Kurtus, Ron. "Mixtures." *School for Champions.* http://http://www.school-for-champions.com/chemistry/mixtures.htm (accessed on February 18, 2008). Basics of mixtures versus compounds.

Lide, David R, ed. *CRC Handbook of Chemistry and Physics, 83rd edition.* Boca Raton, FL: CRC Press, 2002. This authoritative reference provides properties of chemical substances.

"Separating and Purifying." *Journal of Chemical Education.* http://jchemed.chem.wisc.edu/JCESoft/CCA/CCA6/MAIN/1ChemLabMenu/Separating/MENU.HTM (accessed on February 18, 2008). Somewhat technical description of separation techniques.

79

Simple Machines

When most people envision machines, the image probably does not include a simple screwdriver or pencil sharpener. Yet these devices are also machines. A machine is any object that makes work easier by altering the way in which the work is accomplished. Put another way, a machine can use a smaller force to overcome a larger force. In physics, work is defined as force applied over a distance. For example, a person does work when pushing a shopping cart down an aisle, yet does no work when pushing against a closed door.

Simple machines have few moving parts, or sometimes none at all. They are the building blocks for machines of all levels of complexity and all mechanical devices. People have been using simple machines for thousands of years. Zippers, staplers, nails, and scissors are just a few examples of common modern-day machines.

Machines can enlarge and change the direction of a force, yet all machines must follow the principles of the conservation of energy. This principle states that the work or amount of energy coming out of a machine is equal to the amount of energy put into the machine. Work is made up of the amount of force applied and the distance over which the force is maintained. Effort is the force applied. In mathematical terms, work equals force times distance $w = fd$. Put another way, a machine that uses half the force to lift an object, must then double the distance it applies the force.

Simple machines include the inclined plane, wedge, screw, lever, pulley, and wheel and axle.

Incline at work An inclined plane, also called a ramp, decreases the amount of force needed to lift a load or weight by increasing the distance the load travels. For example, an inclined plane that covers twice the distance of the vertical side will need half the amount of effort to lift a

distance of ramp determines amount of

Full Effort

In a ramp or inclined plane, the greater the distance, the less effort. GALE GROUP.

weight than if the weight was lifted straight up. The amount of work remains the same.

Historians theorize that ancient Egyptians used long, shallow ramps to help them carry five-ton stones up pyramids that soared hundreds of feet tall. Driveways, slides, and car ramps are modern-day examples of machines that make use of inclined planes.

A wedge looks like an inclined plane, yet it does work by moving (an inclined plane always remains still). A wedge changes the direction of a force. When a wedge comes into contact with an object, the wedge changes the direction of the force and causes it to move at a right angle. Wedges are often used to push things apart. The force needed for the wedge depends upon the size of the wedge angle. The smaller the angle of the wedge, the less force is needed yet the greater the distance it must be pushed. The pointed end of the nail is an example of a wedge. As the nail is pounded down with a force, the wood is pushed apart sideways. A narrow nail with a small angle must be moved more distance than that of a thick nail with a larger angle. Less force is needed for the thin nail yet it must move a greater distance. Doorstops, the tines on a fork, and knives are other examples of wedges.

A screw is basically an inclined plane wrapped around a cylinder. The length of the screw is the height of the plane, and the distance traveled is determined by the amount of threads on the screw. While turning, a screw converts a rotary motion into a forward or backward motion. The spiral ridges, or threads, around the screw cause the screw to turn many times to move forward a short distance. This is similar to moving an object up an inclined plane or ramp.

The width between the threads, or pitch, is similar to the angle of the inclined plane. The closer together the threads are around the screw, the more it needs to turn to move the same distance, making it less effort to turn. Screws with threads spaced farther apart travel less distance and take more force to turn. The screw's spiral threads act like wedges. Each thread produces a force at right angles to its rotation.

Pulley power A pulley consists of a rope or other cord pulled over a steadied wheel. At one end of the rope is the object or load to be lifted; the other end is where the force is applied.

A single, fixed pulley changes the direction of a force. The force needed to lift the load still equals the weight of the load, yet it can feel easier if a person is pulling down instead of pushing up. Using two or more pulleys connected together can decrease the amount of effort needed to lift the same load. If using two pulleys, the rope leading to each individual pulley can hold half as much weight. With the load weighing half as much, a person need apply only half the force. The tradeoff is that the rope needs to be pulled twice the distance. The force is cut in half but the distance the rope must be pulled has doubled.

Lever lifts A lever is any bar-type object free to move or pivot about at a fixed point. The point at which the lever pivots is called the fulcrum. A downward motion at one end results in an upward motion on the opposite side.

In a lever, the fulcrum's relationship to its load and the force applied, or effort, determines the work of the lever. Levers are categorized by where the fulcrum is located in relation to the load and effort. There are three basic types of levers. A first-class lever has its fulcrum placed between its load and the effort. One end is forced down and the other end moves up. When the fulcrum is in the center of the lever, the amount of effort pushed down on one side equals the amount of load lifted on the

Slides of all kinds are examples of inclined planes. © KELLY-- MOONEY PHOTOGRAPHY/ CORBIS.

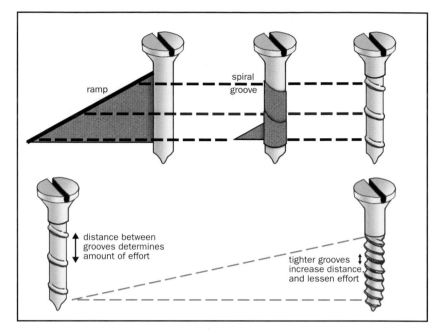

Screws are examples of simple machines. The closer together the threads are around the screw, the more it needs to turn to move the same distance, making it less effort to turn. Screws with threads spaced farther apart travel less distance and take more force to turn. GALE GROUP.

other side. If the distance from the effort to the fulcrum increases by two, then only half as much pushing effort is needed to raise the same load. If the load doubles, then the distance from the fulcrum to the load must also double in order for the same effort to move it. Pliers, a person's jaw, and a seesaw are examples of this type of lever.

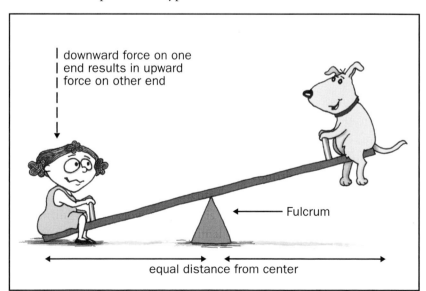

A seesaw is an example of a lever where the fulcrum is equally centered between load and effort. GALE GROUP.

A fulcrum at one end with the load in the middle and the effort at the far end is a second-class lever. This type of lever, such as a wheelbarrow, increases the force needed to lift the load, but decreases the distance it has to move. A third-class lever has the fulcrum at one end, the effort in the middle, and the load at the far end. Tweezers and fishing rods are examples of this type of lever.

A wheel and axle machine rotates around a fixed point and works in a similar way to a revolving lever. The axle is the object that attaches to the wheel. The wheel moves the axle. When the wheel revolves it moves a greater distance than the axle. The larger the diameter of the wheel, the less effort needed to turn it, but the greater distance needed for the same work. In reverse, a greater force applied to the axle will turn the wheel a greater distance. Doorknobs, pencil sharpeners, screwdriver handles, and steering wheels all use a wheel and axle.

A wheelbarrow is an example of a lever where the fulcrum (in this case, the wheel) is at one end with the load (the bucket) in the middle and the effort (person lifting the handles) at the far end. © KELLY A. QUIN.

EXPERIMENT 1

Wheel and Axle: How can changing the size of the wheel affect the amount of work it takes to lift a load?

Purpose/Hypothesis A wheel and axle can be used to do work using less force. In a wheel and axle, both parts move together. In this experiment you will construct a wheel and axle that also incorporates the pulley. You will join two spools together, one the wheel and the other the axle. The axle will hold a load and you will apply force to the wheel. Washers will be the load and also apply the force. This experiment will use three wheels of different diameters. By changing the diameter of the wheel, you will find out how the relationship in size between the wheel and the axle determines how easy it is to lift the load.

Before you begin, make an educated guess about the outcome of this experiment based on your knowledge of work and machines. This

In a pencil sharpener, the wheel turns the axle, which is attached to a blade. The more turns you have to make, the less effort it takes. GALE GROUP.

WORDS TO KNOW

Conservation of energy: The law of physics that states that energy can be transformed from one form to another, but can be neither created nor destroyed.

Control experiment: A setup that is identical to the experiment, but is not affected by the variables that affects the experimental group.

Effort: The force applied to move a load using a simple machine.

Friction: A force that resists the motion of an object, resulting when two objects rub against one another.

Fulcrum: The point at which a lever arm pivots.

Hypothesis: An idea in the form of a statement that can be tested by observation and/or experiment.

Inclined plane: A simple machine with no moving parts; a slanted surface.

Machine: Any device that makes work easier by providing a mechanical advantage.

Pulley: A simple machine made of a cord wrapped around a wheel.

Screw: A simple machine; an inclined plane wrapped around a cylinder.

Simple machine: Any of the basic structures that provide a mechanical advantage and have no or few moving parts.

Variable: Something that can affect the results of an experiment.

Wedge: A simple machine; a form of inclined plane.

Wheel and axle: A simple machine; a larger wheel(s) fastened to a smaller cylinder, an axle, so that they turn together.

Work: Force applied over a distance.

---

educated guess, or prediction, is your hypothesis. A hypothesis should explain these things:

- the topic of the experiment
- the variable you will change
- the variable you will measure
- what you expect to happen

A hypothesis should be brief, specific, and measurable. It must be something you can test through further investigation. Your experiment will prove or disprove whether your hypothesis is correct. Here is one possible hypothesis for this experiment: "Given that the axle stays constant, the larger the wheel, the less force will be needed to lift the load."

In this case, the variable you will change is the diameter of the wheel. The variable you will measure is the amount of force needed to lift the load.

Conducting a control experiment will help you isolate each variable and measure the changes in the dependent variable. Only one variable will change between the control and the experimental setup, and that is the diameter of the wheel. For the control, you will use a wheel that is of equal size to the axle. At the end of the experiment you can compare the results of the control to the experimental trials.

Level of Difficulty Easy to Moderate.

Materials Needed

- 2 small paper or plastic cups
- metal washers all of equal size, at least 20
- dowel (should fit through spools to allow spools to spin)
- masking tape
- ruler
- hole puncher
- marking pen
- string (optional)
- 2 full thread spools of equal size (wheel and axle)
- 3 cylindrical objects of varying sizes: (full thread spools or ribbon spools work well). Use the thread spool as a guide when collecting these objects: find one about half its size, one about twice its diameter, and one about three or four times its diameter).

Approximate Budget $3.

Timetable 20 minutes.

Step-by-Step Instructions

1. Measure and note the diameters of the two equal-size cylinders in a data chart.
2. Set up a wheel and axle control by placing the dowel into the two cylinders of the same size: the wheel and axle. Tape the spools together so they move as one unit.

What Are the Variables?

Variables are anything that might affect the results of an experiment. Here are the main variables in this experiment:

- the diameter of the wheel
- the weight of the cups
- the diameter of the axle
- the load

In other words, the variables in this experiment are everything that might affect the amount of force needed. If you change more than one variable at the same time, you will not be able to tell which variable had the most effect on getting the work done.

How to Experiment Safely

There are no safety hazards in this experiment.

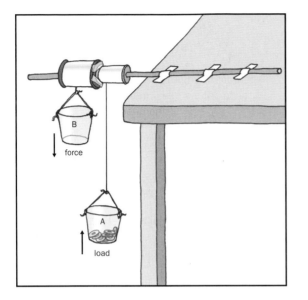

Step 7: Apply force by placing washers in cup B, one at a time, until cup A has been raised and is sitting just below the axle.

GALE GROUP.

Set the dowel on a table with the wheel and axle hanging just over the edge, then tape the dowel firmly to the table at the far end and several points along the dowel. The wheel is the outside cylinder.

3. Label the cups "A" and "B." Punch two holes in each of the cups on opposite sides near the open upper rim. Cut two pieces of string slightly larger than the diameter of the cup. Tie each end of the string to a hole on the outside of the cup so that it is slightly loose.

4. Pull down 20 inches (51 centimeters) of thread from the axle and attach cup A to the thread. Use several inches of the thread from the wheel to attach cup B. (Note: If you are not using thread spools or the thread is weak, then tape a piece of string to the center of the cylinder.)

5. Wrap the thread around the wheel until cup B is sitting just below the thread.

6. Place eight washers in cup A.

7. Apply force by placing washers in cup B, one at a time, until cup A has been raised and is sitting just below the axle. Note the force needed by counting the amount of washers. Record your results.

8. Remove the wheel; cup A will fall back in its starting point.

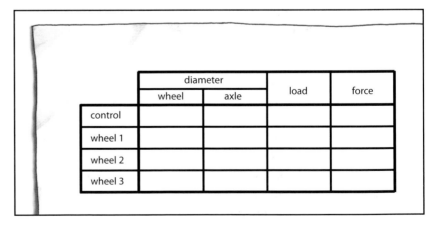

	diameter		load	force
	wheel	axle		
control				
wheel 1				
wheel 2				
wheel 3				

Data chart for Experiment 1.

GALE GROUP.

9. Measure the diameter of a second spool. Slide this wheel on the dowel and firmly attach it to the axle. Pull down the string (or ribbon) and reattach cup B to the new spool, making sure it is at the same starting point just below the spool.

10. Again, apply force by placing washers in cup B, one at a time, until cup A is sitting below the axle. Note the results.

11. Repeat Steps 7 through 10 for the next two wheels.

Summary of Results Examine your chart. Compare the ratio of the diameters between the wheel and axle, and the ratio between the load and force for each wheel. How do they relate to each other, and how do they relate to the control? What size wheel made the work of lifting the load the easiest? In your wheel and axle, look at what other type of machine is in use? How does changing the direction of the force provide an additional mechanical advantage?

Change the Variables To change the variable in this experiment, you can alter the diameter of the axle instead of the wheel. You can also use more or less weights as the load.

EXPERIMENT 2

Lever Lifting: How does the distance from the fulcrum affect work?

Purpose/Hypothesis A lever is a bar that pivots on a fulcrum. The mass placed on a lever is called the load. In a first-class lever, the fulcrum sits in between the two loads. The load presses down on the lever with a force or effort. In this experiment, you will vary the distances between the applied force, or effort, and the fulcrum to determine how to make the load easier to lift. You will use a ruler as the lever, metal washers as the load, and a small narrow object as the fulcrum.

Before you begin, make an educated guess about the outcome of this experiment based on your knowledge of levers and machines.

Troubleshooter's Guide

Below is a problem that may arise during this experiment, a possible cause, and a way to remedy the problem.

Problem: The load only lifted part of the time.

Possible cause: The wheel and axle may have come loose at some point during the experiment. Check to make sure that the two cylinders are firmly attached and they are moving as one unit. You may need to use electrical tape or some other stronger tape. Repeat the experiment.

What Are the Variables?

Variables are anything that might affect the results of an experiment. Here are the main variables in this experiment:

- the mass of the load
- the distance from load to fulcrum

In other words, the variables in this experiment are everything that might affect the work of the lever. If you change more than one variable at the same time, you will not be able to tell which variable had the most effect on the work.

This educated guess, or prediction, is your hypothesis. A hypothesis should explain these things:

- the topic of the experiment
- the variable you will change
- the variable you will measure
- what you expect to happen

A hypothesis should be brief, specific, and measurable. It must be something you can test through further investigation. Your experiment will prove or disprove whether your hypothesis is correct. Here is one possible hypothesis for this experiment: "More force is needed when it is applied closer to the fulcrum than farther from the fulcrum."

In this case, the variable you will change is the distance from the fulcrum. The variable you will measure is the force needed to lift the load.

Level of Difficulty Easy.

Materials Needed

- 12-inch (30-centimeter) flat ruler
- ten metal washers of the same size
- narrow flat object, such as a pencil or domino

Approximate Budget $2.

Timetable 20 minutes.

Step-by-Step Instructions

How to Experiment Safely

There are no safety hazards in this experiment.

1. Make a lever by placing the narrow object that serves as a fulcrum, such as a domino, under a ruler at the 6-inch (15-centimeter) mark.

2. Place four washers at one end of the ruler. Add washers on the opposite end of the ruler until the load is lifted and the lever is

balanced. Note the number of washers and the distance.

3. Remove the washers on the 12-inch (30-centimeter) mark so that the opposite side lies on the table.

4. Place washers one at a time on the 10-inch (25.4-centimeter) mark, until the lever is balanced. Note the number of washers and the distance.

5. Remove the washers on the 10-inch mark and repeat, placing the washers on the 8-inch (20.3-centimeter) mark.

Step 5: Place the washers closer to the fulcrum to determine how many it takes to lift the load. GALE GROUP.

Summary of Results Examine your results and compare the different loads required to accomplish the same amount of work: lifting the load. For each trial, complete the equation work equals force times distance, where force is the number of washers needed to push down one side, and distance is the distance from the fulcrum. Predict how many washers you would need at several different points along the ruler.

Change the Variables To change the variable in this experiment you could alter the position of the fulcrum. Keep the number of washers on one side the same, move the fulcrum, and then determine how much force is needed to lift the load.

EXPERIMENT 3

The Screw: How does the distance between the threads of a screw affect the work?

Purpose/Hypothesis The screw is a simple machine that is a modification of an inclined plane. The threads (or grooves) wrapped around a cylinder are an incline. It is this incline that helps the screw move into an object. The distance between the threads around the cylinder determines the steepness of the incline. The

Troubleshooter's Guide

Below is a problem that may arise during this experiment, a possible cause, and a way to remedy the problem.

Problem: The washers keep falling off.

Possible cause: Your fulcrum may be too high. Use a smaller object, such as a flat pencil, and repeat the experiment.

What Are the Variables?

Variables are anything that might affect the results of an experiment. Here are the main variables in this experiment:

- circumference of screws
- the number of threads
- the diameter of the screwdriver
- the type of screw
- the type of wood

In other words, the variables in this experiment are everything that might affect the work of the screw. If you change more than one variable at the same time, you will not be able to tell which variable had the most effect on the work.

incline affects the distance the screw moves into an object after one full turn.

This experiment will use three screws with different threads. Fewer threads will give a steeper incline. By changing the distance between the threads, you will find out how the steepness of the threads' incline determines the amount of work needed to turn the screw into a piece of wood. You can estimate work through distance and force. Work equals force applied over a distance. All the screws will be moved the same distance. For the purposes of this experiment, you can estimate how much force each screw takes to turn by measuring the number of turns. Some screws may take more effort to turn than others. As you conduct the experiment, consider difficulty of turning each screw compared to one another.

Before you begin, make an educated guess about the outcome of this experiment based on your knowledge of simple machines and screws.

	Screw 1	Screw 2	Screw 3
Thread width			
Number of revolutions			

Step 2: Fill in the distance on a chart. ILLUSTRATION BY TEMAH NELSON.

This educated guess, or prediction, is your hypothesis. A hypothesis should explain these things:

- the topic of the experiment
- the variable you will change
- the variable you will measure
- what you expect to happen

A hypothesis should be brief, specific, and measurable. It must be something you can test through further investigation. Your experiment will prove or disprove whether your hypothesis is correct. Here is one possible hypothesis for this experiment: "More work is needed to turn a screw with fewer threads into an object compared to a screw that has more grooves."

In this case, the variable you will change is the distance between the grooves. The variable you will measure is the work needed to twist the screw.

Level of Difficulty Moderate.

Materials Needed

- 3 screws that are 2-inches (5-centimeters) long, each with a different number of threads; they should all be either flat or Phillips
- 1 block of 2x4 pine wood
- screw driver, flat or Phillips depending on type of screw
- painters tape
- ruler with centimeters and millimeters
- marker or pen

Approximate Budget $8.

Timetable 20 minutes.

Step-by-Step Instructions

1. Use the marker to mark three lines on the wood where the screws will be inserted.
2. Measure the distance between the threads on each screw in centimeters or millimeters. Fill in the distance on a chart similar to the illustration.

Steps 3 and 4: Wrap a piece of tape one-half inch from the point of each screw. Mark a line on the tape to help you count the revolutions. ILLUSTRATION BY TEMAH NELSON.

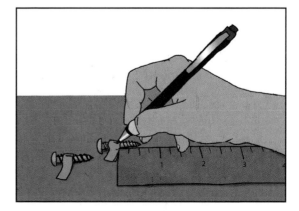

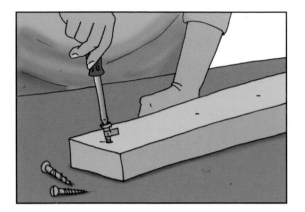

Step 5: Turn the first screw into the wood, counting the rotations. ILLUSTRATION BY TEMAH NELSON.

3. Wrap a piece of tape one-half inch from the point of each screw.

4. Mark a line on the tape to help you count the revolutions.

5. Turn the first screw into the wood. You will need to count the number of rotations made by the screw. Continue with the twisting until the screw is into the wood 0.5 inches (1.3 centimeters), where the mark was placed on the tape matches with the line on the wood.

6. Turn the second and then third screws into the wood. Note the number of turns each screws until it reaches the mark on the tape.

7. Analyze chart to determine which screw required the least amount of revolutions, greatest amount of revolutions.

Summary of Results Consider how easy or hard each screw was to turn. How does the amount of effort relate to the distance between the threads. Using the data on your chart consider when it be better to use a screw with a larger thread distance versus a shorter thread distance? Think about some ways that the principles behind screws are incorporated into common devices.

Change the Variables One way to change the variable in this experiment is to use screws with the same threads but different thicknesses. Try using an extremely wide screw compared to a thin one. You can also use different types of screws and compare the effort involved.

Design Your Own Experiment

How to Select a Topic Relating to this Concept To choose a topic related to simple machines and mechanics you can look at the objects that you use every day. Select several items and identify the type(s) of simple machines that it utilizes. You can use these tools to model the design of your machines. Check the Further Readings section and talk with your science teacher to learn more about machines and mechanics.

Steps in the Scientific Method To conduct an original experiment, you need to plan carefully and think things through. Otherwise, you might not be sure what question you are answering, what you are or should be measuring, or what your findings prove or disprove.

Here are the steps in designing an experiment:

- State the purpose of—and the underlying question behind—the experiment you propose to do.
- Recognize the variables involved and select one that will help you answer the question at hand.
- State your hypothesis, an educated guess about the answer to your question.
- Decide how to change the variable you selected.
- Decide how to measure your results.

Recording Data and Summarizing the Results Your data should include charts and drawings such as the one you did for these experiments. They should be clearly labeled and easy to read. You may also want to include photographs and drawings of your experimental setup and results, which will help other people visualize the steps in the experiment.

If you are preparing an exhibit, you may want to display your results, such as any experimental setup you designed. You may also want to include specimens, in a closed container, so that others can observe what you studied. If you have completed a nonexperimental project, explain clearly what your research question was and illustrate your findings.

Related Projects Because simple machines are all around, finding materials and ideas related to simple machines is relatively simple. As machines

> ### Troubleshooter's Guide
>
> You should not encounter many problems during this experiment. Below is one problem that may arise, and a way to remedy the problem.
>
> **Problem:** The screw won't turn into the wood.
>
> **Possible cause:** You may not be using soft pine or you may be screwing into a particularly hard section of the wood. Try using a fresh piece of pine wood and repeat.

Did you know that your jaw is a simple machine? The jaw acts as a first-class lever when you are chewing food. © KELLY A. QUIN.

are linked with force, you can investigate the principles behind force that are at work in a machine. A project idea can be to take one simple machine and use the same force in many different setups. You can take apart common household simple machines (with an adult's permission, of course) and compare the differences and similarities between machines that use the same principles. Compare one type of simple machine, such as a screwdriver, to its different types. Look at what features each machine has to make its work easier.

You can also build or take apart complex machines, and sketch the simple machines that it uses. For a research project, you can investigate the history of simple machines and how they have impacted people's lives.

For More Information

"Background Information for Simple Machines." *Canada Science and Technology Museum.* http://www.sciencetech.technomuses.ca/english/schoolzone/Info_Simple_Machines.cfm (accessed on February 29, 2008). Informative site explaining various simple machines, including levers, pulleys, and more.

Lafferty, Peter. *Force & Motion.* New York: EyeWitness Books, Dorling Kindersley, 2000. With photographs and many graphics, this book describes the science of force and motion and their applications in simple machines.

Macaulay, David, and Peter Lafferty. *The Way things Work.* Boston: Houghton Mifflin, 1988. Clear text with many illustrations describes the principles behind numerous inventions and tools.

Museum of Science, Boston. *Exploring Leonardo.* http://www.mos.org/sln/Leonardo/LeoHomePage.html (accessed on February 29, 2008). Exhibit on Leonardo da Vinci's work with machines.

"Simple Machines." *BrainPOP.* http://www.brainpop.com/technology/simplemachines/ (accessed on February 29, 2008). Animations, activities, and explanations of simple machines.

University of Utah. "Simple and Complex Machines." *ASPIRE.* http://sunshine.chpc.utah.edu/javalabs/java12/machine/index.htm (accessed on February 29, 2008). Illustrated explanations with lab activities of various machines.

80

Soil

Commonly called dirt, soil is a central ingredient for life on Earth. Soil is the thin, outer layer of material on the surface of Earth, ranging from a fraction of an inch to several feet thick.

Plants depend on soil for their nutrients and growth. These plants are then consumed and used by animals, including people. Soils provide shelter and a home for insects and small animals. Microscopic organisms flourish in soil, breaking down dead matter, which returns nutrients into the soil for new life. People use soils directly as a material to build on and grow crops in. Soils also reveal a historical record of an area's past life and geography. Understanding the properties of a soil is a key to determining how the soil will function for a particular use.

The specific makeup of soil depends on its location, yet all soils share the same basic composition: minerals, water, air, and organic matter, meaning matter that contains carbon and comes from living organisms. Minerals are naturally occurring inorganic or nonliving substances that come from Earth's crust. Different types and combinations of these components form multiple types of soil. In the United States alone, researchers have identified over seventy thousand different soils. Soils are characterized by many features, including their structure, texture, living organisms, and acidity.

The scoop on dirt Soil is a dynamic material that Earth is constantly manufacturing. The highest percent of any given soil is made of minerals, which all come from the same material: rocks. Nature churns rocks into new soil regularly and slowly. A rock is a mixture of minerals that stays together under normal conditions. Rocks can be hard, relatively soft, small, or large. Over time, rocks get weathered or worn down naturally by their environment.

Several factors contribute to how fast the rock weathers. The rock's composition, climate, surrounding organisms, and location are all key

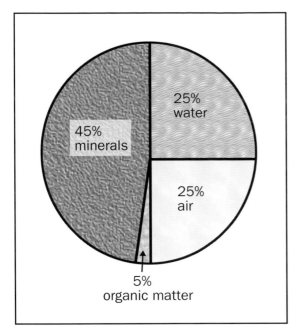

Basic composition of soil. GALE GROUP.

factors. Weathering also needs time. It can take 100 years to more than six hundred years to form one inch of topsoil.

The rocks that form soil are called the parent material. When some rocks weather, their minerals react with other elements to form different chemicals from the original parent material. Other rocks retain the same composition of the parent material. The makeup of the parent material determines many properties of the resulting soil.

The mineral content of the parent material can be acidic, neutral, or alkaline. The acidity of soil is measured on a pH scale from 0 to 14. On this scale, a pH of 7 is neutral, above 7 is alkaline, and below 7 is acidic. The acidity of the soil is a key factor in determining the types of plants and other organisms that thrive there. Iron, for example, is an acidic mineral in which azaleas and blueberries grow well. Elm, yucca, and sycamore grow in nonacidic soils. Soil life also depends upon minerals for essential nutrients, which come from the specific mineral content in the parent material. Calcium, phosphorus, and potassium are examples of familiar minerals soil life needs.

Winds, rain, sunshine, and temperature shifts all play a part in weathering. Water slips into the cracks of a rock. Varying temperatures

Climate and location are two factors that cause rocks to break down and form soil. GALE GROUP.

freeze and thaw the water repeatedly, expanding the cracks and fragmenting the rock. Rain pounds against a rock, wearing it down into increasingly smaller particles. Winds beat against the rock's surface, tearing away its outer layers. In general, a moist, warm climate causes rocks to break down more quickly than a cool, dry climate.

The surface features of an area also impact soil formation and its erosion. Water that flows over land can carry soil with it and expose new rocks to weathering. Soils on slopes and hills have a high rate of water flow. Here, soils are carried by the water flow at a faster rate than soils on flat surfaces, which have more time to form.

Nature churns rocks into new soil regularly and slowly.
CORBIS.

Along with the weather, a warm climate also hastens the weathering process because it provides a comfortable environment for life. Organisms that live in and on the soil affect soil's formation in several ways. Plant roots stretch into the soil and break up small fragments. Burrowing animals wriggle through soil and move rock fragments to cause crumbling. Animals stomp on the soil and split up rock pieces. Some microscopic organisms that produce acid, such as fungi and lichens, break up the minerals within rocks.

Size matters Soils are generally made up of one of three mineral particles: sand, silt, or clay. The type of particles is another major factor in determining the life in and on the soil. Water and air, needed by both plants and animals, sit in the spaces between the particles. Almost all soils have some combination of these particles, and it is the relative percentage of one over the other that determines its category.

Sand particles are relatively large, ranging in size from 0.002 inches to 0.08 inches (0.05 millimeters to 2 millimeters) in diameter. Sandy particles feel gritty to the touch. The particles have large air spaces between them, causing water to run through easily. Because they do not retain moisture, sand is loose and crumbly. Water that runs through sand can cause minerals necessary for growth to drain or leach out of the soil. Leaching is the movement of dissolved particles downward through the soil.

Silt is the next largest soil particle, ranging in size from 0.00008 inches to 0.002 inches (0.002 millimeters to 0.05 millimeters) in diameter. Silt particles are fine and hold in some water. Silt particles feel soft and can hold together well when moist. When they are dry they are easily blown away by wind.

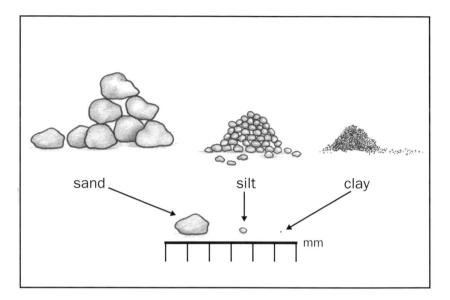

Clay particles are the smallest type of soil. Clay particles have little air space between them. They hold the highest amount of water and keep other soil particles together. Moist clay packs tightly together and can be molded. When clay particles are dry they harden, which can slow the growth of plant roots.

Dirty layers As the weathering process continues over time, it causes soil to develop into layers that have distinct characteristics. A vertical slice of two or more of these layers is known as a soil profile. The layers are known as soil horizons and are named O, A, B, and C. How thick each horizon is depends upon its location. Soil horizon properties differ in their color, texture, consistency, life, and acidity.

The uppermost soil layer, the O layer, is filled with organic matter. As this matter gets decomposed from soil-dwelling creatures it forms a dark-brown, organic material called humus. Most humus comes from plant materials, such as dead leaves, twigs, and stems that fall to the ground. Dead animals in the soil and above it also contribute to humus. Humus retains water and contains nutrients for life to grow.

Sitting right below this layer is the A layer, called topsoil. Topsoil contains decaying plant and animal remains, along with a wealth of microscopic organisms such as bacteria. With all of its humus and organic matter, topsoil is usually the darkest and most fertile layer in the soil. Soil animals, such as earthworms and ants, live comfortably in this layer, using the plant and animal remains for food. Plant roots stretch out in this region to suck up the water and nutrients.

Subsoil is the middle, or B, soil layer. It is usually lighter in color than topsoil because it does not contain as much humus, making it less fertile. Denser and with less nutrients than topsoil, relatively few animals and plants are found here. Some plants with long roots reach down into the subsoil to get at the water stored between the particles.

The C layer, or horizon, contains partially disintegrated parent material and its minerals. It is far less altered and weathered than the layers above it and has none of the organic matter life needs to grow. Beneath this layer is the bottom region below the soil called bedrock. This layer contains bits of rock similar to the parent material.

Life in the dirt lane Soils are teeming with life, from the microscopic bacteria and fungi to the visible small animals and plants. Live organisms promote growth and new life in soil. Once dead, organisms contribute to the amount of decayed organic matter in soil, which influences its characteristics.

Pick up a handful of soil and you are holding billions of microscopic organisms. These microbes decompose organic matter and return vital nutrients into the environment. Plant roots hold soil particles together and prevent them from blowing away. Animals that burrow into the soil, such as squirrels and moles, create holes that allow air and water to enter. Insects such as beetles, ants, spiders, and snails eat organic matter and begin the decaying process. Worms tunnel through the soil, creating air pockets and turning over the soil.

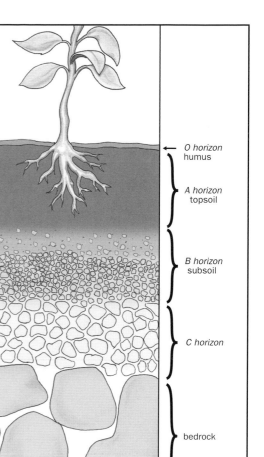

In a soil horizon the soil particles get gradually larger. GALE GROUP.

EXPERIMENT 1

Soil Profile: What are the different properties of the soil horizons?

Purpose/Hypothesis Soil is composed of three main categories of particles: sand, silt, and clay. Each of these particles has distinct properties

Earthworms tunnel through the soil, creating air pockets and turning over the soil. © SALLY A. MORGAN; ECOSCENE/ CORBIS.

including its feel, texture, color, nutrients, and size. While these three particles can form many different combinations in a soil, the proportion of each changes in each horizon.

In this experiment, you will take a soil profile and determine the properties of three different horizons. Because the depth of each soil horizon depends on location, the depth suggested to dig is a guide. You may need to dig farther down than suggested to find three unique horizons, or you may not have to dig as deep.

Once you have the three samples you will examine their characteristics in several ways. Using a kit, you will test each sample for nutrients. By feeling the soil and pressing it together you can determine its texture and feel. You will then estimate the relative proportions of sand, silt, and clay by measuring the point at which each layer settles in water. Larger particles will settle first; the smallest particles will settle last. Another varying characteristic among the horizons is the amount of microorganisms, which decompose organic matter and create the humus. An optional part to this experiment is to determine the amount of microorganisms in each horizon by placing chopped organic matter in each sample and examining the results.

Before you begin, make an educated guess about the outcome of this experiment based on your knowledge of soil horizons and soil particles. This educated guess, or prediction, is your hypothesis. A hypothesis should explain these things:

- the topic of the experiment
- the variable you will change
- the variable you will measure
- what you expect to happen

A hypothesis should be brief, specific, and measurable. It must be something you can test through further investigation. Your experiment will prove or disprove whether your hypothesis is correct. Here is one possible hypothesis for this experiment: "The soil horizons at lower

WORDS TO KNOW

Alkaline: A substance that is capable of neutralizing an acid, or basic. In soil, soil with a pH of more than 7.0, which is neutral.

Bedrock: Solid layer of rock lying beneath the soil and other loose material.

Clay: Type of soil comprising the smallest soil particles.

Control experiment: A setup that is identical to the experiment, but is not affected by the variables that affects the experimental group.

Humus: Fragrant, spongy, nutrient-rich decayed plant or animal matter.

Hypothesis: An idea in the form of a statement that can be tested by observation and/or experiment.

Leach: The movement of dissolved minerals or chemicals with water as it percolates, or oozes, downward through the soil.

Mineral: An nonorganic substance found in nature with a definite chemical composition and structure.

Organic: Made of, or coming from, living matter.

Parent material: The underlying rock from which soil forms.

Rock: Naturally occurring solid mixture of minerals.

Sand: Granular portion of soil composed of the largest soil particles.

Silt: Medium-sized soil particles.

Soil: The upper layer of Earth that contains nutrients for plants and organisms; a mixture of mineral matter, organic matter, air, and water.

Soil horizon: An identifiable soil layer due to color, structure, and/or texture.

Soil profile: Combined soil horizons or layers.

Topsoil: Uppermost layer of soil that contains high levels of organic matter.

Variable: Something that can affect the results of an experiment.

Weathered: Natural process that breaks down rocks and minerals at Earth's surface into simpler materials by physical (mechanical) or chemical means.

---

depths will contain more sand, be grittier, lighter, and have less minerals and organic matter than the soil of the top horizon."

In this case, the variable you will change is the depth of the soil. The variable you will measure is the soil's properties, including its particle makeup, organic matter, color, and mineral content.

Level of Difficulty Difficult (because of the digging and the multiple parts).

Materials Needed

- area with soil that you can dig (another option is to find an area already dug; see also Change the Variables)

What Are the Variables?

Variables are anything that might affect the results of an experiment. Here are the main variables in this experiment:

- the patch of soil you choose
- the depth you dig
- the amount the jar is shaken
- the type of organic matter present

In other words, the variables in this experiment are everything that might affect the soil horizons. If you change more than one variable at the same time, you will not be able to tell which variable had the most effect on the properties of each horizon.

How to Experiment Safely

This is a messy experiment; be sure to wash your hands thoroughly after collecting the soil. Watch out for any insects in the soil.

- shovel
- plastic container that can hold about 2 cups (500 milliliters)
- grasses, flowers, leaves (optional part)
- yardstick
- ruler
- three self-sealing bags
- three 1-quart (about 1-liter) straight jars with lids
- water
- marking pen
- nutrient testing kit (available from garden or hardware stores)

Approximate Budget $18.

Timetable Varies because of digging; 3 hours experiment time; 24 hours waiting. Optional part will take 3 weeks; 15 minutes per week.

Step-by-Step Instructions

1. Find a clear area of soil and dig to a depth of about 30 inches (76 centimeters). Place the ruler in the hole to measure depth.

2. Label the self-sealing bags "Soil A," "Soil B," and "Soil C."

3. Use the plastic containers to collect three samples at different depths. (Examine the soil profile for differences in color and texture and use this as your collection indicators. The following measurements are guidelines.) Collect the first soil sample by placing the top of the container at 2 inches (5 centimeters) down and scooping dirt inside the container. When filled, place the soil in Soil A bag and note the depth on a data chart. Collect the next soil sample at roughly 15 inches (38 centimeters). Place the soil in Soil B bag and note the depth. Collect the third soil sample at 30 inches (76 centimeters). Place the soil in Soil C bag and note the depth. Remove any visible insects from the soil samples.

4. Note the color(s) of each sample on your data chart.

5. Determine the texture of each layer: Collect a small ball of soil in your hand from Soil A and spray it with water so that it is damp. (If it is already damp leave as is.) Rub the soil between your fingers and feel if the texture is floury (silt), sticky (clay), or gritty (sand).

6. Use that same ball to determine if the soil sticks together. Press the soil between your thumb and forefinger to make a ribbon. Note whether the soil forms a ribbon without breaking, forms a ribbon with breaking, or does not form a ribbon.

7. Repeat Steps 5 and 6 for Soil B and Soil C.

8. Estimate the relative percentage of clay, sand, and silt particles: Place 1 cup of Soil A in a labeled jar and add water until the jar is almost full. Repeat with the other two soils, adding the same amount of water in each jar and making sure the jars are labeled. Cover the jars and shake for at least two minutes.

9. After one minute, make a mark on the jar at the level the particles have settled to the bottom. This is the sand. Measure up to the mark with the ruler.

Step 3: Collect soil samples from three horizons. GALE GROUP.

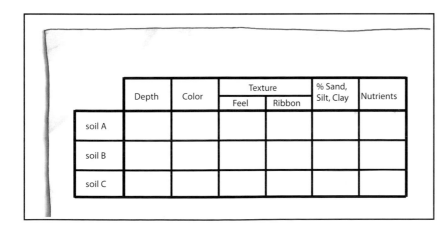

	Depth	Color	Texture		% Sand, Silt, Clay	Nutrients
			Feel	Ribbon		
soil A						
soil B						
soil C						

Data chart for Experiment 1. GALE GROUP.

Steps 9 to 11: Measure each layer of particle. GALE GROUP.

10. Let the jars sit undisturbed. After two to three hours, mark and measure the thickness of the next layer. This is the silt.

11. Wait at least 24 hours to measure the last level, which is the clay.

12. Divide the thickness of each layer by the total height of all three layers. Multiply that number by 100 for a rough percentage of each type of particle. Note the results.

13. Test for nutrients: Follow the directions on the nutrient kit to determine the level of nutrients in each soil sample.

14. (Optional) Determine the relative amount of microorganisms in each sample: Leave 1 cup (about 240 milliliters) of each soil sample in the bag and add enough water to moisten (the rest of the soil can be returned to ground). Seal the bag and poke small holes in the top.

15. Chop up organic matter, such as leaves, grass, and/or flowers. Add 2 tablespoons (30 milliliters) of the chopped organic matter to each bag. Spray each soil so each is the same moistness and place bags in a dark environment, such as a drawer. Every five to seven days add another tablespoon of water (15 milliliters) to each of the soils. Every week for two to three weeks, note the decomposition of the organic matter and any visible life, such as fungi.

Summary of Results Examine your chart of the three soils. What is the most striking difference in soil properties between them? How did Soil A compare to Soil C in texture and color? How do the differences in the estimated soil particles relate to the soils color and whether it sticks together? Determine if any of your soils showed the property of only one type of soil particle? Hypothesize would happen if you grew the same plant in each soil. Based on your results, how does each soil hold water? Write a brief summary of the experiment and your analysis.

Change the Variables The main way to change the variable in this experiment is to alter the type of soil. If digging is not possible in your area, you can purchase different soil types in a garden shop and repeat the same steps for each soil. To change the variable in the microorganisms part, you can use the same type soil and alter the kind of organic matter.

Modify the Experiment You can conduct a simplified version of this experiment that will take less time (and less mess) by comparing the soil composition from two locations. First, consider what two areas you want to collect soil. Try to find soils that have different characteristics, such as color or if plants grow in it. Make a hypothesis if one soil contains more sand, silt, or clay than the other sample.

Using a spade, collect a sample of each soil type. Scrape away the first couple inches of the soil and then place about a cup of the soil in a plastic bag. Make sure to label the bag with the soil location. Spread out each sample and remove any pebbles, leaves, or other debris. You can do this by hand or with a colander. You will need two narrow glass jars with lids, a measuring cup, liquid soap, and a ruler.

Place a cup of soil from one location in the first glass jar and a cup of soil from the second location in the second jar. Add a drop of liquid soap (this will separate the soil particles). Fill the jars with water and shake for at least two minutes. Set the jars down and watch the particles settle to the bottom. After a couple minutes, use a ruler to measure the amount of sand that settled. Sand is the heaviest soil particle. After another 15 minutes, measure the particles that have settled. Measure the buildup of particles over a set time period, comparing the two jars. When you have finished, you can graph the amount of particles that settled in each sample for each time period. Did one sample have more sand? Are there still clay particles floating about in the water? Was your hypothesis correct? Think about how the area and soil life, if anything, relates to the soil sample.

Troubleshooter's Guide

Below are some problems that may arise during this experiment, some possible causes, and some ways to remedy the problem.

Problem: The soil horizons were very similar.

Possible cause: You may not have dug down deep enough when you collected the samples. There should be a change in texture and color marking the different horizons. Repeat the experiment, digging down another 12 inches (30 centimeters) or more.

Problem: The organic matter did not decompose.

Possible cause: You may not have allowed enough time for the microorganisms in the soil to decompose it. It is also possible that you have few microorganisms in any of your soils. Repeat with another sample from the same location, and use a soil as a control that is a rich, dark brown color from the top layer of the soil.

EXPERIMENT 2

Soil pH: Does the pH of soil affect plant growth?

Purpose/Hypothesis A soil's pH is a measure of how acidic or basic it is. A soil that is basic is called alkaline. Alkaline soils are often referred to as sweet; acidic soils are referred to as sour. Soil pH is measured on a pH scale. The pH scale ranges from 1 to 14, with 7 being neutral, neither acid nor alkaline. Water, for example has a pH of 7. Acidic soils have a pH less than 7; the lower the number, the more acidic the soil. Alkaline soils have a pH above 7; the higher the number, the more alkaline the soil.

Most plants prefer a neutral to slightly acidic soil, with a pH between 6 and 7, yet some plants prefer acidity whereas others grow best in alkaline soil. Potatoes, gardenias, and blueberries grow best in acidic soils. Geraniums, asparagus, and mint grow best at higher pH levels. The pH of the soil also affects how available the nutrients are for plants to absorb. For example, nitrogen, potassium, and phosphorous are key nutrients that plants needs to grow. In soil that is highly acidic or alkaline, plants cannot get phosphorus. Potassium is most available in soils with high pH and unavailable at low pH. Nitrogen becomes available to plants with a pH of roughly 5.5 or above.

To ensure proper growth of crops or other plants, it is important to know the pH level of the soil before planting.
FIELD MARK PUBLICATIONS.

In this experiment, you will test how acidity affects plant growth by growing the same type of plant in both an acidic and an alkaline soil. To make soil more alkaline, gardeners add calcium carbonate (limestone). This is referred to as liming. For a quick way to make soil more alkaline you can add baking soda, which is also alkaline. To increase the acidity of the soil you will add vinegar (gardeners use sulfur or aluminum sulfate). To determine the soil pH's effect, you can measure height, number of leaves, how fast the plants grow, leaf color, and number of flowers.

Before you begin, make an educated guess about the outcome of this experiment based on your knowledge of soil and acidity. This educated guess, or prediction, is your hypothesis. A hypothesis should explain these things:

- the topic of the experiment
- the variable you will change
- the variable you will measure
- what you expect to happen

A hypothesis should be brief, specific, and measurable. It must be something you can test through further investigation. Your experiment will prove or disprove whether your hypothesis is correct. Here is one possible hypothesis for this experiment: "The plant will grow best in one type of soil pH; plants grown in the other two pH soils will not be as healthy."

In this case, the variable you will change is the pH of the soil. The variable you will measure is the health of the plant.

Conducting a control experiment will help you isolate each variable and measure the changes in the dependent variable. Only one variable will change between the control and the experimental setup, and that is the soil pH. For the control, you will use a neutral potting soil, between pH of 6 and 7. At the end of the experiment you can compare the results of the control to the experimental trial.

Level of Difficulty Moderate.

What Are the Variables?

Variables are anything that might affect the results of an experiment. Here are the main variables in this experiment:

- the type of soil
- the nutrients in the soil
- the type of plant
- the pH of the soil

In other words, the variables in this experiment are everything that might affect the growth of the plant. If you change more than one variable at the same time, you will not be able to tell which variable had the most effect on the plant's growth.

Materials Needed

- 15 seeds of one plant type
- 3 plant pots, such as plastic containers
- potting soil
- white vinegar
- baking soda
- cheesecloth
- small bucket that cheesecloth can fit over
- rubber band or string (to fit around container)
- ruler
- container that holds 8 cups (about 2 liters), such as a soda bottle
- pH test kit or strips (available at garden or hardware store)
- measuring spoons
- measuring cup
- marking pen

Approximate Budget $10.

Timetable Varies depending on the plant selected and soil; an estimated 1 hour for setup, then 10 minutes every five days for six weeks.

Step-by-Step Instructions

1. Measure the pH of the Control soil and note the results. It should be somewhere between 6 and 7.
2. Prepare acidic soil: The soil should be dry to moist. Make a solution of 1 tablespoon (15 milliliters) vinegar with 8 cups (about 2 liters) of water in the bottle or container and shake it.

Steps 7 and 8: Measure how pH affects the plants' health. GALE GROUP.

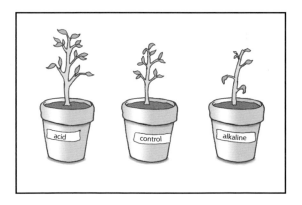

3. Secure the cheesecloth over the top of the small bucket with a rubber band or string. Put the soil on top of the cheesecloth. One cup at a time, pour the vinegar-water solution over the soil until it is saturated, then test the pH. Have the soil reach a pH of roughly 5.0. Depending on the soil, you may need to add more of the vinegar solution. If more acidity is needed, wait until the soil becomes dry to moist (try putting it in the Sun), then again pour the vinegar-water solution over the soil. Retest the pH

of soil. When the pH is at the right level for the experiment, note the pH on a chart.

4. Prepare alkaline soil: The soil should be dry to moist. Make up a solution of 1 tablespoon baking soda with 4 cups (about 1 liter) of water and shake it.

5. Repeat Step 3, replacing the vinegar-water solution with the baking soda-water solution. Have the soil reach a pH of roughly 8.0. Depending on the soil, you may need to make the soil more alkaline. Wait until the soil becomes dry to moist, then pour more of the baking soda-water solution over the soil. Retest the pH of soil and when it is alkaline enough note the number.

6. Label each of the containers: "Alkaline," "Acidic," and "Control."

7. Plant five seeds in each container, using the indicated soil, and care for as indicated.

8. Every five days (this may vary depending on your plant) measure the height of the plant, number of leaves, flowers/buds, or any other characteristic of your plant.

Troubleshooter's Guide

Below is a problem that may arise during this experiment, a possible cause, and a way to remedy the problem.

Problem: The soil did not turn very acidic or alkaline.

Possible cause: The soil may not have been dry enough for it to soak up the vinegar or baking soda. Make sure you wait long enough so that when you press the soil together it falls apart, then add the solution.

Summary of Results When the control plants have reached full height, examine your results. Was your hypothesis correct? How did each of the other plants compare to the control? Are there specific characteristics of the plant that were especially different than the control? Once you have determined the best pH of your plant, research what nutrients are available to your plant in that soil. What nutrients are lacking?

Change the Variables There are a few ways that you can change the variables in this experiment. You can alter the type of plant you grow, or you may want to grow several different types at once. (Some plants display interesting differences in a range of soil pHs, such as hydrangeas, which have a visible petal-color change.) You can also choose a soil with a low amount of nutrients, then add different nutrients to the soil to determine each one's effect on plant growth. Nutrient-testing kits are available at garden or hardware stores.

Design Your Own Experiment

How to Select a Topic Relating to this Concept Whether it is bought or dug, soil offers many possible project ideas. Check the Further Readings section and talk with your science teacher to learn more about soil. You may want to visit a garden store or greenhouse to look at the different varieties of soils available. Look around at the types of soils in your area and the kinds of plants that grow in them.

Steps in the Scientific Method To conduct an original experiment, you need to plan carefully and think things through. Otherwise, you might not be sure what question you are answering, what you are or should be measuring, or what your findings prove or disprove.

Here are the steps in designing an experiment:

- State the purpose of—and the underlying question behind—the experiment you propose to do.
- Recognize the variables involved and select one that will help you answer the question at hand.
- State your hypothesis, an educated guess about the answer to your question.
- Decide how to change the variable you selected.
- Decide how to measure your results.

Recording Data and Summarizing the Results Your data could include charts and graphs to display your data. If included, they should be clearly labeled and easy to read. You may also want to include photographs and drawings of your experimental setup and results, which will help other people visualize the steps in the experiment.

If you are preparing an exhibit, you may want to bring samples of any soil samples you used, and display your results, such as any experimental setup you designed. If you have completed a nonexperimental project, explain clearly what your research question was and illustrate your findings.

Related Projects Soils' diversity and significance offer a range of project ideas. You could further compare the properties of soil particles by measuring how different types of soils hold water. The amount of water soils hold relates to pesticides and fertilizers that people put in the soil. A project could explore what happens to these products when they are placed in soils of various types. This could lead to a project on leaching and nutrient deficiencies in the soil.

You could also explore the properties of parent materials and the process of weathering. A project could look at why certain parts of the world have distinct soils, such as deserts. You may be able to collect or purchase rock samples and compare their characteristics with one another. How does the soil composition in certain geographic areas impact their economy, environment, and agriculture? You could also look at the methods scientists have developed to replenish the soil of minerals, nutrients, and other vital properties.

Compare the properties of soil particles by measuring how different types of soils hold water. The amount of water soils hold relates to pesticides and fertilizers that people put in the soil. ILLUSTRATION BY TEMAH NELSON.

For More Information

Bial, Raymond. *A Handful of Dirt*. New York: Walker and Company, 2000. Explains what soil is made of and what lives in it.

"The Dirt on Soil: What's Really Going on Under the Ground?" *Discovery Education.* http://school.discoveryeducation.com/schooladventures/soil/ (accessed on March 11, 2008). Information and pictures of soil layers and life, along with a game.

Soil Science Education Home Page. http://soil.gsfc.nasa.gov/index.html (accessed on March 11, 2008). Basic information, featured soils, and learning activities about soil.

Stell, Elizabeth P. *Secrets to Great Soil*. Pownal, VT: Storey Publishing Book, 1998. Comprehensive book on soil properties and how to create fertile soil.

81

Solar Energy

Sunlight has been recognized as a powerful source of energy since ancient times. "Burning glasses" that dated back to 7 B.C.E. have been found in the ruins of Nineva (now part of Iraq). These glasses were similar to magnifying lens and could concentrate sunlight into a beam hot enough to start a fire. Each day, Earth receives about 4 quadrillion kilowatt-hours of solar energy, generated by nuclear reactions deep inside the Sun's mass. While we receive a lot of solar energy, it is not easy to harness. Environmental concerns and our limited supply of fossil fuels make finding ways to gather and concentrate solar energy efficiently an urgent challenge.

Hot! Hot! Hot! Think of the Sun as a constantly active hydrogen bomb: a swirling, mass with eruptions that give off great amounts of energy. Within the Sun's center, the temperature is about 25,000,000°F

Solar eruptions like this one could provide us with enough power for thousands of years— if we could harness the energy.
GALE GROUP.

These solar collectors turn to catch the Sun's rays throughout the day. PHOTO RESEARCHERS INC.

This plant in the Pyrenees Mountains in France uses mirrors to capture solar energy. PHOTO RESEARCHERS INC.

(14,000,000°C). About 700 million tons (635 million metric tons) of hydrogen fuse into 695 million tons (630 million metric tons) of helium each second. What happens to the missing five million tons of material? It is converted into solar energy. Besides heating and illuminating the Sun itself, some of this energy travels to Earth as sunlight.

How is some of this energy collected? One way is through the use of solar collectors, flat devices made of aluminum, copper, or steel panels painted black. The black color helps to absorb the heat energy. The glass or plastic covering these panels enables light to enter, but prevents most of the heat from bouncing back into the atmosphere. The heat is then stored in a layer of pebbles or salt surrounded by a thick layer of insulation behind the black panel.

This type of solar energy collection is an active solar energy system. An active system requires a separate collector, as well as a storage device and pumps or fans that draw heat when needed. Passive solar energy systems use the design of the building or natural materials to collect the Sun's energy. One example is buildings with large windows that face south, allowing the Sun's heat to spread throughout the structure during the day. This process is similar to the greenhouse effect, in which the Sun's energy gets trapped near Earth's surface by gases and other atmospheric matter.

Various forms of passive solar energy systems have been applied for centuries. For example, buildings were constructed with thick walls of stone, sod, and adobe to absorb the Sun's heat during the day and release it at night. Greenhouses were used in the early 1800s to capture the Sun's heat so plants could be grown during cold weather.

Solar reflections The Pyrenees Mountains, near Odeille in southern France, seem like an unlikely place for a solar reflector, but one has existed there since the 1950s. It towers over a meadow of wildflowers and features 63 separate mirrors that reflect sunlight onto a curved, mirrored wall. Electric motors move the mirrors to track sunlight and direct it to a central receiving tower. This method generates the intense heat

WORDS TO KNOW

Active solar energy system: A solar energy system that uses pumps or fans to circulate heat captured from the Sun.

Efficiency: The amount of power output divided by the amount of power input. It is a measure of how well a device converts one form of power into another.

Greenhouse effect: The warming of Earth's atmosphere due to water vapor, carbon dioxide, and other gases in the atmosphere that trap heat radiated from Earth's surface.

Hypothesis: An idea in the form of a statement that can be tested by observation and/or experiment.

Passive solar energy system: A solar energy system in which the heat of the Sun is captured, used, and stored by means of the design of a building and the materials from which it is made.

Photoelectric effect: The phenomenon in which light falling upon certain metals stimulates the emission of electrons and changes light into electricity.

Photovoltaic cells: A device made of silicon that converts sunlight into electricity.

Solar collector: A device that absorbs sunlight and collects solar heat.

Solar energy: Any form of electromagnetic radiation that is emitted by the Sun.

Variable: Something that can affect the results of an experiment.

needed for industrial use. It also produces steam in boilers, which is used to produce electricity.

Other solar energy collectors include photovoltaic (pronounced photo-vol-TAY-ic) cells, developed by three Bell Telephone scientists in 1954 as a way to produce electric power from sunlight. Also known as solar cells, they convert sunlight energy into electrical energy. They have been used to provide electric power during space exploration, but are most commonly used to light billboards and power irrigation pumps. Because the energy output of solar cells is small, many are needed to produce a significant amount of electricity. However, newer cells now operate at about a 40% efficiency, a good rate compared to the efficiency of burning fossil fuels, which is about 34%. As the demand for less expensive and sustainable solar energy increases, scientists are developing new ways to create more efficient solar cells. sola

In the experiments and project that follow, you will learn about two uses of solar energy: helping plants grow, powering electric motors, and heating a home. The experiments and project will help you appreciate all the ways that solar energy can—or could—affect our lives.

EXPERIMENT 1

Capturing Solar Energy: Will seedlings grow bigger in a greenhouse?

Purpose/Hypothesis A greenhouse is a passive solar collector, allowing light energy to pass through while blocking the escape of heat. The locked-in heat and moisture from watering create a warm, humid environment similar to a rain forest. In this experiment, you will build a greenhouse and determine whether it helps seedlings grow faster and bigger. Clear plastic will be used as the walls of the greenhouse because it allows the light in and traps the heat.

To begin the experiment, use what you have learned about solar energy to make a guess about how the greenhouse will affect the seedlings. This educated guess, or prediction, is your hypothesis. A hypothesis should explain these things:

- the topic of the experiment
- the variable you will change
- the variable you will measure
- what you expect to happen

A hypothesis should be brief, specific, and measurable. It must be something you can test through observation. Your experiment will prove or disprove whether your hypothesis is correct. Here is one possible

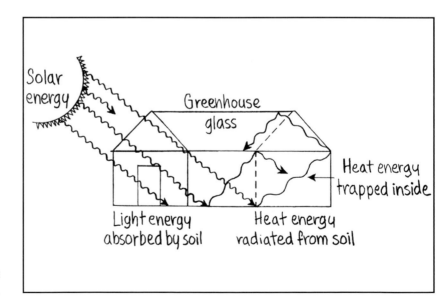

Greenhouse model. GALE GROUP.

hypothesis for this experiment: "The trapped solar energy in a greenhouse will cause seedlings to grow faster and larger than identical seedlings grown in the same environment without a greenhouse."

In this case, the variable you will change is whether seedlings are inside or outside the greenhouse, and the variable you will measure is the growth rate of the seedlings. If the seedlings inside the greenhouse grow more than those outside the greenhouse, your hypothesis is correct.

Level of Difficulty Easy/moderate.

Materials Needed

- 4 wooden boards, roughly 1 × 6 × 20 inches (2.5 × 15 × 50 centimeters)
- 1 piece of transparent plastic or glass, 24 × 24-inch (60 × 60-centimeter) and 0.25 inch (0.5 centimeter) thick
- Eight 2-inch (5-centimeter) nails
- 10 marigold or radish seeds
- 10 small plastic pots, or 10 plastic yogurt containers, or 10 bottoms cut from 1-quart (1-liter) milk cartons
- soil
- hammer
- goggles
- gloves

What Are the Variables?

Variables are anything that might affect the results of an experiment. Here are the main variables in this experiment:

- the amount of sunlight reaching all the seedlings
- the type of plants
- the temperature outside the greenhouse
- the color of the material under the greenhouse
- the water and care given to the seedlings

In other words, the variables in this experiment are everything that might affect the growth of the seedlings. If you change more than one variable at a time, you will not be able to determine which variable had the most effect on the growth rate.

How to Experiment Safely

Goggles and adult supervision are required when hammering the nails. Wear gloves when handling the glass.

Approximate Budget $12. (Use any lumber that is cost-effective. When formed into a box, the lumber must be tall enough for the pots to fit under the glass or plastic and still have room for the seedlings to grow.)

Timetable 2 to 3 weeks. (This experiment requires 30 minutes to assemble the greenhouse and 2 to 3 weeks to monitor the plant growth.)

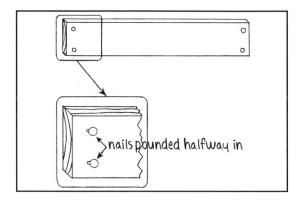

Step 1: Nails positioned on wood for assembling the greenhouse. GALE GROUP.

Step-by-Step Instructions

1. Hammer two nails through each end of a piece of wood, as illustrated. Repeat with a second piece of wood. Place the wood into a square with the two pieces with nails opposite each other.

2. Hold the wood in position and assemble the box by carefully driving the nails into the ends of the two remaining pieces of wood.

3. Place the piece of plastic or glass over the wood box. Be sure it completely overlaps the wood box so there are no gaps around the edges.

4. Place the greenhouse outside in a sunny spot or inside near a sunny window.

5. Plant the seedlings in the ten pots. Place five pots inside the greenhouse and five next to the greenhouse. Water each pot when the soil feels dry.

6. Measure and record the growth rate of each group of seedlings every day on a chart similar to the one illustrated. Continue your experiment for 2 weeks or longer.

Growth Chart

Time	Seedlings in greenhouse	Seedlings outside greenhouse
3 days		
4 days		
5 days		
6 days		
7 days		
8 days		

Step 6: Growth chart for Experiment 1. GALE GROUP.

Summary of Results Study the results on your growth chart. Can you see a difference between the seedlings inside and outside the greenhouse? Which ones are growing faster? Which ones look healthier? Was your hypothesis correct? Did the heat and humidity in the greenhouse affect the plants' growth rate? Write a paragraph summarizing and explaining your findings.

Change the Variables You can vary this experiment by using different kinds of seeds or using small, identical plants. You can also try growing plants under a "ceiling" of plastic, with the sides open to the air. Does this arrangement still trap enough heat to make a difference in the growth? Does the difference in humidity affect plant growth?

PROJECT 2

Solar Cells: Will sunlight make a motor run?

Purpose/Hypothesis In this project, you will be working with photovoltaic cells, or solar cells, which utilize the photoelectric effect to convert solar energy into electricity. This project will allow you to determine if you can operate a small electric motor with solar cells. It will also let you determine how many cells and how much sunlight it takes to operate the motor.

Level of Difficulty Easy/moderate.

Materials Needed

- 3 solar cells (.5-volt rating each)
- 1 DC motor (1.5-volt rating)
- 4 jumper wires with alligator clips on each end—three about 4 inches (10 centimeters) long, and one about 12 inches (30 centimeters) long

Troubleshooter's Guide

Below are some problems that may arise during this experiment, some possible causes, and ways to remedy the problems.

Problem: The seedlings inside and outside the greenhouse are growing slowly.

Possible causes:

1. The time of year makes a difference, especially in the northern area of the country. During the winter, the Sun's rays are less intense, and all the seedlings will grow more slowly. You will still see a difference. It will just take a little more time.
2. The spot does not get enough sun. Move the greenhouse and the other seedlings to a sunnier spot.
3. There is a gap between the box and the glass or plastic, which allows the warm air and humidity inside the greenhouse to escape. Seal the gap with tape.

Problem: The seedlings inside the greenhouse withered and died after they sprouted.

Possible cause: During the summer, the temperature inside the greenhouse can soar to 110°F (43°C) or more in direct sun. Move the greenhouse and all ten pots to a less sunny location or cover the glass or plastic with a large sheet of thin white paper to block some of the Sun's rays.

How to Experiment Safely

Handle solar cells carefully. They are fragile and break easily.

Troubleshooter's Guide

Below is a problem that may arise during this project, a possible cause, and a way to remedy it.

Problem: The motor does not rotate under any condition.

Possible cause: The connections may be loose. Check them connections and try again.

- stopwatch or clock
- marking pen
- posterboard or a small table to support the experiment
- cardboard to provide shade, about 24 inches (60 centimeters) square

Approximate Budget $25. (Supplies can be purchased at an electronics store.)

Timetable About 30 minutes.

Step-by-Step Instructions

1. Place the jumper wires with alligator clips on the + and - terminals of the solar cells, as illustrated. Attach the other ends to the motor terminal. Be careful to match the + or - connections. Place the experiment on a piece of posterboard or a small table so you can move it around.

2. Make a small mark on the shaft of the electric motor with the marking pen.

3. Test the ability of the solar cells to power the motor under different lighting conditions, such as the following: outside on a sunny day; outside on a sunny day, but shaded by the cardboard; inside on a sunny day, but out of direct sunlight; inside in a dark room; inside at night under an incandescent and/or fluorescent light bulb.

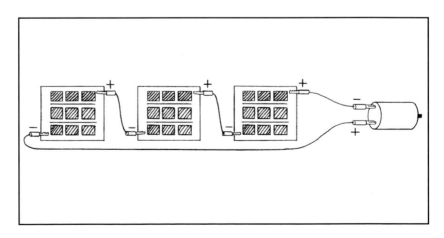

Step 1: Set-up of three-cell circuit. GALE GROUP.

Performance Chart

Condition	Response
Outside on a sunny day	Number of rotations in 10 seconds: Other notes:
Inside on a sunny day	Number of rotations in 10 seconds: Other notes:

Step 4: Sample performance chart for Project 2. GALE GROUP.

4. Record how many rotations the motor makes in 10 seconds—or if it runs at all—under each condition, using a chart similar to the one illustrated.

Summary of Results Study your results. Under which conditions did the solar cells operate the motor? How many rotations could you record? Write a paragraph summarizing and explaining your findings.

What Are the Variables?

Variables are anything that might affect the results of an experiment. Here are the main variables in this experiment:

- the amount of heat generated from the heat lamp
- the amount of time the container is left under the heat lamp
- the length of black plastic tubing and therefore the volume of the substance put into the tube.

In other words, the variables in this experiment are everything that might affect the air temperature in the containers. If you change more than one variable at a time, you will not be able to determine which variable had the most effect on the temperature.

EXPERIMENT 3

Retaining the Sun's heat: What substance best stores heat for a solar system?

Purpose/Hypothesis Solar energy is often used in homes as a source of heat. The solar energy system (solar panels) captures and stores the heat of the sun during the sunny hours. The heat is then re-circulated in the home when needed, during the night or on cloudy days. Storing the heat of the sun is a major component of a solar energy system.

Some storage devices use Glauber's salt (sodium sulfate decahydrate) in their storage systems. Glauber's salt has the ability to store more heat in its liquid state than water or other substances.

In this experiment you will test Glauber's salt along with two other substances to measure which one stores heat longer and would be most useful in a solar energy system. A heat lamp will provide the "Sun's" energy. You will place three different substances: water, Glauber's salt, and iodized salt in three clear plastic containers and place under a heat lamp for 12 hours. Once the heat lamp is turned off, you can begin to measure which substance best retains heat.

To begin the experiment, use what you have learned about solar energy to make a guess about what substance will retain heat the longest. This educated guess, or prediction, is your hypothesis. A hypothesis should explain these things:

- the topic of the experiment
- the variable you will change
- the variable you will measure
- what you expect to happen

A hypothesis should be brief, specific, and measurable. It must be something you can test through observation. Your experiment will prove or disprove whether your hypothesis is correct. Here is one possible hypothesis for this experiment: "The Glauber's salt will retain heat longer than the water and table salt after being placed under a heat lamp."

In this case, the variable you will change is the substance in the plastic containers. The variable you will measure is the air temperature in each of the containers. If the air temperature in the container with the substance containing the Glauber's salt remains higher than the other containers, your hypothesis is correct.

How to Experiment Safely

The heat lamp can get hot. Be careful when handling the lamp; you may want an adult to help.

Level of Difficulty Moderate to Advanced (because of the time and detail involved).

Materials Needed

- 3 clear plastic containers with lids, approximately $2 \times 6 \times 6$ inches
- 1 heat lamp (150 watts) with a clip
- 60 grams (about one-quarter cup) of water
- 60 grams iodized salt (table salt)
- 60 grams Glauber's salt (sodium sulfate decahydrate, available from a science supply store; you may need to ask your teacher for help ordering)
- a container big enough to hold all three containers, an empty aquarium works well
- tape
- 3 digital thermometers small enough to be placed inside plastic container. If testing one substance at a time, then only 1 thermometer is needed (if you only have 1 thermometer, you can test each item separately)

Approximate Budget $15 (assuming you have or can borrow a heat lamp and large container).

Timetable approximately 30 minutes to set-up; 12 hours waiting; 2 hours monitoring results

Step-by-Step Instructions

1. Place 60 grams of Glauber's salt (in crystal form) in one plastic container. Label the container "Glauber's."
2. Place 60 grams of water in the second container, and 60 grams of iodized salt in the third container. Label each container with the substance it contains.

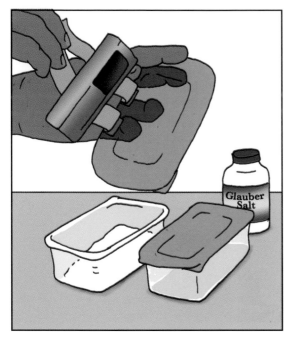

Step 3: Tape one thermometer on the side of each container so that the temperature readings are visible. ILLUSTRATION BY TEMAH NELSON.

Step 6: Turn on the heat lamp. Leave the lamp on for 12 hours. ILLUSTRATION BY TEMAH NELSON.

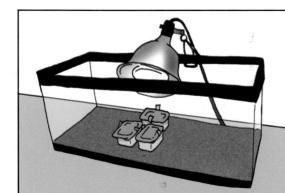

3. Tape one thermometer on the side of each container so that the temperature readings are visible.

4. Place all three labeled containers in the large container and clip the heat lamp onto the side of container. Make sure the heat lamp shines on all three containers evenly.

5. Record the starting temperature of containers on a chart.

6. Turn on the heat lamp. Leave the lamp on for 12 hours.

7. Turn off the heat lamp and record the temperature every 15 minutes for two hours. You can keep recording every 30 minutes until the air returns to the starting temperature.

Summary of Results Study the results of your temperature readings. You may want to graph the data. Can you see a difference between the rate at which the Glauber's salt and table salt cooled? How did these substances compare to the water temperature reading? Which substance cooled down the fastest and which took the longest to cool? Was your hypothesis correct? Write a paragraph summarizing and explaining your findings.

Change the Variables You can change the variables in this experiment several ways. You can vary the substances within the containers to measure what stores heat more than others. Instead of using a heat lamp, you could place the containers out in the sun. Depending upon where you live and the season, you can place the containers in a sunny spot, and record the temperatures after the sun has gone down. How does this compare with using a heat lamp? How high do the temperatures get?

Design Your Own Experiment

How to Select a Topic Relating to this Concept First, define what aspect of solar energy you are interested in, such as ways to use this energy. You might want to investigate whether pollution is changing the effects of solar energy on our world.

Check the Further Readings section and talk with your science teacher or school or community media specialist to start gathering information on solar energy questions that interest you. As you consider possible experiments, be sure to discuss them with a knowledgeable adult before trying them. Some of the materials or processes may be dangerous.

Steps in the Scientific Method To do an original experiment, you need to plan carefully and think things through. Otherwise you might not be sure which question you are answering, what you are or should be measuring, and what your findings prove or disprove.

Here are the steps in designing an experiment:

- State the purpose of—and the underlying question behind—the experiment you propose to do.
- Recognize the variables involved, and select one that will help you answer the question at hand.
- State a testable hypothesis, an educated guess about the answer to your question.
- Decide how to change the variable you selected.
- Decide how to measure your results.

Recording Data and Summarizing the Results Every good experiment should be documented so that other people can understand the procedures and results. Keep diagrams, charts, and graphs of any information

---

Troubleshooter's Guide

It's common for experiments to not work exactly as planned. Learning from what went wrong can also be a good experience. Below are some problems that may arise during this experiment, some possible causes, and ways to remedy the problems.

Problem: Temperature changes between the three substances did not differ.

Possible causes: The heat lamp may not be hot enough. Check your heat lamp; it should be at least 150 watts. If it is 150 watts, the containers may not be receiving the same amount of heat. Try heating one container at a time with the heat lamp directly over the container.

Problem: The thermometer is not taking readings.

Possible causes: The thermometer may have fallen into the liquid in the container and is wet. Make sure the thermometer is anchored to the container and check that the thermometer is working. Repeat the experiment.

Problem: The Glauber's salt did not melt completely.

Possible cause: The salt may not be getting enough heat. Try heating one container at a time with the heat lamp directly over the container. You also can increase the number of hours you leave on the heat lamp. If you increase the hours, make sure to keep it the same for the other substances. Even in a partial liquid state Glauber's salt will retain heat. You can take your temperature readings and see the outcome.

---

that is useful. Your experiment, whether successful or not, is important information to be shared with others.

Related Projects Solar energy is available on a daily basis (except on cloudy days), so take advantage of this free resource. For example, you could design and build a solar oven for cooking, a solar battery to run toys, or a radiometer to measure solar intensity. Explore the possibilities!

For More Information

Aldous, Scott. "How Solar Cells Work." *HowStuffWorks.* http://www.howstuffworks.com/solar-cell.htm (accessed on March 18, 2008). Explanation of solar cells.

Asimov, Issac. *The Sun and Its Secrets.* Milwaukee, WI: Gareth Stevens Publishing, 1994. Discusses the Sun's origins, content, and historical facts.

Edelson, Edward. *Clean Air.* New York: Chelsea House Publishers, 1992. Explores the devastating effects of population growth and industry on air quality and ways to clean up the air including using solar energy as a solution.

Energy Information Administration. "Solar Energy: Energy from the Sun." *Energy Kid's Page.* http://www.eia.doe.gov/kids/energyfacts/sources/renewable/solar.html (accessed on March 18, 2008). Basic information on solar energy.

"Energy Story: Solar Energy." *Energy Quest.* http://www.energyquest.ca.gov/story/chapter15.html (accessed on March 18, 2008). Information and science projects related to solar energy.

"Solar Energy Animation." *Ocean Motion.* http://oceanmotion.org/html/resources/solar.htm (accessed on March 18, 2008). Information demonstrates how the intensity of the energy from the sun varies with location and time.

82

Sound

You hear sound when vibrations enter your ears and send signals through your nerves to your brain. These vibrations are caused by disturbances in the air. For example, when you hit a drum, the top of it vibrates, causing a disturbance in the molecules in the air. This vibration, or sound wave, travels through the air in all directions, eventually reaching your ears.

If you could see sound waves, they would look much like the waves you see when you drop a stone onto a calm water surface.

How do we hear? Sound waves travel through air at about 1,088 feet (332 meters) per second. When the sound waves or vibrations reach your ears, they push on your eardrums and cause them to vibrate. Each eardrum pushes against a series of three tiny bones in your middle ear. These tiny bones push against another membrane, which causes waves in a fluid inside your inner ear. Here, special cells pick up the differences in pressure from the waves and transform them into electrical signals that travel along nerves to your brain. When these signals reach the brain, you hear the sound and usually recognize its source.

How is sound measured? Sound waves are usually described with two measurements: frequency and amplitude. Frequency means the number of waves passing a given point in a given period of time. This is usually measured in hertz, abbreviated Hz. One hertz equals 1 cycle per second. Humans can usually hear sounds with frequencies from 20 Hz to 20,000 Hz. The faster a wave vibrates, the higher its frequency and the higher a sound it produces. The highness or lowness of a sound is its pitch. A high-frequency sound has a high pitch.

The amplitude of the sound is its power or loudness. The taller the sound wave, the higher

Sound waves are usually described with two measurements: frequency and amplitude. GALE GROUP.

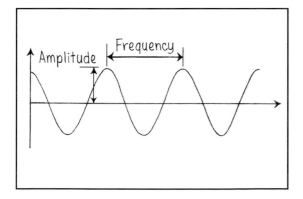

1095

As the drum vibrates, it pushes on molecules in the air, causing them to vibrate in the same way. This vibration, or sound wave, travels through the air in all directions, eventually reaching your ears. PETER ARNOLD INC.

its amplitude and the louder the sound it produces. We usually measure amplitude in decibels. For example, leaves rustling in the wind might produce a sound of about 20 decibels, while a jet taking off creates a sound of at least 140 decibels, loud enough to damage your hearing. Listening to very loud sounds for a long time, including loud music, will damage the tiny nerves in your ears and can lead to a permanent hearing loss. Many rock musicians have discovered that they already have hearing problems.

How long have people wondered about sound? People have been experimenting with sound for a long time. Pythagoras (572–497 B.C.E.) experimented with strings to determine how sounds changed with changes in the lengths of the strings. Historians credit him with the development of the musical scale.

In about 1700, French physicist Joseph Sauveur first used the word acoustics to describe music and the way sound works. He worked on the mathematics of sound and studied how strings made different sounds depending on their length.

Hermann von Helmholtz (1821–1894) discovered much about sound in the 1800s, especially the connections between mathematics and music. He also built one of the first sirens.

Sound, and the way humans and other animals perceive it, is a fascinating topic. What kind of questions do you have about sound? You will have an opportunity to explore different aspects of sound in the following experiments.

EXPERIMENT 1

Wave Length: How does the length of a vibrating string affect the sound it produces?

Purpose/Hypothesis In this experiment, you will find out how the length and tightness of a plucked string affects the sounds it produces. Before you begin, make an educated guess about the outcome of the experiment

WORDS TO KNOW

Acoustics: The science concerned with the production, properties, and propagation of sound waves.

Amplitude: The maximum displacement (difference between an original position and a later position) of the material that is vibrating. Amplitude can be thought of visually as the highest and lowest point of a wave.

Decibel (dB): A unit of measurement for the amplitude of sound.

Frequency: The rate at which vibrations take place (number of times per second the motion is repeated), given in cycles per second or in hertz (Hz). Also, the number of waves that pass a given point in a given period of time.

Hertz (Hz): The unit of measurement of frequency; a measure of the number of waves that pass a given point per second of time.

Hypothesis: An idea in the form of a statement that can be tested by observation and/or experiment.

Pitch: A property of a sound, determined by its frequency; the highness or lowness of a sound.

Wave: A regular disturbance that carries energy through matter or space without carrying matter.

Variable: Something that can affect the results of an experiment

Vibration: A regular, back-and-forth motion of molecules in the air.

Volume: The amplitude or loudness of a sound.

---

based on your knowledge of sound. This educated guess, or prediction, is your hypothesis. A hypothesis should explain these things:

- the topic of the experiment
- the variable you will change
- the variable you will measure
- what you expect to happen

A hypothesis should be brief, specific, and measurable. It must be something you can test through observation. Your experiment will prove or disprove your hypothesis. Here is one possible hypothesis for this experiment: "The longer the string, the higher the pitch of the sound produced by that string."

In this case, the variable you will change will be the length of the string, and the variable you will measure will be the pitch of the sound. You expect a longer string to produce a higher pitch sound.

Waves spread out from the source of the disturbance in wider and wider circles. KELLY A. QUIN.

What Are the Variables?

Variables are anything that might affect the results of an experiment. Here are the main variables in this experiment:

- the kind of string
- the length of the string
- the tightness or tension of the string
- the strength with which the string is plucked
- the pitch of the sound
- the experimenter's ability to detect different pitches

In other words, the variables in this experiment are everything that might affect the perceived pitch of the sound. If you change more than one variable, you will not be able to tell which variable had the most effect on the pitch.

How to Experiment Safely

Be careful handling the scissors.

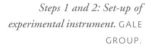

Steps 1 and 2: Set-up of experimental instrument. GALE GROUP.

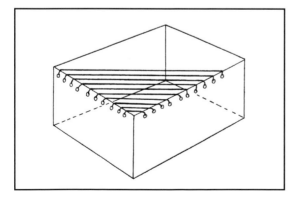

Level of Difficulty Easy.

Materials Needed

- a sturdy cardboard box, such as one for copy paper
- thin, strong string
- scissors
- hole-puncher
- ruler

Approximate Budget $5, if you need to buy string; other materials should be available in the average household.

Timetable 1 hour.

Step-by-Step Instructions You will be working with the top edge of two sides of the box; the edges join to make a V.

1. Use the hole puncher or the tip of your scissors to make ten small holes along each side of the V, placing the holes opposite from each other, as shown.
2. Tie a length of string through each pair of holes, pulling it tightly before tying it to the other edge of the box. You should end up with strings of 10 lengths, as illustrated.
3. Using your ruler, measure the length of each string from knot to knot. Record these lengths on your data sheet.
4. Pluck each string several times and listen carefully. What do you hear? Describe it on your data sheet. You may want to play the strings for other people, so you are not depending on only your own ears.
5. If possible, bend the cardboard angle a little outward to pull the strings tighter and increase the tension. Repeat sStep 4. How do the sounds change?

6. Try plucking the strings harder and softer. Record what you hear on your data sheet.

Summary of Results Study the results on your chart. Did the longer strings produce higher pitches or lower pitches? Why? Was your hypothesis correct? Did increasing the tension change the pitch of the sound? Write a paragraph summarizing and explaining what you have found.

Change the Variables You can vary this experiment. Try using different materials, such as piano wire, fishing line, thicker string, or rubber bands. See how the pitch of the sound is affected.

EXPERIMENT 2

Pitch: How does the thickness of a vibrating string affect sound?

Purpose/Hypothesis In this experiment, you will explore how the thickness of the vibrating object affects the pitches it produces. You will use different sizes of rubber bands to test this effect. Before you begin, make an educated guess about the outcome of this experiment based on your knowledge of sound. The educated guess, or prediction, is your hypothesis. A hypothesis should explain these things:

- the topic of the experiment
- the variable you will change
- the variable you will measure
- what you expect to happen

A hypothesis should be brief, specific, and measurable. It must be something you can test through observation. Your experiment will prove or disprove your hypothesis. Here is one possible hypothesis for this experiment: "Thicker bands will produce lower pitches."

Troubleshooter's Guide

Experiments do not always work out as planned. Even so, figuring out what went wrong can definitely be a learning experience. Here are some problems that may arise during this experiment, some possible causes, and ways to remedy the problems.

Problem: You cannot hear a clear sound from the strings.

Possible cause: Your strings are not tied tightly enough. Try again, trying them tightly.

Problem: All the strings sound the same.

Possible cause: Your cardboard box is not big enough to allow markedly different lengths of strings. Find a bigger box so the lengths of the strings vary more and try again.

Step 3 and 6: Data sheet for Experiment 1. GALE GROUP.

String length	Sound produced
1 inch	
2 inches	

What Are the Variables?

Variables are anything that might affect the results of an experiment. Here are the main variables for this experiment:

- the thickness of rubber bands
- the length of bands
- the strength with which the band is plucked
- the sound produced by plucking
- the experimenter's ability to detect different pitches

In other words, the variables in this experiment are everything that might affect the pitch of the sound. If you change more than one variable, you will not be able to tell which variable had the most effect on the pitch.

How to Experiment Safely

Try not to snap yourself with the rubber bands.

In this case, the variable you will change will be the thickness of the rubber band, and the variable you will measure will be the pitch of the sound. You expect a thicker band to produce a lower pitch sound.

Level of Difficulty Easy.

Materials Needed

- 8-inch-square (20-centimeter square) metal baking pan with straight sides
- 5 rubber bands of different thickness but the SAME length
- ruler

Approximate Budget $5, if you need to purchase rubber bands; other materials should be available in the average household.

Timetable 1 hour.

Step-by-Step Instructions

1. Arrange the rubber bands in order from thinnest to thickest.
2. Measure the width of each rubber band with your ruler. Record these numbers on your data sheet, as illustrated.

Thickness of band	Sound produced
3 mm	
6 mm	
etc.	

Step 2 and 5: Data sheet for Experiment 2. GALE GROUP.

3. Keep the bands in order, stretch each one over the pan, which acts as a sound box. Be sure to stretch them the same amount so the portion of the band over the open part of the pan is under the same tension as the rest of the band. See illustration.

4. Pluck each band, beginning with the thickest one, and listen carefully to the pitch it produces.

5. Describe each tone as you pluck the band and record on your data sheet what you hear.

Summary of Results Study the results on your chart. How did the thickness of the band affect the pitch it produced? Did a thick band produce a lower pitch or a higher pitch? Thick bodies vibrate more slowly than small ones, and slower vibrations produce lower pitches. Is this what happened in your experiment? Was your hypothesis correct? Write a paragraph summarizing what you learned.

Troubleshooter's Guide

Here are some problems that may arise during this experiment, some possible causes, and ways to remedy the problems.

Problem: You cannot hear the differences in the pitches.

Possible cause: Your rubber bands are too similar in size. Try to find bands that are several millimeters different in width. Check an office supply store or an art supply store.

Problem: You cannot hear much sound at all.

Possible cause: The pan is absorbing the vibrations. Be sure the pan is metal, with straight sides, and deep enough so the bands are free to vibrate.

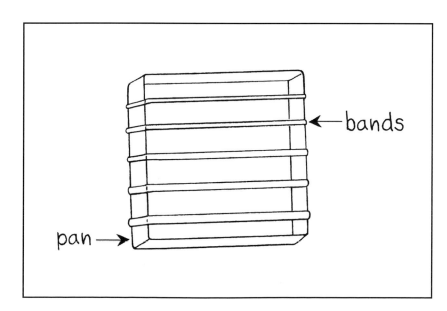

Step 3: Keeping the rubber bands in order, stretch each one over the pan, which acts as a sound box. GALE GROUP.

What Are the Variables?

Variables are anything that might affect the results of an experiment. Here are the main variables in this experiment:

- the loudness of the sound
- the distance of the sound from the experimenter
- the material covering the sound device
- the thickness of the material covering the sound device
- the enclosure of the sound device
- the experimenter's ability to detect the loudness

In other words, the variables in this experiment are everything that might affect the perceived loudness of the sound. If you change more than one variable, you will not be able to tell which variable had the most effect on the sound.

Change the Variables You can vary this experiment in several ways. Try using bands with even greater differences in thickness. Record their width and see what happens. Try putting the same size bands on a larger pan and plucking the two instruments next to each other. What do you hear? Experiment with different size pans and you can create an entire orchestra. What is the effect of length on the sounds you produce? You can also use a box made from something else, such as wood or plastic. Repeat the experiment and record what you learn.

EXPERIMENT 3

Soundproofing: How do different materials affect sound?

Purpose/Hypothesis How sound waves travel through a gas, liquid, or solid depends upon the properties of the matter. When sound waves pass through materials, they may move easily through the material, be absorbed, or be reflected. It is likely that some combination will happen. The more a sound is absorbed, the better the material is at sound insulation.

In this experiment, you will measure how different solid materials affect sound. You can test several materials, including cardboard, plastic, aluminum foil, Styrofoam, felt, and rubber. The thickness of a material also affects the amount of sound waves that pass through the material. For this reason, you will need to have all the materials at about the same thickness. Which of the materials will best absorb the sound waves?

You will need a helper to carry out this experiment. Your helper will make sure the listener does not see the materials being tested, which will help avoid bias. Your helper will also serve as a second listener, so you can have two sets of data to draw upon.

Before you begin, make an educated guess about the outcome of the experiment based on your knowledge of sound and the materials. This educated guess, or prediction, is your hypothesis. A hypothesis should explain these things:

- the topic of the experiment
- the variable you will change
- the variable you will measure
- what you expect to happen

A hypothesis should be brief, specific, and measurable. It must be something you can test through observation. Your experiment will prove or disprove your hypothesis. Here is one possible hypothesis for this experiment: "The rubber material will absorb the sound more than the other materials."

In this case, the variable you will change will be the material covering the sound, and the variable you will measure will be the loudness of the sound.

In this experiment, your control will be the reference for you to compare each sound. The control in this experiment will be the metronome sound moving through air, not enclosed by any solid material. Throughout the experiment you will compare the control against the experimental test materials.

Level of Difficulty Moderate.

Materials Needed

- piece of cardboard, about 1/8 inch thick, large enough to cover the box opening
- aluminum baking sheet, about 1/8 inch thick, large enough to cover the box opening
- felt fabric
- Styrofoam (available at hardware or craft stores)
- rubber floor mat (car mats work well)
- masking tape
- scissors
- metronome, you could also use an alarm clock, watch that ticks loudly, or other device with a constant sound
- shoe box, large enough to fit the metronome or other sound device
- ruler
- helper
- headphones (optional)

Approximate Budget $10, most materials should be available in a household.

Step 2: Place the shoebox on a table or countertop and set the metronome (or other device) inside. ILLUSTRATION BY TEMAH NELSON.

Step 5: Completely cover the box opening with one of the materials. ILLUSTRATION BY TEMAH NELSON.

Timetable 45 minutes.

Step-by-Step Instructions

1. Using the ruler, make sure the felt and Styrofoam are the same thickness as the other materials. You may need to fold over the felt and cut the Styrofoam.

2. Place the shoebox on a table or counter-top and set the metronome (or other device) inside.

3. Stand back several feet from the box, at a distance where you can hear the sound. Use the tape to mark the spot on the floor where you are standing.

4. Place the shoebox on a table or countertop and set the metronome (or other device) inside. Stand at the tape and turn around so you cannot see the box. Have your helper start the metronome. This is the loudness you will compare the test materials against.

5. While you cover your ears with headphones (if available), have your helper completely cover the box opening with one of the materials. You should not know which of the materials your helper is using. The material may need to be taped to the box so that the opening is sealed.

6. After your helper has given you a signal, uncover your ears and listen. Note how the loudness compares to the Control sound in a chart (see the sample chart).

7. Still keeping your back turned, have your helper listen to the sound device uncovered before moving on to the next material. This will help you compare the sound against each test material.

8. Repeat Steps 6–8, using all the materials. Make sure you cover your ears while your helper places the material over the box opening. Do not turn around. After you listen to each sound, write down how the loudness compares to the Control.

9. When you have tested all the materials, you and your helper switch places. Make another chart. Have your helper stand at

the tape mark on the floor, facing away from the box. Repeat the process, with you placing each material over the box opening in any order.

Summary of Results Look at the results on the two charts. Are they the same? Was there one material that you both thought significantly affected the loudness of the sound? Were there any materials that made the sound louder? Were you or was your helper surprised at the results? While analyzing your results, consider the properties of each material. Write a paragraph summarizing and explaining what you have found.

Change the Variables There are many ways you can vary this experiment to explore soundproofing. You can focus on one of the materials, such as the fabric, and test different types. You can test velour, silks, and felt. You can test different types of metals. If you test different types of one material, make sure the thicknesses are about the same. But you also can use one material and change the thickness. You could try combining certain materials together to test for soundproofing. You may want to research the materials that buildings or musicians use to soundproof rooms, and test how these materials affect sound.

Troubleshooter's Guide

Here are some problems that may arise during this experiment, some possible causes, and ways to remedy the problems.

Problem: You had different results than your helper.

Possible cause: It is likely that there will be some difference in how you and your helper perceive the loudness. If the results are extremely different, it may be that one of you is not completely covering the box opening. Compare how you are both placing the material against the box opening? Are you both sealing the box completely? When you have found a consistent setup, try again.

Problem: The sounds were all muffled about the same amount.

Possible cause: You may be standing too far away from the sound to make a noticeable difference. Stand far enough away that you can hear the sound clearly without anything covering the box opening, and repeat the experiment.

Design Your Own Experiment

How to Select a Topic Relating to this Concept Are you interested in the frequency of vibrations and the pitches they produce, how to amplify sound to make it louder, or how to direct where the sound waves go? Maybe you are interested in how sound waves travel through different materials, such as gases, water, and solids. Would you like to make your own instruments and experiment with the sounds they make?

Check the Further Readings section and talk with your science teacher or school or community media specialist to start gathering information about sound questions that interest you.

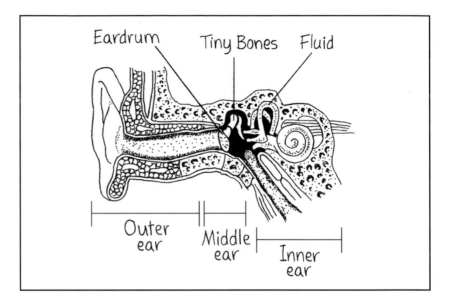

Structure of the human ear.
GALE GROUP.

Steps in the Scientific Method To do an original experiment, you need to plan carefully and think things through. Otherwise you may not be sure what question you are answering, what you are or should be measuring, or what your findings prove or disprove.

Here are the steps in designing an experiment:

- State the purpose of—and the underlying question behind—the experiment you propose to do.

- Recognize the variables involved, and select one that will help you answer the question at hand.

- State a testable hypothesis, an educated guess about the answer to your question.

- Decide how to change the variable you selected.

- Decide how to measure your results.

Recording Data and Summarizing the Results Your data should include charts, such as the one you did for these experiments. They should be clearly labeled and easy to read. You may also want to include photos, graphs, or drawings of your experimental set-up and results.

If you are preparing an exhibit, display the sound-producing devices you create to help explain what you did and what you discovered. Observers could even test them out themselves. If you have done a nonexperimental project, you will want to explain clearly what your research question was and illustrate your findings.

Related Projects There are many uses of sound in modern technology. You could investigate how acoustics work in a large concert hall or how speakers and amplifiers work in your home sound system. You could also see how sound is used in modern medicine, in ultrasound machines, for example. These machines help doctors observe things that are difficult to see by turning sound into pictures.

For More Information

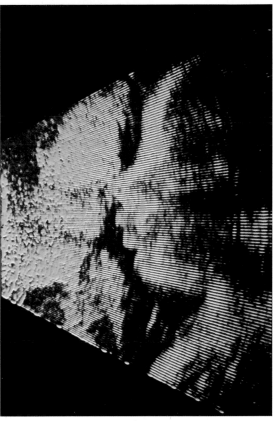

Ultrasound scan of a fetus.
PHOTO RESEARCHERS INC.

Dale, Jeremy W., and Simon F. Park. *Molecular Genetics of Bacteria.* New York, NY: John Wiley & Sons, 2004.

De Pinna, Simon, and Chris Fairclough. *Sound (Science Projects).* Austin, TX: Raintree/Steck Vaughn, 1998. Provides ideas for science fair projects involving the principles of sound.

Harris, Tom. "How Hearing Works." *HowStuffWorks.* http://www.howstuffworks.com/hearing.htm (accessed on March 13, 2008). Clear explanation of hearing and sound.

Kaner, Etta. *Sound Science.* Toronto: Kids Can Press, 1991. Explores the nature of sound using games, puzzles, fun facts and experiments.

"Science of Music." *Exploratorium.* http://www.exploratorium.edu/music/ (accessed on March 13, 2008). The science of the sounds of music.

Trun, Nancy Jo, and J.E. Trempy. *Fundamental Bacterial Genetics.* Oxford, UK: Blackwell Science, 2003.

Van Cleave, Janice. *Physics for Every Kid: 101 Easy Experiments in Motion, Heat, Light, Machines, and Sound.* New York: John Wiley & Sons, 1991. Presents step-by-step experiments using household materials and scientific explanations.

"ZoomSci." *PBS Kids.* http://pbskids.org/zoom/activities/sci/ (accessed on March 13, 2008). Simple science experiments on sound.

Budget Index

Chapter name in brackets, followed by experiment name. The numeral before the colon indicates volume; numbers after the colon indicate page number.

Experiment Central, 2nd edition

Experiment Central, 2nd edition

Level of Difficulty Index

Chapter name in brackets, followed by experiment name. The numeral before the colon indicates volume; numbers after the colon indicate page number.

EASY

Easy means that the average student should easily be able to complete the tasks outlined in the project/experiment, and that the time spent on the project is not overly restrictive.

EASY/MODERATE

Easy/Moderate means that the average student should have little trouble completing the tasks outlined in the project/experiment, and that the time spent on the project is not overly restrictive.

MODERATE

Moderate means that the average student should find tasks outlined in the project/experiment challenging but not difficult, and that the time spent on the project/experiment may be more extensive.

MODERATE/DIFFICULT

Moderate/Difficult means that the average student should find tasks outlined in the project/experiment challenging, and that the time spent on the project/experiment may be more extensive.

DIFFICULT

Difficult means that the average student wil probably find the tasks outlined in the project/experiment mentally and/or physically challenging, and that the time spent on the project/experiment may be more extensive.

Timetable Index

Chapter name in brackets, followed by experiment name. The numeral before the colon indicates volume; numbers after the colon indicate page number.

30 TO 45 MINUTES

2 HOURS

3 HOURS

Experiment Central, 2nd edition

General Subject Index

The numeral before the colon indicates volume; numbers after the colon indicate page number. **Bold** page numbers indicate main essays. The notation (ill.) after a page number indicates a figure.

A

A groups (periodic table), *4:* 829
A layer (soil), *5:* 1066–67, 1067 (ill.)
Abscission, *1:* 192
Absolute dating, *3:* 525
Acceleration
    bottle rocket experiment, *3:* 493–501, 495 (ill.), 498 (ill.), 499 (ill.)
    build a roller coaster experiment, *5:* 934–38, 935 (ill.), 936 (ill.), 937 (ill.)
    centripetal force experiment, *3:* 501–5, 503 (ill.)
    centripetal force in, *3:* 493, 493 (ill.)
    Newtonian laws of motion on, *3:* 492, 492 (ill.)
    of planetary orbits, *3:* 579–80
Acetate, *3:* 509, 511–14, 511 (ill.), 512 (ill.), 513 (ill.)
Acetic acid, *1:* 165, *4:* 820–23, 820 (ill.), 821 (ill.), 822 (ill.)
Acetone, *3:* 511–14, 511 (ill.), 512 (ill.), 513 (ill.)
Acid/base indicators, *4:* 860
    cave formation experiment, *1:* 134, 134 (ill.)
    pH of household chemicals experiment, *4:* 861–65, 861 (ill.), 863 (ill.)
Acid rain, *1:* **1–17,** 17 (ill.)
    brine shrimp experiment, *1:* 5–8, 7 (ill.)
    damage from, *1:* 1–3, *4:* 860–61
    design an experiment for, *1:* 15–16
    formation of, *1:* 1, 164
    pH of, *1:* 1, 2 (ill.), 3 (ill.), *4:* 860–61, 861 (ill.)

    plant growth experiment, *1:* 9–12, 11 (ill.)
    structure damage experiment, *1:* 12–15, 14 (ill.), 15 (ill.), 16
Acidity
    in food preservation, *3:* 452
    in food spoilage, *3:* 478
    measurement of, *1:* 1
    neutralization of, *1:* 4
    for separation and identification, *5:* 1033, 1034 (ill.)
    of soil, *5:* 1064
    soil pH and plant growth experiment, *5:* 1074–77, 1074 (ill.), 1076 (ill.), 1079 (ill.)
    See also pH
Acids
    acid-copper reduction experiment, *4:* 813–17, 814 (ill.), 815 (ill.)
    cave formation experiment, *1:* 132–35, 134 (ill.)
    chemical properties of, *1:* 164
    chemical titration experiment, *4:* 865–68, 865 (ill.), 866 (ill.), 867 (ill.)
    copper color change experiment, *4:* 820–23, 820 (ill.), 821 (ill.), 822 (ill.)
    electricity conduction by, *2:* 334
    pH of, *4:* 859–61
    uses for, *4:* 859, 860
    See also Lemon juice; Vinegar
Acoustics, *5:* 1096
Acronyms, *4:* 700
Actions, reactions to every, *3:* 492, 494

cxxi

B

C

I

N

Tensile strength
    of materials, *4:* 687
    polymer strength experiment, *5:* 914–19, 917 (ill.), 918 (ill.)
    of polymers, *5:* 912
    tape strength experiment, *4:* 687 (ill.), 688–91, 689 (ill.), 690 (ill.)
Terraces, soil, *2:* 386
Tetra fish, *3:* 407–9, 409 (ill.), 410
Textiles, *4:* 686, 696
Thales of Miletus, *2:* 325
Theophrastus, *3:* 565, *6:* 1283–84
Theory of special relativity, *6:* 1179, 1180 (ill.)
Thermal energy. *See* Heat
Thermal inversion, *1:* 47, 47 (ill.)
Thermal pollution, *1:* 49
Thermal properties, *4:* 687
Thermometers, *1:* 151
Thiamine, *4:* 760
Thickness, *5:* 1099–1102, 1100 (ill.), 1101 (ill.)
Thigmotropism, *6:* 1192, 1205 (ill.)
Third law of motion, *3:* 492, 492 (ill.), 494, 580
Thomas, Robert Bailey, *6:* 1284
Thorax, *3:* 632
Threads, *5:* 1048–49, 1050 (ill.), 1057–60, 1058 (ill.), 1059 (ill.), 1060 (ill.)
Thunder, *6:* 1148–49
Thunderstorms, *6:* 1147–49, 1149 (ill.), 1150, 1151, 1151 (ill.)
Thyme, *2:* 392–95, 394 (ill.), 395 (ill.)
Thymine, *2:* 286–87
Tides, *3:* 580, *4:* 777 (ill.), 784, *5:* 992 (ill.)
    Earth's rotation effect, *5:* 983–84
    moon's effect on, *4:* 774, 775 (ill.), *5:* 983–84
    Sun's impact on, *5:* 983–84, 993–94
Time, *6:* **1175–89,** 1176 (ill.), 1178 (ill.)
    design an experiment for, *6:* 1188–89
    devices for measuring, *6:* 1177–78, 1177 (ill.)
    history of, *6:* 1175–78
    pendulum oscillation time experiment, *6:* 1180–85, 1182 (ill.), 1183 (ill.)
    space-time, *6:* 1179–80, 1180 (ill.)
    water clock experiment, *6:* 1185–88, 1187 (ill.)
Time zones, *6:* 1178–79, 1179 (ill.)
Titan Arum, *3:* 423, 427

Titration, *4:* 860, 865–68, 865 (ill.), 866 (ill.), 867 (ill.)
Tomatoes, *1:* 164
Tools, *2:* 390–92, 400, *5:* 969
Topsoil, *5:* 1064, 1066–67, 1067 (ill.)
    erosion of, *2:* 375, 375 (ill.)
    soils for fossil casts experiment, *3:* 526–29, 528 (ill.)
    See also Soil
Tornadoes, *6:* 1149–51, 1149 (ill.), 1150 (ill.), 1155 (ill.), 1284 (ill.)
    water vortex experiment, *6:* 1155–58, 1157 (ill.)
    weather forecasting of, *6:* 1286
Torricelli, Evangelista, *1:* 34, *6:* 1284
Tortoises, *5:* 1019
Toughness of materials, *4:* 687
Toxicity, *1:* 164
Trace fossils, *3:* 524
Trace minerals, *6:* 1226
Traits, genetic, *3:* 554–55, 556–59, 558 (ill.), 559 (ill.), 562
Transfer of energy, *5:* 930, 930 (ill.)
Transformation of energy, *5:* 929
Transforming factor (DNA), *2:* 285–86
Transpiration
    transpiration rate and environment experiment, *5:* 904–7, 906 (ill.)
    of water, *5:* 885, 890, 892 (ill.), 893 (ill.), 898, 899
Tree resins, *3:* 523–24
Trees
    angiosperm, *6:* 1295, 1296 (ill.)
    annual growth of, *1:* 71–72, 72 (ill.), 73 (ill.)
    coniferous, *1:* 103, 104 (ill.), *6:* 1295
    deciduous, *1:* 107–8, 107 (ill.), 192
    growth pattern experiment, *1:* 74–79, 78 (ill.)
    lichen on, *1:* 79
    rainforest, *1:* 105–6
    structure of, *6:* 1295–96, 1297 (ill.)
    wood from, *6:* 1295
    See also Forests
Troglobites, *1:* 130
Troglophiles, *1:* 130–31
Trogloxenes, *1:* 130
Tropical forests, *2:* 376

W